# EWTN:  A Network Gone Wrong

# EWTN: A Network Gone Wrong

How the Eternal Word Television Network is contributing to the spread of "silent apostasy" in the Roman Catholic Church

Christopher A. Ferrara

Good Counsel Publications
Pound Ridge, New York

# EWTN: A Network Gone Wrong

First Edition

ISBN: 0-9663046-7-5

For all correspondence, contact:

Good Counsel Publications
P.O. Box 203
Pound Ridge, New York 10576

1-800-954-8737 • www.networkgonewrong.com

To

Our Lady Conqueror of All Heresies, who warned us of the
coming apostasy, and promised to restore the Church
through the Triumph of Her Immaculate Heart

and

Pope Saint Pius X, the last canonized Pope, who defeated the
Modernists of his day. May the Church soon be blessed with
a Pope of equal greatness, who will rescue her from
the scourge of darkness that calls itself light.

"Were one to attempt the task of collecting together all the errors that have been broached against the Faith and to concentrate the sap and substance of them all into one, he could not better succeed than the Modernists have done. Nay, they have done more than this, for... their system means the destruction not of the Catholic religion alone but of all religion."

. . .

"Though they express astonishment themselves, no one can justly be surprised that We number such men among the enemies of the Church... [T]hey proceed to disseminate poison through the whole tree, so that there is no part of Catholic truth from which they hold their hand, none that they do not strive to corrupt."

-- POPE SAINT PIUS X on the errors of the Modernists,
in his encyclical *Pascendi*

# Preface

With the death of Pope John Paul II and the election of his successor, Benedict XVI, a new era has begun in the history of the Roman Catholic Church. But the crisis that has wracked the Church since the Second Vatican Council (1962-1965) goes on, even if the faithful hope that during the present pontificate measures will at last be taken to bring the crisis to an end.

Over the past forty years a growing number of Catholics have come to recognize what is manifest: that the post-conciliar crisis began with, and has resulted from, a host of previously unheard-of ecclesial innovations, imposed in the name of the Council, which have provoked confusion and disorder and led to a massive turning away from the Faith—an apostasy—in the Catholic Church.

The theme of this book is that the Eternal Word Television Network (**EWTN**) both exemplifies and promotes these ruinous novelties, and thus has contributed to the crisis itself. It is the author's burden to demonstrate that with the departure of its foundress, Mother Angelica, from a leadership role, EWTN has taken a sharp turn toward what Pope St. Pius X condemned as the heresy of Modernism, as it attempts to combine Catholicism with rock and roll, show business and the worst novelties of the era after Vatican II.

While EWTN was once a sign of hope for a Catholic restoration, it has become instead a major factor in the Modernist innovation of the Church since the Council: a mixture of truth and error, orthodoxy and heresy, the sacred and the profane. EWTN now functions as an organ of what is aptly dubbed "New Church"—a kind of *faux* church that exists parasitically within the host organism, which is the unchanged and unchangeable Roman Catholic Church of all time. The author will show that the unprecedented emergence of "New Church" is the very essence of the post-conciliar crisis, and that this development was predicted in the Third Secret of Fatima, as Pope Pius XII indicated in a stunning prophecy that figures largely in this book.

The author also shows that even as EWTN promotes all manner of destructive ecclesial innovation, EWTN also presents itself as the standard of authentic Catholicism and calls for the shunning of Catholics who defend the perennial Faith without alteration. EWTN is thus not merely a passive adopter of novelty, but an active promoter of ecclesial revolution.

For these reasons, the author concludes, EWTN—a worldwide television, radio and Internet presence—must now be considered one of the foremost agents of Modernist apostasy in the Church and a positive danger to the welfare of souls, despite certain good elements in its programming. Thus, it is not Catholics who defend the perennial Faith who must be shunned, but rather EWTN and the rest of the "New Church" establishment, which has been leading the Church toward ruin over the past forty years of ecclesial decay and decline.

Should anyone take the trouble to respond to this book, let him begin here, where the author stresses that he does not intend to suggest that any of the EWTN directors or celebrities mentioned critically in the following pages are all necessarily subjectively guilty of apostasy, Modernism, formal heresy or any other deliberate offense against the Faith. Such guilt is a matter of Divine Judgment, and the personal piety and sincerity of individuals is not in question here. Words, however, have their objective meanings, and deeds their objective consequences. It is the duty of every Catholic to oppose words and deeds that undermine the Faith, give scandal, disturb the good order of the Church and endanger the welfare of souls—especially when those words and deeds are televised throughout the world to audiences of millions of Catholics and non-Catholics by a lay-run organization that has absolutely no authority in the Church, yet creates the impression that it represents the best of what the Church is. The honest critic must confront the evidence presented in the following pages, rather than turn the matter into an outraged defense of the alleged subjective motives of this or that person. Let the critic address what a person is shown to have said or done, not what he "meant" to say or do according to some hidden intention elaborated after the fact.

Nor should anyone who might wish to respond to this book waste his time demonstrating that certain elements of what EWTN presents are soundly Catholic. That this is so is not only stipulated at the beginning of the book, but is in fact the crux of the problem with EWTN: that it combines things of the Faith with things inimical to the

Faith, thus attacking the integrity of what Pope St. Pius X called "the Catholic name." The combination of the orthodox with the heterodox is the essence of Modernism. As Pius X declared in condemning the writings of the Modernists: "Hence in their books you find some things which might well be expressed by a Catholic, but in the next page you find other things which might have been dictated by a rationalist." Let the critic, therefore, address the evidence of things inimical to the Faith, rather than attempting to prove what is not in dispute.

Those who direct EWTN may believe they are doing a service to the Church and that they have the right to engage in their public mission. It is the author's conviction, however, that if they consider attentively the evidence of what they are promoting, they will no longer have the refuge of good faith. Having taken upon themselves a public religious mission, those responsible for EWTN become subject to public criticism from fellow Catholics who, out of their own sense of duty, oppose what EWTN is doing. And it is an act of charity, not unkindness, to oppose errors—from whatever source— that threaten the integrity of the Faith and therefore the welfare of souls. It is in this spirit of fraternal correction, however forcefully expressed, that this book was written.

January 6, 2006
Feast of the Epiphany

**Abbreviations:**

CCC        Catechism of the Catholic Church
CIC         Code of Canon Law (Latin)
DS          Denzinger-Schönmetzer
Dz.         Denzinger

# CONTENTS

PREFACE .................................................................................. vii

OVERVIEW
*The Banishment of Mother Angelica* ............................................ 1

## PART I
## The Modernist Crisis in the Church

CHAPTER 1
*The Silent Apostasy* ................................................................ 19

CHAPTER 2
*A Great Façaule of Novelty* ...................................................... 28

CHAPTER 3
*The Scope of the Crisis* ............................................................ 32

CHAPTER 4
*What Does it Mean to Be a Catholic?* ...................................... 41

CHAPTER 5
*Modernism: The Synthesis of All Heresies* ................................ 45

## PART II
## EWTN's Role As Promoter of Modernism

CHAPTER 6
*EWTN's "Moderate" Modernism* ............................................... 53

CHAPTER 7
*EWTN's Promotion of Liturgical Destruction* ............................ 56

CHAPTER 8
*Abandoning the Dogma "No Salvation Outside the Church"* .......... 70

CHAPTER 9
*Abandoning the Return of the Dissidents to Rome*....................................... 85

CHAPTER 10
*Promoting the Return of the Judaizers* ....................................... 117

CHAPTER 11
*Promoting Paganism and Sacrilege*........................................ 151

CHAPTER 12
*Quasi-Idolatry of the Pope's Person* ........................................ 158

CHAPTER 13
*Promoting Destruction of the Traditional Rosary*........................... 164

CHAPTER 14
*Promoting Sexual Gnosticism and the NFP Cult* ....................... 174

CHAPTER 15
*"Cool" Catholicism*....................................................... 204

CHAPTER 16
*The Assault on Fatima*....................................................... 209

**PART III**
**Summing Up**

CHAPTER 17
*Did They Love You, John Paul II?*.................................... 235

CHAPTER 18
*What the Evidence Shows*.................................................... 245

CHAPTER 19
*What Should We Do?* ........................................................ 253

Index .............................................................................. 263

# Overview

## The Banishment of Mother Angelica and EWTN'S Promotion of Modernism

Having been silenced by the Vatican since 1960, the year the Third Secret of Fatima was to be revealed to the Church and the world, Sister Lucy of Fatima went to her eternal reward on February 13, 2005. On April 2, 2005 the long reign of John Paul II ended with his own death, and Catholics now pray for the repose of his soul.

But the crisis in the Church rages on—just as predicted in the Third Secret. Millions of Catholics remain unconvinced that the Vatican's disclosure of the obscure vision of a "bishop dressed in white" being executed outside a half-ruined city is all there ever was to the Secret that had been kept under lock and key in the Vatican for more than forty years. Speaking for members of the faithful all over the world, Mother Angelica, the feisty and tradition-minded foundress of the Eternal Word Television Network (**EWTN**), made the following declaration on her live television show of May 16, 2001:

> As for the Secret, well *I happen to be one of those individuals who thinks we didn't get the whole thing.* I told ya! I mean, you have the right to your own opinion, don't you, Father? There, you know, that's my opinion. *Because I think it's scary...*

Some seven months later, following the first of two strokes (and a series of previously undetected mini-strokes), Mother Angelica left the airwaves as EWTN's live television host. As noted in a biography of Mother Angelica by EWTN personality Raymond Arroyo, "By the end of 2001, Mother Angelica's detachment from EWTN was complete."[1] Mother's role at EWTN is now reduced to leading the Rosary in short pre-recorded segments and the broadcast of some of her old television shows—censored for "theological correctness" by EWTN's current management, which, as we shall see, has become decidedly Modernist in its orientation.[2]

One might say that Mother Angelica has been "Sister Lucy-ized"—but not on account of the strokes. While EWTN says the strokes have rendered Mother Angelica unable to appear on television, in truth she had already been driven from her position of control over the network she founded by an episcopal power play orchestrated with the assistance of a Vatican congregation.

It all began in November 1997 with Mother's unforgettable televised denunciation of the infamous Cardinal Mahony, that celebrity prelate who is the very embodiment of post-conciliar Modernism and decay in the Church. Mother rightly denounced Mahony's "pastoral letter" on the Holy Eucharist as a Modernist obfuscation of the true doctrine of the Mass. Under pressure from Mahony's friends in the Vatican apparatus, Mother made an on-the-air apology; but the "apology" was even more defiant than the original commentary. For nearly an hour Mother "served up a point-by-point critique of the pastoral letter,"[3] demonstrating that Mahony had slighted and thus undermined the doctrine of transubstantiation. An infuriated Mahony filed a canonical complaint in Rome. Arroyo quotes one elderly curial Cardinal as admitting that "Mother Angelica has the guts to tell him [Mahony] what we do not."[4] Mahony's canonical complaint ultimately went nowhere, but he had already begun to agitate the Vatican apparatus to take action against Mother. Arroyo quotes Mahony's director of media relations as stating "The Cardinal wants the Holy See to do something about Mother Angelica's whole attitude that she is not responsible to the National Conference of Catholic Bishops or to any of the individual bishops."[5]

---

[1]Raymond Arroyo, *Mother Angelica: The Remarkable Story of a Nun, Her Nerve and a Network of Miracles*, (New York: Doubleday, 2005), page 317 (hereafter "Mother Angelica").

[2]The heresy of Modernism, famously condemned by Pope St. Pius X in his monumental encyclical *Pascendi* (On the Doctrines of the Modernists), is explained in the concluding chapter of Part I.

[3]*Mother Angelica*, page 262.

[4]Ibid., page 264.

[5]Ibid., page 267.

Then Mother Angelica tangled with another liberal prelate, Bishop David Foley, the ordinary of her diocese in Alabama. Foley had no real authority over Mother's apostolate, the Poor Clares of the Perpetual Adoration. Nevertheless, he insisted that in the new Shrine to the Blessed Sacrament Mother was building in Hanceville, Alabama, no Masses were to be said in the traditional "ad orientem"[6] manner—that is, facing the altar and God in an eastward direction, rather than facing the people.[7] When Mother refused to knuckle under to this illegal demand, in October 1999 Foley issued a preposterous decree stating that Mass facing the altar—an unbroken tradition of the Church from her earliest days—was an "illicit innovation or sacrilege" and that anyone "guilty" of this "sacrilege" would be subject to "suspension or removal of faculties." All Masses in his diocese, Foley declared, would "henceforth be celebrated at a freestanding altar and... the priest would face the people."[8]

In a courageous act of resistance to this abuse of power, Mother Angelica boycotted the dedication of the new Shrine in December 1999, presided over by none other than Foley himself, who celebrated Mass facing the people. Arroyo reports that a clearly humiliated Foley called Mother to the podium to say a few words, but "in silent protest" she remained with her nuns in the cloistered area behind the altar, refusing to serve as Foley's prop.[9] Clearly determined to get revenge, Foley went to the Vatican as the representative of the National Conference of Catholic Bishops to demand action against Mother Angelica (no doubt with Mahony's blessing). Foley, with the advice of Cardinal Medina, head of the Vatican's Congregation for Divine Worship and the Discipline of the Sacraments, promulgated "norms" that banned any televised Mass facing East (i.e. the altar) in his diocese and requiring Mass facing the people. EWTN complied with these "norms," even though they were as preposterous and illegal as Foley's earlier decree, for Foley had no authority to ban the Church's immemorial practice, on television or otherwise.

But the matter did not end there. Foley also induced the Congregation for the Institutes of Consecrated Life and Societies of

---

[6]Latin for "toward the East."

[7]Contrary to popular perception, no legislation from Rome has ever prohibited Mass facing the altar. Rather, the option of Mass facing the people has been introduced, with the "option" becoming only a *de facto* (not legal) norm.

[8]*Mother Angelica*, pages 287-288.

[9]Ibid., page 292.

Apostolic Life to send an Apostolic Visitor, Archbishop Roberto Gonzalez of San Juan, Puerto Rico, to Alabama to investigate the entire EWTN operation.[10] It quickly became apparent that the aim of the visitation (which took place in February-March 2000) was to establish that Mother Angelica's order, the Poor Clares, owned EWTN's assets, including the new Shrine, and not EWTN's civil corporation board of directors, of which Mother was CEO with full veto power over the board's decisions. If it could be established that Mother's order owned the assets, then the whole EWTN enterprise could be subjected to ecclesiastical control, including the possible appointment of a "progressive" replacement for Mother Angelica herself.

In desperation, Mother made a prudential decision that in retrospect was a huge mistake: Fearing that Archbishop Gonzalez's report to the Vatican would recommend an ecclesiastical takeover of her apostolate, Mother surrendered all control over EWTN to the lay people who run it today. At an emergency board meeting in March of 2000, she resigned as CEO of EWTN, relinquishing her veto power, and with it her control over EWTN's affairs. At the same meeting EWTN's board amended the corporate by-laws to insure lay control and preclude any control in the future by a bishop, priest or religious.[11] Thus, instead of continuing her direct resistance to liberal prelates, Mother Angelica thought she could defeat them by a strategic retreat.

One reviewer of Arroyo's biography opines that "by resigning, Mother Angelica had defeated her enemies within the Church and entrusted her network to lay people who shared her orthodox views...."As we will see, however, Mother's retreat was actually a complete rout. For it was precisely Mother's "enemies within the Church" who had gained the victory by driving her from her position of control over EWTN, leaving the network entirely in the hands of lay people, many of them ex-Protestants, who did not have her traditional pre-Vatican II spiritual formation and old-fashioned Catholic militancy. The nun Arroyo calls "the undisputed matriarch of Catholic communications"[12] had been neutralized.

Mother would hang on as EWTN's live television host until December 2001, but the process by which EWTN would be fatally

---

[10]The entire affair is recounted in great detail in *Mother Angelica,* Chapter 18, pages 298ff.
[11]Ibid., pages 307-309.
[12]*Mother Angelica,* page 215.

compromised in its mission of presenting the integral Catholic Faith was already in motion. With Mother Angelica's departure as the network's signature personality by the end of 2001, the original vision of the network as a counter-Modernist force for a Catholic restoration was quickly lost and has never been recovered. Mother's vision has been replaced by an "ecumenical," watered-down blandness, delivered largely by ex-Protestant ministers, combined with lame attempts at "cool" Catholicism with a heavy emphasis on rock music.[13]

The new and "slicker" EWTN appears to be in large part the work of its vice president for production, Doug Keck, who had for twenty years headed operations at a cable TV conglomerate whose programming included The Playboy Channel. It was Keck who, as Arroyo writes, was responsible for "transforming the on-air look and content of the network." And it was Keck who offered the opinion that "proved to be decisive" in Mother's decision to turn over control of the network to Keck and the other lay board members: "Mother, I think you're right. I think you need to step back to protect the network," said Keck at the fateful board meeting.[14] And so she did.

Less than six years later, EWTN's programming now exhibits the same emasculation and liberalization of the Church militant that we see everywhere today in the wake of the Second Vatican Council. The robust Roman Catholicism the fiery Italian nun (formerly Rita Rizzo) exemplified is almost entirely gone from the network. As we will see, EWTN has even gone so far as to promote the Judaization of Catholic worship by a movement whose members insist upon calling themselves "Hebrew Catholics."

No longer, then, does EWTN exhibit the kind of anti-Modernist fervor we witnessed when Mother blasted not only Cardinal Mahony, but all the American bishops for allowing a woman to perform the role of Christ during the Stations of the Cross at World

---

[13]None of this is to suggest that Mother Angelica represented utter perfection in her presentation of traditional Roman Catholicism. Her dalliance with the "charismatic renewal" and the Medjugorje "apparitions" is well known, and it was she who first gave prominence to many of the current EWTN celebrities whose theological views are criticized in this book. Nevertheless, Mother Angelica represented the network's best hope for becoming a vehicle of Catholic restoration (as we shall see further into this overview). Now with her removal from any position of control over EWTN there was nothing to restrain the liberalizing tendency that has subverted its mission.

[14]*Mother Angelica*, pages 303-304.

Youth Day in Denver in 1993. "This is it. I've had all I'm going to take," she said in disgust.[15] A few days later she blasted the bishops on her live television show. Arroyo recounts that after reciting a long train of abuses arising from the governance of liberal prelates, including disrespect for the Blessed Sacrament and mandatory sex education in Catholic schools, she continued:

> It's blasphemous that you dare to portray Jesus as a woman. You know, as Catholics we've been quiet all these years…. I'm tired, tired of being pushed in the corners. I'm tired of your inclusive language that refuses to admit that the Son of God is a man. I'm tired of your tricks. I'm tired of you making a crack, and the first thing you know there's a hole, and all of us fall in. No, this was deliberate… you made a statement that was not accidental. I am so tired of you, liberal Church in America. You're sick…. You have nothing to offer. You do nothing but destroy. You don't have vocations, and you don't even care—your whole purpose is to destroy… You can't stand Catholicism at its height, so you try to spoil it, as you've spoiled so many things in these thirty years….

I saw that broadcast, and I will never forget the sight of Mother shaking with righteous anger before the cameras as she uttered these and so many other words that reflected the suffering of Catholics throughout the entire nation. In that very broadcast Mother vowed that in reaction to the increasingly dissolute state of the Church in America, she and her fellow Poor Clare Sisters would return to the wearing of full habits, which they did immediately. In March of 1994 one of the most staunchly Catholic newspapers in America, *The Remnant* (for which I am privileged to be a columnist), expressed its admiration for Mother's decision to return to the full habit, taking it as a sign that

> the restoration (or perhaps we should say Catholic revival) is beginning to take place in the Church today. It is no longer only the 'traditionalists' who have come to the sad and desperate realization that we must go back

---

[15]Ibid., page 240.

> to our Catholic past in order to see the path of our
> Catholic future…. Mother Angelica and her wonderful
> sisters are to be congratulated for their courage and
> fortitude, but also we should pray that they go even a
> step further…. It is our hope that along with all her other
> courageous work, Mother Angelica will one day
> consider calling for the unconditional return of the
> historical Latin Mass and strike the ultimate blow
> against the modernist onslaught of the Catholic
> Church.[16]

In another hard-hitting commentary, Mother seemed to be
moving in precisely the direction hoped for by *The Remnant* when she
drew a long and quite ironic comparison between the actions of the
Protestant "reformers" in destroying the Catholic liturgy in the
sixteenth century and what the post-conciliar "reformers" did to the
traditional Latin Mass after Vatican II.

But that was all before the sacking of Mother Angelica, her
departure from the airwaves, and EWTN's subsequent change of
direction. As this book will make clear, post-Mother Angelica EWTN
has not only accommodated itself to the Modernist revolution in the
Church after Vatican II, abandoning all opposition to its excesses for
the sake of maintaining "good standing" with the powers that be (the
likes of Foley and Mahony), but has also become a positive promoter
of that same revolution. And it has done so *under the guise of being
traditionally Roman Catholic*, continuing to capitalize on Mother
Angelica's name while providing none of her militantly Catholic
spirit or her common-sense Catholicism.

Worse, owing to the very nature of the television medium EWTN
has evolved into something much more insidious than the overtly
liberal organs of the revolution, such as the *National Catholic Reporter*.
As Bishop Foley had correctly perceived in the controversy over the
eastward-facing altar in the Shrine, Mother Angelica was wielding
"an instrument that is more powerful than anything else in the world
[humanly speaking]. I mean, it's *television*…"[17] It is television indeed.
The sad story to be told by this book is that Foley, Mahony and their
collaborators in the "Modernist Mafia," from the Vatican on down,
have insured that this same powerful instrument would henceforth

---

[16]"What's In a Habit?" *The Remnant*, March 15, 1994.
[17]*Mother Angelica*, page 289.

broadcast and thus inculcate, via EWTN, not only the liturgical revolution which turned the altar around, but all the other basic elements of the post-Vatican II revolution as a whole.

It must be stipulated at the outset that even after the victory of Modernist prelates over Mother Angelica, EWTN still retains certain elements of good Catholic programming. Yet it is the very presence of these good elements that poses a spiritual hazard for EWTN "fans," who are induced by what is good in the content to expose themselves to numerous elements that undermine the Faith.

Here it is necessary to address a threshold objection that will certainly be raised to any suggestion that EWTN is less than the "gold standard" of Roman Catholicism today. The objection goes something like this: "Why criticize EWTN, when EWTN is the most Catholic thing out there?" Let me reply immediately that Catholics, as confirmed soldiers of Christ, have a duty before God not to settle for "the most Catholic thing out there," but rather to *demand* the Catholic Faith in all its integrity from anyone who undertakes to present the Faith to the public. If "the most Catholic thing out there" turns out, upon close examination, to be a mixture of truth and error, orthodoxy and heresy, Tradition and appalling novelty, the sacred and the profane—and I will show here that this is exactly what EWTN has become—then one must avoid "the most Catholic thing out there" like the plague, because one's faith will tend inevitably to be undermined by exposure to this heterodox mixture. It is just such a mixture that has provoked chaos and defection from the Faith since the clearly disastrous and totally unprecedented "updating" of the Church that began at Vatican II.

I am not denying that many Catholics have managed to preserve their faith and to practice it with great piety even in the midst of the changes. That individual Catholics have kept the Faith, however, is not the point in contention here. The point of this discussion is to demonstrate that, in both theory and practice, what now passes for "the most Catholic thing out there"—or what is called a "conservative implementation" of Vatican II—is, objectively speaking, a massive departure from the perennial Faith. The unprecedented and supposedly "officially approved" innovations stemming from the Council, all of which EWTN promotes and defends today, have (as I discuss further below) provoked enormous damage to the life of the Church as a whole. This is seen in the sudden post-conciliar decline in baptisms, conversions, marriages, vocations and Mass attendance, and in the growing lack of adherence to Catholic doctrine, dogma, liturgical tradition and morals on the part of those who still call themselves Catholic. It is right to speak of a veritable *apostasy* in the Church since the Council, and both the late Pope John Paul II and his personal theologian, Cardinal Luigi Ciappi (also now deceased), have used that very word to describe the state of the Church today, as will be shown presently.

Indeed, the idea that Catholics ought to be content with "the most Catholic thing out there" instead of the unaltered and unalterable Faith of our fathers is the very thing that has prolonged the crisis in the Church and led to a widening apostasy among her members. The process at work in the Church since Vatican II is very much akin to the drastic dilution of the meaning of the word "conservative" in politics. Just as today's political "conservative" would have been considered a raving liberal only fifty years ago, so also today's "conservative" Catholic would have been viewed as a heretic, or at least suspect of heresy, by the great Popes of the Catholic Church of all time. Just as in politics we are expected to settle for less and less conservative "conservatives," so too in the Church we are expected to settle for a less and less Catholic version of our holy religion. The only difference is that in politics the "sliding scale" of what it means to be "conservative" has temporal consequences, whereas in the Church the consequences are both temporal and eternal. Our very souls are at risk.

What we need to remember is that there is an objective and unchanging standard of Roman Catholicism, and that for the first time in Church history—and this is the essence of the crisis that afflicts us now—the faithful are losing sight of that standard. But it is easy to recall this objective standard if one thinks for a moment about what the Church has always taught and practiced. Just imagine, for example, Saint Pius X attending the New Mass in a so-called "conservative" parish of today. The sainted Pontiff would probably scream in horror and demand that the spectacle be stopped. *Never before have we seen such a situation in the Church.*

Speaking of the new liturgy alone—and the crisis involves far more than that—the renowned liturgical scholar Msgr. Klaus Gamber has rightly observed:

> A Catholic who ceased to be an active member of the
> Church for the past generation and who, having decided

to return to the Church, wants to become religiously
active again, probably would not recognize today's
Church as the one he had left. Simply by entering a
Catholic church, particularly if it happens to be one of
ultra-modern design, he would feel as if he had entered
a strange, foreign place. He will think that he must have
come to the wrong address and that he accidentally
ended up in some other Christian religious
community.[18]

After forty years of ecclesial confusion and decline, therefore, we
should be mindful that it is a treacherous business indeed to settle for
"the most Catholic thing out there." For today, the "most Catholic
thing out there" may not be very Catholic at all. As I will
demonstrate, EWTN purveys a version of Catholicism that is inimical
to the Faith, a danger to souls and destructive of the good order of
the Church.

What will become crystal clear in the succeeding chapters is that
with Mother Angelica gone from the scene and the network in the
hands of lay people, most of whom have no memory of the Catholic
Church before Vatican II, EWTN now actively supports and defends
against all criticism every element of the "new" Catholicism that
supposedly arose during and after the Council: the new Mass, the
new ecumenism, the new "dialogue" and "interreligious dialogue,"
the new "opening to the world," the new attitude toward the
conversion of the Jewish people, and even a new version of the
Message of Fatima. The result of all the changes is what I have
already described as "New Church"—a pseudo-Church existing
within the official structure of the Roman Catholic Church in a kind
of parasitical relationship to the host organism. As we shall see, *not a
single one of these novelties has ever been imposed upon Catholics as a duty
of their religion*. Yet EWTN promotes them all as if they were
obligations of the Faith.

I will employ the term "New Church" throughout this book in
order to distinguish its features and its proponents from authentic
Roman Catholicism, which was not and *could not* be replaced by any
"reformed" version at Vatican II. Authentic Roman Catholicism is

---

[18]Monsignor Klaus Gamber, *The Reform of the Roman Liturgy: Its Problems and
Background* (Harrison, New York: Foundation for Catholic Reform, 1993), page
107.

commonly referred to by the collective term "Tradition." A few words about the meaning of this crucial term are in order.

By "Tradition" is meant the totality of the perennial doctrine, dogma, liturgy, spirituality and practice of the Catholic Faith as handed down from century to century with unbroken continuity before the start of the Second Vatican Council. Stated more simply, it means what Catholics have always believed and the way they have always worshipped. It is to Tradition that a Catholic looks to determine whether all is right with the Church. The ancient Church Father St. John Chrysostom expressed this principle most succinctly: "Is it tradition? Ask no more!" The word "tradition" is derived from the Latin verb *tradere*, meaning to "hand over, deliver, entrust."[19] The function of the leaders of the Church is not to change what has been handed over, delivered and entrusted to them, but rather to hand over, deliver and entrust to their successors exactly what they received. "Therefore, brethren" says St. Paul, "stand fast: and hold the traditions, which you have learned, whether by word or by our epistle." (2 Thess. 2:14) As one of the great early Church Fathers, St. Vincent of Lerins explained, Tradition is our only refuge at a time of confusion in the Church, as it was during the Arian heresy, which in St. Vincent's day was an event of the rather recent past. As St. Vincent declared:

> And if some new contagion should seek to poison, not only a little part of the Church, but the whole Church at once then his [the Catholic's] greatest care should once again be to adhere to antiquity, which obviously cannot be seduced by any deceitful novelty.[20]

As the very nature of Tradition would imply, the only object of true reform in the Church is the *restoration* of Tradition. The Church underwent this true reform in the great Catholic Counter-Reformation following the Council of Trent, when Catholic dogma, doctrine, morals, spiritual life, and the traditional Latin liturgy were strongly reaffirmed against the Protestant rebels, local liturgical abuses were curbed, and the strict discipline of the priesthood was reestablished wherever it had fallen into neglect. This true reform is even more urgently needed in the Church today.

---

[19]*American Heritage Dictionary*, Fourth Edition.
[20]*Commonitorium*, Chapter 3, Section 7.

In this discussion I will *not* employ such terms as "traditionalist," "conservative" or "neo-Catholic" to distinguish different "strains" of Catholicism in the post-conciliar Church. As useful as such terms may have been in the past, the ecclesial crisis has advanced to the point where one must speak frankly of who is, and who is not, adhering to the Roman Catholic religion in its integrity. This is also necessary because the proponents of New Church have not hesitated to render judgments on the Catholicity of those who have held fast to Tradition during this crisis, denouncing these faithful Catholics simply because they will not embrace the unheard-of novelties of the past forty years.

For the good of the Church, this absurd situation must be corrected. As Holy Scripture warns us: "Woe to you that call evil good, and good evil: that put darkness *for* light, and light *for* darkness: that put bitter for sweet, and sweet for bitter."[21] For too long EWTN and other "mainstream" aiders and abettors of the post-conciliar revolution have been allowed to adorn themselves with the cloak of respectability, while they impugn faithful Catholics who defend Tradition and refuse to follow them down the path of compromise. The cloak must come off so that the truth about these people can be revealed—not for their disgrace, but for their own good and, above all else, for the good of the Church. For as I will demonstrate here, whether or not they understand subjectively that they are Modernists, this is what EWTN and the other post-conciliar purveyors of novelty are, objectively speaking. It is, therefore, *they*, not traditional Roman Catholics, who are theologically suspect. It is they, as the evidence to be presented here will prove, who are advancing novelties that are objectively contrary to the Faith, sacrilegious, scandalous and even offensive to good morals. It is their "new" version of Catholicism, not the perennial practice of the Faith, that ought to be condemned. It is the proponents of New Church, not the adherents of the Catholic Church of all time, who should be examined for their views.

Let me emphasize at the outset that this entire discussion presumes, for the sake of charity, that those responsible for EWTN's Modernist content do not subjectively intend to depart from the Faith. They may even think in their distorted view of the situation—a

---

[21]Isaias 5:20. Most biblical quotes are from the Douay-Rheims Bible (Rockford, Illinois: TAN Books and Publishers, 1971).

view which leads them to condemn faithful Roman Catholics as "extreme traditionalists" — that they are actually defending the Faith. Some may even possess that state of mind Our Lord warned His disciples would be that of the Pharisees: "yea, the hour cometh, that whosoever killeth you will think that he doth a service to God." (John 16:2) But if they are acting in good faith or out of blindness at present, they will have no excuse for continuing in their course of conduct once they consider (or if they refuse to consider) with an open mind the evidence presented here in this book; and they will no longer be entitled to the presumption that they do not understand that they are promoting Modernism.

In any case, justice, the good of the Church and the good of souls demand that Catholics who are only endeavoring to practice the Faith without alteration not allow themselves to be framed by the accusation, so often leveled by EWTN and other New Church organs, that they are "extreme traditionalists," "disobedient" and even "schismatic." It is time for the accusers, not the accused, to stand trial. For as the evidence will show, it is the accusers, not the accused, who are implicated in the collapse of faith and discipline in the Church since Vatican II.

This book is divided into three parts. In Part I, I lay the groundwork for an understanding of the current crisis in the Church, which the late John Paul II described as "a silent apostasy." I show that this crisis is essentially a resurgence of the Modernist heresy condemned by Pope St. Pius X early in the twentieth century — a heresy that seeks to alter the very meaning of Catholic doctrine and dogma according to a process of "evolution," to overturn the Church's dogmatic faith and liturgical tradition, to attack the very identity of the Church, and indeed to destroy the very concept of objective truth itself. Others have referred to this process as a "creeping apostasy," which by slow degrees induces Catholics to accept corruptions of the true Faith under the pretense of authentic Catholic teaching "updated" for the times. This, we will see, is the dominant tendency of EWTN's content.

In Part II, I discuss in considerable detail EWTN's role in contributing to this Modernist crisis since Mother Angelica's coerced departure. The evidence will show:

- First, that EWTN promotes, defends and advances the "New Mass" and all the other "officially" approved

"reforms" of the liturgy which have broken with
Tradition in precisely the ways demanded by the
Protestant rebels of the sixteenth century, and practically
destroyed Catholic worship and Eucharistic faith over
the past forty years, as even high-ranking Cardinals
have admitted;

- Second, that EWTN has, under the guise of a "new
  understanding" of Catholic dogma since Vatican II,
  helped to undermine Catholic adherence to (a) the
  infallibly defined dogma that outside the Roman
  Catholic Church no one can be saved; (b) the closely
  related constant teaching of the Roman Pontiffs that the
  only means of achieving Christian unity is the return of
  the Protestant and schismatic dissidents to the Catholic
  Church; and (c) the abolition of the Old Covenant in
  favor of the New Covenant in Christ Jesus, and the
  consequent objective necessity of Jewish conversion for
  the salvation of the Jews;

- Third, that EWTN has promoted and encouraged a
  Judaizing tendency in the Church not unlike that which
  confronted the original Jewish Apostles in the first
  century;

- Fourth, that EWTN has excused, defended and
  promoted sacrilege in Catholic holy places in the name
  of "interreligious dialogue";

- Fifth, that EWTN is contributing to a tendency to replace
  Roman Catholicism with a common-denominator
  natural religion that deemphasizes adherence to
  revealed truth as necessary for salvation;

- Sixth, that EWTN has advocated a senseless and un-
  Catholic quasi-idolatry of the Pope's person that does a
  grave disservice to the Pope, his office and the Faith;

- Seventh, that EWTN is leading the destruction of the
  traditional Rosary;

- Eighth, that EWTN promotes a cult of sexual gnosticism

and "Natural Family Planning" (NFP);

- Ninth, that EWTN has generally corrupted the Faith by trying to combine it with rock music and show business in a vain effort to make Catholicism "cool" (EWTN's own word) and appealing to the base instincts of a mass audience;

- Tenth, that EWTN attacks and attempts to ostracize from the Church the defenders of Roman Catholic Tradition, and especially those, such as Father Nicholas Gruner, who defend the traditional Catholic understanding of the Message of Fatima and its prophetic relation to the crisis in the Church.

In short, I will show that post-Mother Angelica EWTN has become a "moderate" (and therefore more dangerous) Modernist enterprise that presents a corruption of authentic Roman Catholicism passed off as solid orthodoxy, and that as such EWTN is now a serious and highly insidious threat to the integrity of the Faith and a major obstacle to the restoration of the Catholic Church.

In Part III, I will sum up the case against EWTN and New Church in general, in the context of the death of John Paul II and the election of Benedict XVI as his successor. And, to conclude, I will suggest ways in which we members of the lay faithful can, with the Message of Fatima in view, work according to our stations in life for an end to the ecclesial crisis over which New Church (including EWTN) presides.

With our overview of the matter complete, let us proceed to the first stage of the case against EWTN: an understanding of the current crisis in the Church. Only with that understanding can one fully appreciate the magnitude of the problem EWTN poses for faithful Catholics.

# Part I

# The Modernist Crisis
# in the Church

# Chapter 1

# The Silent Apostasy

The Code of Canon Law of the Catholic Church defines "apostasy" as "the total repudiation of the Christian faith."[22] The law of the Church treats apostasy as a canonical offense because abandonment of the Faith is the greatest calamity that can befall a man on this earth. As St. Paul declared, "without faith it is impossible to please God" (Heb. 11:6) and thus impossible to attain life everlasting.

One of history's most remarkable examples of the consequences of apostasy is Julian the Apostate (331-363), nephew of Constantine the Great. Constantine's conversion in 312 A.D. had marked the end of the Roman persecution of the Church and the emergence of Rome as a Catholic city, whose official religion Constantine declared to be Catholicism. But Julian, who briefly succeeded Constantius II (Constantine's son and Julian's cousin), abjured his own Catholic faith and returned to the worship of pagan gods. Julian died railing against both the false god Helios and the true God in the Person of Jesus Christ. His last recorded words were: "Helios, thou hast ruined me." And, indeed, the end of apostasy *is* ruin—eternal ruin. That is why the law of the Church regards it with such severity.

But it must not be imagined that apostasy is limited to formal and public abjuration of the Faith, as we see in the case of Julian. The concept of apostasy, more broadly understood, includes also a *falling away* from the Faith. As St. Thomas Aquinas teaches, "Apostasy denotes a backsliding from God. This may happen in various ways according to the different kinds of union between man and God."[23] For the priest or religious who has taken vows, apostasy involves specifically "withdrawing from the religious life to which he was bound by profession, or from the Holy Order which he had received." But, says Aquinas, there is a second and broader form of

---

[22]1983 Code of Canon Law, §751.
[23]*Summa Theologica*, II-II, Q. 12, Art. 1.

apostasy: "a man may also apostatize from God by rebelling in his mind against the Divine commandments..." This second form of apostasy "denotes an act of the will in rebellion against God's commandments, an act that is to be found in every mortal sin."[24] In this sense, even those who profess to be Catholics may (objectively speaking) be apostates because of their rebellion against the Church's teaching on the divine commandments. It is in this broader objective sense that I use the term "apostasy" in this book, rather than the formal canonical sense of a "total repudiation of the Christian faith."

The Book of the Apocalypse links a general falling away from the Catholic Faith to the emergence of Antichrist, which is the prelude to the Second Coming of Our Lord on Judgment Day. Chapter 12 speaks of the "tail of the dragon" (i.e. the devil) sweeping one-third of the stars—the consecrated souls of the Church, both priests and religious—from Heaven. This loss of consecrated souls to apostasy occurs during the dragon's battle with the "Woman clothed with the sun," the Woman who gives birth to the Messiah Who will ultimately vanquish the dragon. As St. Paul teaches, this Great Apostasy provoked by the dragon is "a revolt first, and the man of sin (then will) be revealed, the son of perdition". (2 Thess. 2:3) Hence, as Our Lord Himself asked His disciples: "When the Son of man comes, do you think He will find faith on the earth?" (Luke 18:8)

Not long before his passing, no less than Pope John Paul II suggested that we have already entered into the time of the Great Apostasy. In his sermon on the occasion of the beatification of Jacinta and Francisco Marto, the child seers of Fatima, on May 13, 2000, our late Pope referred explicitly to Chapter 12 of the Apocalypse and the "tail of the dragon":

> The message of Fatima is a call to conversion, alerting humanity to have nothing to do with the "dragon" whose "tail swept down a third of the stars of heaven, and cast them to the earth" (Apoc. 12: 4). Man's final goal is Heaven, his true home, where the heavenly Father awaits everyone with His merciful love. God does not want anyone to be lost; that is why 2,000 years ago He sent His Son to earth, "to seek and to save the lost" (Luke 19: 10)... In Her motherly concern, the Blessed Virgin came here to Fatima to ask men and women "to stop offending God, Our Lord, who is

---

[24]Ibid.

already very offended." It is a mother's sorrow that
compels Her to speak; the destiny of Her children is at
stake. For this reason She asks the little
shepherds: "Pray, pray much and make sacrifices for
sinners; many souls go to hell because they have no one
to pray and make sacrifices for them."

This was clearly a papal warning concerning widening apostasy
in the Church—an apostasy that is leading countless souls to hell
under the influence of the dragon.

In his apostolic exhortation *Ecclesia in Europa* ("The Church in
Europe"), issued in January 2001 to assess the Synod of European
bishops in 1999, the Pope again referred explicitly to the Book of the
Apocalypse in observing that Europe has succumbed to "a vision of
man apart from God and apart from Christ." The Pope lamented "*the
loss of Europe's Christian memory and heritage*, accompanied by a kind
of practical agnosticism and religious indifference whereby many
Europeans give the impression of living without spiritual roots and
somewhat like heirs who have squandered a patrimony entrusted to
them by history." That patrimony is, of course, Roman Catholicism—
the same faith abandoned by Julian the Apostate in the fourth
century Roman Empire.

The Pope, surveying the state of Europe today, declared that
"European culture gives the impression of '*silent apostasy*' on the part
of people who have all that they need and *who live as if God does not
exist*." The fruits of this silent apostasy are "the diminishing number
of births, the decline in the number of vocations to the priesthood
and religious life, and the difficulty, if not the outright refusal, to
make lifelong commitments, including marriage." Here the Pope
clearly described that rebellion against divine commandments that
St. Thomas Aquinas articulated is apostasy in the broader sense; it is
a silent—as distinct from an open and formal—apostasy.

The Pope returned to this quasi-apocalyptic theme yet again in
July of 2003. Speaking at Castelgandolfo, he reiterated his dire
observation of January 2001 that "European culture gives the
impression of a 'silent apostasy' on the part of men who are sated,
who live as if God did not exist."[25] Adopting the same theme only a
few days later, Cardinal Paul Poupard, head of the Pontifical Council

---

[25]Vatican Information Service, July 17, 2003. See also "Europe Needs to
Rediscover Christ, Says John Paul II: Warns That Continent's Foundation Could
Erode"; Zenit.org, July 13, 2003.

for Culture, observed that "Unbelief is no longer a phenomenon reduced to a few individuals but *a mass phenomenon*" that is seen especially "in countries where a secular cultural model prevails"—in other words, all of Europe. Poupard dismissed claims of a "return to the sacred" with his comment "the emergence of a new weak religiosity, without reference to a personal God, something more emotional than doctrinal. We are witnessing the de-personalization of God. This new religiosity does not coincide with a return to the Faith..." And while militant atheism may have subsided, it has been replaced by "a phenomenon of practical unbelief which is growing in cultural realms penetrated by secularism. It is a cultural form that I would describe as 'neo-paganism,' in which religion is an idolatry of material goods, a vague religious feeling that is rather pantheistic, which is at ease with cosmological theories, such as those of New Age." This phenomenon, said Poupard, "is typical of the secularized cultures of the West."[26]

The context of the Pope's remarks concerning the "silent apostasy" was his spiritual assessment of a Europe that was *once Catholic*, and the majority of whose inhabitants still identify themselves nominally as Catholics. Thus, the silent apostasy is explicitly a departure from the Catholic Faith even though the Faith is still nominally professed and even outwardly practiced in parish churches.

But the Pope's assessment can hardly be limited to Europe. The situation is no different in North America, where opinion polls show that the overwhelming majority of nominal Catholics no longer heed the Church's teaching on contraception, abortion, divorce and remarriage or any other matter (such as "gay rights" legislation) on which predominant American opinion diverges from Church teaching. The same polls also show that the great majority of Catholics no longer believe in such fundamental Catholic doctrines as the Real Presence of Christ in the Holy Eucharist. Consequently, in North America we see precisely what the Pope lamented in Europe: "the diminishing number of births, the decline in the number of vocations to the priesthood and religious life, and the difficulty, if not the outright refusal, to make lifelong commitments, including marriage."[27]

---

[26]"Religious Unbelief in the World: Cardinal Poupard Draws a Sobering Sketch of Rising Secularism"; interview with Zenit.org, July 14, 2004.
[27]See, e.g. "A Gallup Survey of Catholics Regarding Holy Communion," January 1992.

If this is true in both Europe and North America, then *the whole of the Western Church* is afflicted by "silent apostasy," without any formal abjuration of the Faith. The bulk of nominal Catholics in the West generally live, to recall the Pope's own words, "as if God does not exist." Or, as St. Thomas Aquinas put it, they live "in rebellion against God's commandments, an act that is to be found in every mortal sin." (Of course, we are speaking here, as the Pope did, of the objective condition of this mass of people, without any judgment of the subjective state of individual souls.) That is, apostasy in this sense of the word consists in a *revolt* against God's law as expounded by His Church. The very word revolt denotes: "To turn away; to abandon or reject something...."[28]

Before the Second Vatican Council ended in 1965, no Pope had spoken of a widespread *apostasy* among once-faithful Catholics, even if there were many pre-conciliar papal statements concerning the increasingly disastrous state of the world in general and the threat this situation posed to the Church. There were no papal lamentations about plummeting Catholic birth rates or the drastic decline in vocations to the priesthood. Quite the contrary, in the very document convoking Vatican II Pope John XXIII declared that the Church was in the midst of "the rise and growth of the immense energies and of the apostolate of prayer, of action in all fields. It has seen the emergence of a clergy constantly better equipped in learning and virtue for its mission; and of laity which has become ever more conscious of its responsibilities within the bosom of the Church, and, in a special way, of its duty to collaborate with the Church hierarchy."[29] Indeed, by every measurable vital sign of the Church's activity, she had never been healthier than in the years leading up to the Council: conversions were at an all-time high; the seminaries and convents were turning away vocations for lack of space; the Catholic schools were flourishing; the parish churches were filled each Sunday, and there were long lines at the confessional.

Pope John famously envisioned his Council as a metaphorical opening of the window of the Church to the outside world to let in what he believed was some much-needed "fresh air." Within a few years of the Council's conclusion, however, Pope Paul VI was already lamenting that "the opening to the world became a veritable invasion of the Church by worldly thinking. We have perhaps been too weak

---

[28]*Merriam-Webster Unabridged Dictionary.*
[29]Apostolic Constitution *Humanae Salutis*, December 25, 1961.

and imprudent."[30] Only three years after the Council, Pope Paul was forced to admit that the robust Church described by his predecessor "is in a disturbed period of self-criticism, or what could better be called self-demolition." And in 1972, in perhaps the most astonishing remark ever made by a Roman Pontiff, Paul VI declared that "from somewhere or other the smoke of satan has entered the temple of God."

What happened? Or, as the late Msgr. Ruldolph Bandas put the question in 1967, a mere two years after the Council: "How could our Church be so profoundly blighted in so short a time?"[31] It is now widely believed, even if only imprecisely understood, that the Second Vatican Council and the changes in the Church it engendered had something to do with the massive falling away of Catholics in the post-conciliar epoch and the widespread collapse of faith and discipline in the Church. What exactly is the connection?

From Pope Paul's own historic admission, it would appear that the "somewhere or other" from which the smoke of satan suddenly entered the Church was the very "window" John XXIII had opened to the world. Even John Paul II, whose entire pontificate was one long tribute to the "opening" created by the Second Vatican Council, was constrained to issue the warning, in his 1986 enyclical *Dominum et vivificantem*, that when assessing the Council's supposed fruits "one must learn how to 'discern' them carefully from everything that may instead come originally from the 'prince of this world.' This discernment in implementing the Council's work is especially necessary in view of the fact *that the Council opened itself widely to the contemporary world*, as is clearly seen from the important Conciliar Constitutions *Gaudium et Spes* and *Lumen Gentium*." Thus the Pope himself depicted Vatican II—precisely because of its "opening to the world"—as a council whose fruits must be carefully distinguished from what comes from the devil! No other ecumenical council in the history of the Church has carried such a papal caveat.

As the very words of the conciliar Popes themselves would suggest, then, the silent apostasy of Catholics decried by John Paul II resulted directly from the "opening to the world" rued by Paul VI, and that opening resulted from the Second Vatican Council. The "opening to the world" did indeed become an invasion of the Church by worldly thinking, followed by what everyone can see were unprecedented and disorienting changes in virtually every aspect of

---

[30]Speech of November 23, 1973.
[31]*The Wanderer*, August 31, 1967, page 7.

the Church's life—most especially in her liturgy, her theology and her very status as the foundation of a proper social order.

And it is precisely *apostasy*—a turning away from the Catholic Faith—that describes this situation. Cardinal Luigi Ciappi, the late personal theologian to four Popes, including Pope John Paul II, revealed after having read the Third Secret of Fatima that

> In the Third Secret it is foretold, among other things, that the great apostasy in the Church will begin at the top.[32]

John Paul II's own reference to a "silent apostasy" in Europe reflects this predicted failure of the Church's leadership at the highest levels.

Our Lady of Fatima could only have been referring to the coming apostasy in the famous words comprising what Fatima scholars unanimously conclude is the opening line of the Third Secret: "In Portugal *the dogma of the Faith* will always be preserved etc." Although the Vatican has yet to reveal the words of Our Lady indicated by the "etc." that Sister Lucy inserted to hold the place for the contents of the Secret, the words that *are* written would make no sense outside the context of a prediction about the failure to preserve the dogma of the Faith in many other places in the Church. The Third Secret does not predict a failure of the Church herself, but does foretell a failure of her human members, a number of whom are at the top of the Catholic hierarchy.

This interpretation of the Third Secret is confirmed by an historical incident little known in the Catholic world. In 1931 the future Pope Pius XII, when he was still Msgr. Pacelli, serving as Vatican Secretary of State under Pius XI, made an astonishingly accurate prophecy of the coming upheaval in the Church, a prophecy he expressly linked to the Fatima Message:

> I am worried by the Blessed Virgin's messages to little
> Lucy of Fatima. This persistence of Mary about the
> dangers which menace the Church is a divine warning
> against the suicide of altering the faith, in her liturgy,
> her theology and her soul.... I hear all around me

---

[32]Cited in *The Devil's Final Battle*, edited and compiled by Father Paul Kramer, (Terryville, Connecticut: The Missionary Association, 2002), pages 33 and 169 (see http://www.devilsfinalbattle.com/ch4.htm and http://www.devilsfinal battle.com/ch13.htm).

innovators who wish to dismantle the Sacred Chapel, destroy the universal flame of the Church, reject her ornaments and make her feel remorse for her historical past.[33]

That the future Pope linked his prediction to the Message of Fatima is just as astonishing as what he predicted. This was clearly a reference to the Third Secret of Fatima, as the first two Fatima secrets had said nothing of the events Pacelli described in 1931. As he continued, Pius XII made another, even more astonishing, prediction:

> A day will come when the civilized world will deny its God, when the Church will doubt as Peter doubted. She will be tempted to believe that man has become God. In our churches, Christians will search in vain for the red lamp where God awaits them. Like Mary Magdalene, weeping before the empty tomb, they will ask, "Where have they taken Him?"[34]

The prophecy of Pius XII concurs with the statement of Cardinal Ciappi mentioned above: that the Third Secret warns of impending apostasy in the Church that would begin at the top. That apostasy would necessarily involve "the suicide of altering the faith, in her liturgy, her theology and her soul." And what have we seen since Vatican II if not precisely an attempt to alter the liturgy, the theology, and indeed the very soul of the Church? Speaking of the changes in the liturgy in particular, no less than Cardinal Joseph Ratzinger, now Pope Benedict XVI, has written that the Church "*is calling its very being into question* when it suddenly declares that what until now was its holiest and highest possession [the traditional Latin Mass] is strictly forbidden and when it makes the longing for it seem downright indecent."[35] How can such a course of action be anything but a sign of apostasy?

As I will discuss further on in more detail, what we are seeing today is indeed an assault on the liturgy, theology and soul of the Church. That assault has drastically eroded adherence to what true Catholics have always believed according to the infallible dogmatic definitions of the Church. Remove the defined dogmas and the very

---

[33]Roche, *Pie XII Devant L'Histoire*, page 52.
[34]Ibid., page 53.
[35]Ratzinger, *Salt of the Earth*, page 176.

foundations of the Catholic religion disappear, and with them the Faith itself. Speaking at Fatima on May 13, 1982, and alluding perhaps to Our Lady's own reference to an attack on the dogmas of the Faith, Pope John Paul II declared:

> Can the Mother, who with all the force of the love that She fosters in the Holy Spirit and desires everyone's salvation, can She remain silent when She sees the very bases of Her children's salvation undermined? No, She cannot remain silent.

And She did not remain silent at Fatima. She warned us of what was coming, and what we see most clearly today.

Nor can *we* remain silent in the face of apostasy, regardless of who authors it. As St. Paul teaches in Holy Scripture: "But though we, or an angel from heaven, preach a gospel to you besides that which we have preached to you, let him be anathema." (Gal. 1:8) Thus God Himself, speaking through St. Paul, warned us to oppose and condemn *anyone*, no matter how high his office or how great his prestige—even the very Apostles and the angels themselves—if they should try to teach us a Gospel other than the one announced by Christ and preserved intact for 2,000 years by the infallible teaching authority of His Church. No one—absolutely no one—has the authority to change what the Church has always professed, believed and defined infallibly. No one has the authority to lead us into apostasy.

If, as Cardinal Ciappi has told us, the Third Secret predicts an apostasy in the Church that begins at the top, that apostasy will have its collaborators below. And if, as St. Paul teaches, we must oppose even the Church's leaders (Cardinals, bishops, "prestigious" priests) should they try to alter the Gospel, so also must we oppose their collaborators. As Part II will demonstrate, **EWTN** is now one of those collaborators—and a leading one, at that—whether or not its individual directors and television celebrities subjectively intend it to be. That is, EWTN is actively participating in the assault on the Church's liturgy, theology and very soul as the one ark of salvation outside of which no one is saved.

# Chapter 2

# A Great Façade of Novelty

Upon reflection, it becomes apparent that a Catholic is perfectly free to practice the Faith as if the "renewal of Vatican II" had never happened, for the Council did not, in fact, require Catholics to believe or to do a single thing they had not always believed or done before 1962. That is why those who accuse loyal Catholics of "dissenting from Vatican II" can never answer this simple question: "What are the Catholic doctrines of Vatican II from which we are accused of dissenting?" Of course, there are no such doctrines, nor could there be. As the *First* Vatican Council solemnly declared: "For, the Holy Spirit was not promised to the successors of Peter that by His revelation they might disclose new doctrine, but that by His help they might *guard* sacredly the revelation transmitted through the apostles and the deposit of faith, and might faithfully set it forth."[36]

Not even the New Mass, supposedly the greatest fruit of the Council, was ever legally imposed upon the Church in place of the traditional Latin Mass. The Vatican itself now admits that the traditional Latin Mass *was never legally forbidden*, for Pope Paul's promulgation of his Novus Ordo Missae in 1970 did not equate with a prohibition of the traditional Missal. The cat was let out of the bag in 1995 when Cardinal Alfons Stickler (in response to a written question from Father Nicholas Gruner) told the audience at a Catholic conference in New Jersey that a commission of nine Cardinals (namely, Ratzinger, Mayer, Oddi, Stickler, Casaroli, Gantin, Innocenti, Palazzini, and Tomko) had been convened by Pope John Paul II in 1986 to determine the legal status of the traditional Mass. By a vote of 8 to 1 the commission agreed that Paul VI *never legally suppressed the traditional Mass* as opposed to simply promulgating the Novus Ordo. By a vote of 9 to 0, the commission

---

[36]First Vatican Council, *Dogmatic Constitution I on the Church of Christ*, Chapter 4; Denzinger (Dz.), 1836.

agreed that *every priest remained free to use the old Missal*. That the Pope required such a commission to inform him on the legal effect of what his own predecessor had done is quite a commentary on the confused state of the Church today.

Cardinal Stickler further disclosed that in view of the commission's findings, the Pope was presented with a document for his signature, declaring that any priest of the Roman Rite was free to choose between the traditional Missal and the new Missal. The Cardinal also confirmed reports that the Pope was dissuaded from signing the document by certain cardinals who claimed it would cause "division."[37] The Pope later settled on the *Ecclesia Dei* indult of 1988, thus in effect granting permission for what had never actually been forbidden in the first place.

In an address given on the tenth anniversary of *Ecclesia Dei*, no less than the currently reigning Pope (when he was Cardinal Joseph Ratzinger) finally admitted the obvious: that the traditional Latin Mass had never been forbidden and that, indeed, it would be unheard-of for the Church even to attempt such a thing:

> It is good to recall here what Cardinal Newman observed, that the Church, throughout her history, has never abolished nor forbidden orthodox liturgical forms, which would be quite alien to the Spirit of the Church.... The authority of the Church has the power to define and limit the use of such rites in different historical situations, but she never just purely and simply forbids them. Thus the Council ordered a reform of the liturgical books, but it did not prohibit the former books....[38]

In May of 2004 *Inside the Vatican* revealed that Paul VI himself acknowledged he had never forbidden the traditional Mass. In an interview with Father Jean Marie Charles-Roux, age 90, one of the priests who celebrated Mass for Mel Gibson in Rome during the

---

[37]The Cardinal's revelations, to which I was an eyewitness, took place at the Christifideles Conference in Fort Lee, New Jersey on May 20, 1995. The revelations were widely reported in *The Latin Mass*, *Catholic Family News*, *The Remnant* and other Catholic publications and have never been denied by the Vatican.

[38]Address by Cardinal Joseph Ratzinger, Prefect of the Congregation for the Doctrine of the Faith, Ergife Palace Hotel, Rome, Saturday, October 24, 1998.

filming of *The Passion of the Christ*, we learn that "Charles-Roux said to Paul: 'For 18 months I have celebrated the new Mass, but I cannot continue. I was ordained to celebrate the old Mass, and I want to return to it. Will you permit me to do so?' And Paul said: 'Certainly, *I never forbade celebration of the old Mass*; I have only offered an alternative.'"

As for "ecumenism," "dialogue," and "interreligious dialogue," no teaching of the Church requires that the Catholic faithful engage in these post-conciliar novelties, whose meaning is far from clear. No Catholic is obliged to attend prayer meetings with assorted non-Catholic religionists or to join "dialogue" commissions with them, for example. Here we are dealing with "pastoral" initiatives and policies that are in no way imposed on the faithful as binding Catholic doctrine requiring any kind of assent, much less an assent of faith (i.e., the assent required with such articles of the Faith as the Immaculate Conception).

Thus, the Great Façade of novelty that was erected after Vatican II is just that: a façade which merely conceals, but does not change—because it cannot change—the doctrinal and liturgical patrimony which is our birthright as baptized Catholics. Catholics have every right to hold fast to the Faith precisely as it was lived and practiced before the Council. And who can doubt not only our right, but also our duty to do so, given the disastrous results of the conciliar "aggiornamento"? As noted in the Overview, by every empirical measure, and according to every available statistic, the "reforms" of Vatican II have led immediately to drastic declines in the vital signs of the Church's existence: baptisms, conversions, vocations, and adherence to Catholic doctrine. Whatever the "reforms" have touched has immediately begun to decompose: from the liturgy, to the seminaries, to catechesis, to the Catholic schools. The argument that these declines are a mere "coincidence" having nothing to do with the introduction of the post-conciliar novelties is utter nonsense. If the merely human wisdom of the directors of a soft drink company could see that the "new" Coca Cola was harming the company, Catholics should be able to see that the post-conciliar experiment in "new" Catholicism is harming the Church. The evidence of this is simply overwhelming.[39]

---

[39]It is an empirical fact, demonstrated by every available statistic, that the post-conciliar commencement of programmatic ecumenism and dialogue was followed by a sudden and precipitous decline in Church attendance, the number

As the Code of Canon Law states, in the Church "the salvation of souls... must always be the supreme law."[40] The salvation of our souls, not adherence to non-binding novelties, is our first obligation as Catholics. Yet, as I will show, **EWTN** would have us believe that the novelties of the past forty years take precedence over the traditions of the past 2,000 years, even if those novelties have manifestly compromised the Church's primary mission of saving souls.

---

of priests, the number of new ordinations, the number of seminarians and the number of conversions and baptisms. In his book *Index of Leading Catholic Indicators: The Church since Vatican II*, Kenneth C. Jones lays to rest (at least for the sensible person) the truly silly argument that all of these immediate declines following the Council were just coincidental. For a fascinating (however grim) mathematical analysis of the statistics compiled by Jones, see "Springtime Decay," by the mathematician David L. Sonnier, at: http://www.seattlecatholic .com/article_20040119.html.

[40] The Code of Canon Law, Canon 1752.

# Chapter 3

# The Scope of the Crisis

The chronicle of the Church's precipitous decline following the "reforms" engendered by Vatican II has already been set forth in numerous abundantly documented and unimpeachable sources, from the seminal works of Michael Davies to the monumental study *Iota Unum* by Romano Amerio, who was a *peritus* (theological expert) at Vatican II. Informed Catholics need no further proof that the post-conciliar "renewal" has been a disaster. Our own eyes inform us that the introduction of unheard-of novelties into the life of the Church has provoked an unprecedented ecclesial crisis.

For our present purposes it suffices to consider some key admissions of the scope of the crisis by two sources **EWTN** and other New Church apologists cannot pigeonhole with the bogus label "extreme traditionalist": Cardinal Joseph Ratzinger, now Pope Benedict XVI, and Msgr. Klaus Gamber. Forty years after the Second Vatican Council, the candid admission of Cardinal Ratzinger in 1984 is truer than ever:

> The results of the Council seem cruelly to have contradicted the expectations everybody had, beginning with John XXIII and Paul VI.... [W]e have been confronted instead with a continuing process of decay that has gone on largely on the basis of appeals to the Council, and thus has discredited the Council in the eyes of many people.[41]

Although the Cardinal tries to absolve the Council of any blame, claiming that we need to "discover the real Council"[42] (whatever that is), the question remains: Why should the Council *not* be discredited

---

[41]*L'Osservatore Romano*, November 9, 1984.
[42]Ratzinger, *Principles of Catholic Theology*, page 390.

in the eyes of the faithful, seeing that it gave us no new doctrine and no new definitions, but only a collection of ambiguity-laden documents which have caused no end of confusion in the Church, and a supposed "opening to the world" that was immediately followed by what Paul VI himself lamented as "an invasion of the Church by worldly thinking"?[43]

"By their fruits you shall know them," said Our Lord. (Matt. 7:16) The Fathers of Vatican II clearly did not produce the fruits the Church had usually subsequently received from previous ecumenical councils: strong affirmations of doctrine and dogma, condemnations of error, the reestablishment of Church discipline. This time, as Cardinal Ratzinger himself has admitted, the opposite has occurred: a "process of decay." This was a Council that, in fact, expressly *refused to claim for itself the note of infallibility.*[44] Moreover, it was a Council that expressly refused to issue any condemnations of error. As Pope John declared in the Council's opening address: "Nowadays... the spouse of Christ prefers to make use of the medicine of mercy rather than the arms of severity. She considers that she meets the needs of the present day by demonstrating the validity of her teaching rather than by issuing condemnations...."[45] But where, it must be asked, is the mercy in refusing to condemn errors that lead souls to hell? Instead of dogmatic definitions and condemnations of error, the Council wished to have the freedom to indulge in non-traditional "pastoral" formulations whose very novelty alarmed a number of the Council Fathers, leading to the *nota praevia*. On this point we have the posthumously revealed testimony of Bishop Thomas Morris, a Council Father: "I was relieved when we were told that this Council *was not aiming at defining or giving final statements on doctrine*, because a statement of doctrine has to be very carefully formulated and I would have regarded the Council

---

[43]Speech of November 23, 1973.

[44]"In view of the conciliar practice and *pastoral purpose* of the present Council, the sacred Synod defines matters of faith and morals as binding on the Church only when the Synod itself openly declares so." Addenda to *Lumen Gentium*, Explanatory Note of the Theological Commission, in Walter M. Abbott, S.J., ed., *The Documents of Vatican II* (New York: America Press, 1966), pages 97-98. In disobedience to the command of Paul VI, the Preliminary Note was demoted to the status of an addendum to *Lumen Gentium* in some published editions of Council documents.

[45]*Council Daybook*, National Catholic Welfare Conference, Washington, D.C., vol. 1, pages 25, 27.

documents as *tentative and liable to be reformed.*"[46]

When a Council refuses to do what other Councils have done—affirm dogma, condemn error, and restore discipline—the faithful can hardly be surprised when such a council produces confusion and disorder, even if the Holy Ghost prevented outright error from being promulgated as binding Catholic doctrine at Vatican II.

Over the past four decades the Council has been invoked incessantly by the heralds of the post-conciliar "renewal," but the more it is invoked, the more we are urged to pursue its never-quite-explained "opening to the world", the more the "process of decay" accelerates. At this point the faithful are surely entitled to wonder how much longer this pursuit of the "real Council" will go on before the leaders of the Church recognize the manifest truth that the Council provoked an ecclesial disaster.

And besides, if what the former Cardinal Ratzinger called "the real Council" is no more faithful to Catholic truth than what he has presented as the "authentic" Message of Fatima, then the "real Council" is not something we should ever hope to find. In his June 2000 commentary on the Third Secret of Fatima, the Cardinal claimed that the triumph of the Immaculate Heart of Mary occurred 2,000 years ago at the Annunciation (even though Our Lady of Fatima refers to this triumph as a future event, following the conversion of Russia), reduced the Immaculate Heart to any heart that achieves spiritual union with God, and stripped the Message of Fatima of all prophetic content, leaving only a generic prescription for prayer and penance. Ratzinger's commentary cited in support of its "interpretation" of the Fatima Message none other than Edouard Dhanis, a Modernist Jesuit who refused to examine the Fatima archives which utterly refuted his public speculation that Sister Lucy essentially concocted the Fatima prophecies, including those concerning Russia. No wonder the *Los Angeles Times* remarked that Ratzinger's commentary had "gently debunked the cult of Fatima."[47] The Church has no more need of a Modernist "real Council" than it

---

[46]*Catholic World News,* January 22, 1997. This testimony was confided to Catholic journalist Kieron Wood with the understanding that it would not be published until after Bishop Morris' death, which occurred recently.

[47]Cfr. *The Devil's Final Battle*, Chapter 8 (see also http://www.devilsfinal battle.com/ch8.htm); "Catholic Church Unveils Third Secret: The Vatican's Top Theologian Gently Debunks a Nun's Account of Her 1917 Vision That Fueled Decades of Speculation," *Los Angeles Times*, June 27, 2000.

does a Modernist "real" Message of Fatima. The faithful should have nothing to do with either, nor has either ever been imposed by the Church as binding on her members.

As Cardinal Ratzinger has further admitted, at Vatican II something happened in the Church that has never happened before: For the first time ever, the false impression was created that the Church was starting over again; that her historical clock, as it were, had been reset to zero and, for all intents and purposes, the first council of the Church was Vatican II and her first Pope was John XXIII. Here, too, Cardinal Ratzinger confirms our worst suspicions:

> The Second Vatican Council has not been treated as part of the entire living Tradition of the Church, but as an end of Tradition, a new start from zero.... That which was previously considered most holy—the form in which the liturgy was handed down—suddenly appears as the most forbidden of all things, the one thing that can safely be prohibited. It is intolerable to criticize decisions which have been taken since the Council; on the other hand, if men make question of ancient rules, or even of the great truths of the Faith... nobody complains or only does so with great moderation.... *All of this leads a great number of people to ask themselves if the Church of today is really the same as the Church of yesterday, or if they have changed it for something else without telling people....*[48]

Thus, the late Pope's own right hand man, who is now Pope Benedict XVI, acknowledged that the liturgical revolution after Vatican II, combined with the other "decisions taken since the Council"—*decisions*, not Catholic doctrine as such—have led people to believe that somehow the "Church of today" is no longer the same as the "Church of yesterday." Never before in the history of the Church have Catholics had such a perception.

Speaking of the post-Vatican II changes in the liturgy, it was the same Cardinal Ratzinger who wrote: "I am convinced that the ecclesial crisis in which we find ourselves today depends in great part on the collapse of the liturgy."[49] Never before in Church history

---

[48]Statement to the Bishops of Chile (1988).
[49]Ratzinger, Joseph Cardinal, *La Mia Vita*, quoted by Michael Davies in *The Latin Mass*, Fall 1997.

could it be said that the liturgy had "collapsed." And why did the liturgy collapse, if not due to the unprecedented "implementation" of Vatican II via the New Mass of Paul VI? Obviously, there can be no other reason.

Even more dramatic is Cardinal Ratzinger's observation that the imposition of Pope Paul's new Missal in place of the traditional Missal was "a breach into the history of the liturgy whose consequences could only be tragic."[50] What good reason was there to subject the Church to this tragedy? Cardinal Ratzinger went on to ask a question perhaps more devastating than any directly critical assessment of our situation: "[W]hen the community of faith, the worldwide unity of the Church and her history, and the mystery of the living Christ are *no longer visible in the liturgy*, where else, then, is the Church to become visible in her spiritual essence?"[51] So, even Cardinal Ratzinger suggests that the Faith *is no longer visible* in the "reformed" liturgy of the post-conciliar Church. How can such a development be anything but the result of what Sister Lucy called a "diabolical disorientation" of the Church's leaders, beginning "at the top" as Cardinal Ciappi said concerning the contents of the Third Secret? Clearly, Cardinal Ratzinger's own admissions confirm that the Church is undergoing an assault on her liturgy, her theology and her very soul, precisely as Pope Pius XII predicted in 1931.

Yet one cannot fail to note that Cardinal Ratzinger himself was deeply involved in the very process of decay that he lamented. Indeed, while issuing profoundly negative judgments on the outcome of the Council, Cardinal Ratzinger *defended* the new orientation of the Church. It was none other than he who declared in 1987 that the Council documents *Gaudium et Spes* (on the Church in the "modern world") and *Dignitatis Humanae* (on religious liberty) constituted "*a revision of the Syllabus of Pius IX, a kind of countersyllabus*" that "corrected" what the Cardinal dared to call the "*one-sidedness* of the position adopted by the Church under [Blessed] Pius IX and [Saint] Pius X in response to the situation created by the new phase of history inaugurated by the French Revolution..."[52] Cardinal Ratzinger also opined that the age-old model of the Catholic

---

[50]Ratzinger, Joseph Cardinal, *Milestones: Memoirs: 1927-1977* (San Francisco: Ignatius Press, 1998), page 148.
[51]Ibid., page 149.
[52]Joseph Ratzinger, *Principles of Catholic Theology* (San Francisco: Ignatius Press, 1989), pages 381-82.

state in union with the Holy See, as enshrined in the Spanish, Italian and other concordats still in effect at the time of the Council, embodied "a view of the world that no longer corresponded to the facts" and "an obsolete Church-state relationship." Cardinal Ratzinger depicted Vatican II as "an attempt at an official reconciliation with the new era inaugurated in 1789."[53] And it was Cardinal Ratzinger who employed rhetoric reminiscent of the French Revolution when he wrote that "'the demolition of bastions' [in the Church] is a long-overdue task.... She [the Church] must relinquish many of the things that have hitherto spelled security for her and that she has taken for granted. *She must demolish longstanding bastions* and trust solely the shield of faith."[54]

In short, Cardinal Ratzinger has approved of the Church's "attempt" to adopt the very view the *Syllabus* of Blessed Pius IX condemns: namely, that "the Roman Pontiff can and ought to reconcile himself and come to terms with progress, liberalism and modern civilization." Pius IX condemned any such conciliation with "the modern world" because he knew that "progress, liberalism and modern civilization" seek to destroy the Faith by destroying Catholic social order. "Progress, liberalism and modern civilization" are the very program of international Freemasonry, which Pius IX's immediate successor, Pope Leo XIII, described in his monumental encyclical condemning Freemasonry, *Humanum Genus*: "[T]hey especially desire to assail the Church with irreconcilable hostility... [T]hey will never rest until they have destroyed whatever the Supreme Pontiffs have established for the sake of religion."

As Professor James Billington, the former Librarian of Congress, demonstrated in his renowned study *Fire in the Minds of Men*, the French Revolutionaries, inspired by the German "illuminist" philosophy of Adam Weishaupt, plotted in their Masonic lodges to overthrow Catholic social order and replace the Catholic religion with "the revolutionary faith." What Cardinal Ratzinger calls "the new phase of history inaugurated by the French Revolution" is precisely what Leo XIII described as "the destruction of whatever the Supreme Pontiffs have established for the sake of religion" — beginning, first of all, with Catholic social order in a Catholic state, which Cardinal Ratzinger dismissed as "obsolete."

---

[53]Ibid., page 381.
[54]Ratzinger, *Principles of Catholic Theology*, page 391.

Once Catholic social order was overthrown in France, Italy and the rest of Europe, all that remained for the keepers of the revolutionary faith was to carry the principles of the French Revolution into the very citadel of the Church and, to the extent humanly possible, overthrow her. With the conciliar "opening to the world" that aim was accomplished, leaving Pope Paul himself famously to lament, as already noted, that that opening had allowed the invasion of the Church by worldly thinking. Worldly thinking invaded not only the sacred liturgy, reducing it to the Protestantized rubble we see today, but also the very thinking of Churchmen, who changed their entire approach to the world from one of militant opposition and evangelical zeal to a submissive accommodation to "the modern world" — the very thing Cardinal Ratzinger describes as "an attempt at an official reconciliation with the new era inaugurated in 1789."

Perhaps no one has summed up the results of the conciliar "opening to the world" better than the perceived "moderate," Monsignor Klaus Gamber, the renowned liturgist whose short work *The Reform of the Roman Liturgy*, to which Cardinal Ratzinger himself wrote an approving preface, is unsparing in its criticism of the liturgical reforms of Paul VI. Here, with Cardinal Ratzinger's approval, is what Monsignor Gamber wrote of the state of the Church in 1993:

> Is this the spring people had hoped would emerge from the Second Vatican Council? Instead of a genuine renewal in our Church, we have seen *only novelties.* Instead of our religious life entering a period of new invigoration, as has happened in the past, what we see now is *a form of Christianity that has turned towards the world.*[55]

Only novelties and a form of Christianity that has turned towards the world: this, in a nutshell, is the legacy of the Council. Cardinal Ratzinger agrees with Msgr. Gamber's lamentation of this legacy, for he endorsed Gamber's book. Yet the Cardinal has also defended the Council's clearly disastrous attempt at a "reconciliation" of the Church with the "modern world," which is only part of the conciliar "opening to the world" that is precisely what has given us the legacy Cardinal Ratzinger laments.

---

[55]Msgr. Klaus Gamber, *The Reform of the Roman Liturgy*, page 102.

Concerning the new Mass, Monsignor Gamber, even more clearly than Cardinal Ratzinger, rightly described it as a completely unprecedented break with the Church's entire liturgical tradition: "there has never actually been *an actual break with Church tradition, as has happened now*, and in such a frightening way, where almost everything the Church represents is being questioned."[56] Indeed, to overthrow the liturgy is to open the way to the overthrow of everything else; for the sacred liturgy of the Church is her most redoubtable rampart against heresy. As Pope Pius XII declared in his monumental encyclical *Mediator Dei*, defending the traditional Latin liturgy against innovation, "The use of the Latin language, customary in a considerable portion of the Church, is a manifest and beautiful sign of unity, as well as an effective antidote for any corruption of doctrinal truth."[57] Likewise, in *Veterum Sapientia*, John XXIII, literally weeks before the Council, declared: "In the exercise of their paternal care they [the bishops] shall be on their guard lest anyone under their jurisdiction, *eager for revolutionary changes*, writes against the use of Latin in the teaching of the higher sacred studies or *in the liturgy*, or through prejudice makes light of the Holy See's will in this regard or interprets it falsely."[58] It can hardly be a sign of the working of the Holy Ghost that this Apostolic Constitution was discarded within months of the close of Vatican II.

Surveying the results of what Paul VI had done, Monsignor Gamber concluded that "the traditional Roman rite, more than one thousand years old and until now the heart of the Church, was destroyed."[59] The effects of that destruction, wrote Gamber, threaten the existence of the Faith itself:

> The real destruction of the traditional Mass, of the traditional Roman Rite with a history of more than one thousand years, *is the wholesale destruction of the faith on which it was based*, a faith that had been the source of our piety and of our courage to bear witness to Christ and His Church... Many Catholics agonize over the question: what can be done about the loss of our faith and of our liturgy?[60]

---

[56] Ibid., page 109.
[57] *Mediator Dei*, n. 60.
[58] *Veterum Sapientia*, February 22, 1962.
[59] Gamber, *op. cit.*, pages 98-99.
[60] Ibid., pages 98-99.

But as Chapter 7 will show, EWTN does not agonize over this question. Rather, EWTN defends and promotes the new liturgy and opposes restoration of the traditional Latin Mass.

This then, is the legacy of Vatican II: the liturgy has collapsed, no one knows where the priests for the next generation will come from because there are almost no vocations, and the missions are practically dead. Only 25% of baptized Catholics even bother to attend Mass any longer, and of these the majority see nothing wrong with contraception, divorce and remarriage, or even abortion in at least some cases. Catholics have become virtually indistinguishable from liberal Protestants in their moral beliefs. John Paul II and Sister Lucy are dead; Russia, which is now a neo-Stalinist dictatorship, has yet to be converted; while the once-Christian West endures the "silent apostasy" lamented by John Paul II. This is the scope of the crisis that confronts the Church today. As we shall see in due course, EWTN's promotion of New Church novelties of all kinds, broadcast to the entire world as if they were authentic Catholicism, has contributed greatly to that very crisis.

# Chapter 4

# What Does it Mean to Be a Catholic?

In the Overview I mentioned Cardinal Ciappi's revelation that the Third Secret of Fatima predicts that "the great apostasy in the Church will begin at the top." In the following pages I will show that **EWTN** not only defends and promotes the very things that have induced this apostasy, but also takes the position that Catholics who do not adhere to the post-conciliar novelties are less than orthodox, disloyal to "the Magisterium," and even "schismatic." That is, EWTN (along with all the other leaders of the New Church establishment) dares to claim that *Catholics who have simply continued to practice the Faith of our fathers without alteration* are suddenly no longer to be considered loyal members of the Church.

This, of course, is a monstrous lie—a total inversion of the proper order of things, and thus a sure sign of diabolism at work. It is itself an element of apostasy in the Church, a manifestation of the very phenomenon Pope Paul VI himself noted when he admitted: "from somewhere or other the smoke of satan has entered the temple of God."[61] For indeed, the attack on Roman Catholic Tradition by many of the leaders of the Church since Vatican II, the attempt to make the adherents of Tradition into outcasts in their own Church, is precisely what the current ecclesial crisis involves.

As I will discuss in Part II, EWTN and the other self-appointed arbiters of what I call post-conciliar correctness, both within and without the hierarchy, are trying to drive the Catholic defenders of Tradition into the deserts of the post-conciliar landscape. The members of the New Church establishment would have us believe they alone are the guardians of orthodoxy, while the "pre-Vatican II" Catholics, who simply hold fast to what has been handed down to them by their ancestors—just as Catholics have always done—are

---

[61]Speech of June 30, 1972.

suspect and must be shunned.

But who is the Catholic party in this time of confusion, and who is not? What does it *mean* to be a Catholic? To be a Catholic is to profess and practice the Catholic Faith whole and entire. As the Church declares in the Athanasian Creed: "Whoever wishes to be saved, needs above all to hold the Catholic Faith; unless each one preserves this *whole and inviolate*, he will without a doubt perish in eternity."[62]

But to be a Catholic means something else that has been all but forgotten over the past four decades of ceaseless innovation in the Church: it means not only adherence to all of the Church's dogmatic teachings, without exception, but also to her *received and approved rites for the administration of the sacraments and all of the other elements of her ecclesiastical tradition*. The Church's "received and approved" rites are those which have been transmitted down through the centuries—handed over, delivered, entrusted for safekeeping—as part of the Church's unbroken Tradition. Concerning the Church's received and approved rites the Council of Trent declared:

> If anyone says that the *received and approved* rites customarily used in the Catholic Church for the solemn administration of the sacraments can be changed into other new rites by any pastor in the Church whosoever, let him be *anathema*.[63]

The Council of Trent also anathematized those who would discard or tamper with the received and approved rites:

> If anyone says that the *received and approved* rites of the Catholic Church, accustomed to be used in the administration of the sacraments, may be despised or omitted by the ministers without sin and at their pleasure, or may be changed by any pastor of the churches to other new ones, let him be anathema.[64]

And, as Pope St. Pius X reminded us in *Pascendi*, his monumental encyclical against the Modernists:

---

[62]"The Creed 'Quicumque'"; Denzinger, 39.
[63]Council of Trent, Session VII, Canon 13 on "The Sacraments in General".
[64]Ibid.

> But for Catholics nothing will remove the authority of the second Council of Nicea, where it condemns those "who dare, after the impious fashion of heretics, to deride the *ecclesiastical traditions*, to invent novelties of some kind… or endeavor by malice or craft to overthrow *any one of the legitimate traditions* of the Catholic Church"…. Wherefore the Roman Pontiffs, Pius IV and Pius IX, ordered the insertion in the profession of faith of the following declaration: "I most firmly admit and embrace the apostolic *and ecclesiastical* traditions and *other observances* and constitutions of the Church."

As we can see from these pronouncements of the Church, to be a Catholic means to hold fast not only to everything Christ and the Apostles personally taught and which has been handed on by the Church, but also everything the Church's teaching office (Magisterium) has taught since the Apostolic Age in keeping with the Gospel: the Creeds, decrees of ecumenical councils and Popes, the papal encyclicals and so forth. But being Catholic *also* means holding fast to the sacred liturgy and the innumerable other traditions and observances of the Church mentioned by St. Pius X.

In sum, to be Catholic means to believe *and practice* the Faith in accordance with the doctrines, dogmas, morals, liturgy, rituals, customs and observances handed down by the Church in the unbroken continuity of Tradition, which embraces both traditions of apostolic origin and those ecclesiastical traditions approved over the ages by the Church since the time of the Apostles.

Conversely, to be a Catholic means *not* to adhere to novelties that would undermine any part of Tradition—either apostolic or ecclesiastical. Rather, Catholics must abhor and reject such novelties. As St. Teresa of Avila once said, she would die a hundred deaths for the smallest ritual of the Catholic Church. And notice that St. Pius X, in the above-quoted passage from *Pascendi*, refers to the teaching of his predecessors Pius IX and Pius IV, and also refers all the way back to the Second Council of Nicea (787). Pius X did this to demonstrate the absolute historical continuity of the Church's teaching that Catholics must adhere to the whole of *both* components of the Church's overall Tradition: apostolic and ecclesiastical.

This is why, as Pius X observed, both Pius IV and Pius IX made such adherence part of the *professions of faith* they prescribed for the universal Church. And, as noted, the Councils of Florence and Trent anathematized—held to be accursed and excluded from the Church—those who would refuse to embrace the received and approved rites of the Church for the administration of the sacraments, including the traditional rite of Mass. When Popes or Councils (headed by Popes) prescribe something as part of the Faith and require Catholics to profess their belief in it, or when they anathematize some error against the Faith, *they are infallible in doing so*, and such teaching *can never be reformed*.[65] That is, a later Pope or Council could never declare that Catholics are *not* bound to "firmly admit and embrace the apostolic *and ecclesiastical traditions* and *other observances* and constitutions of the Church."

This means, for example, that no Pope could ever require Catholics to reject the approved and received rite of Mass in the Church: the traditional Latin Mass, canonized in perpetuity by Pope St. Pius V in his Bull *Quo Primum* (1570).[66] As already shown, however, Pope Paul VI *never did so*, contrary to the false impression created over the 35 years since promulgation of his new Missal. It is now conceded that Paul VI never revoked *Quo Primum*. The Holy Ghost would never allow any Pope to do such a thing.

Therefore, only one who holds fast to all of the Church's doctrines, dogmas, received and approved rites "and *other observances* and constitutions of the Church" is truly and properly Catholic. That EWTN does not meet this definition of Catholicity will be manifest from the evidence presented in Part II.

---

[65]See, *Catholic Encyclopedia* (1907), "Infallibility," § 5.

[66]"Furthermore, by these presents [this law], in virtue of Our Apostolic authority, We grant and concede in perpetuity that, for the chanting or reading of the Mass in any church whatsoever, this Missal is hereafter to be followed absolutely, without any scruple of conscience or fear of incurring any penalty, judgment, or censure, and may freely and lawfully be used. Nor are superiors, administrators, canons, chaplains, and other secular priests, or religious, of whatever title designated, obliged to celebrate the Mass otherwise than as enjoined by Us. We likewise declare and ordain that no one whosoever is forced or coerced to alter this Missal, and that this present document cannot be revoked or modified, but remain always valid and retain its full force..."

# Chapter 5

# Modernism: The Synthesis of All Heresies

The most succinct way to describe the entire crisis in the Church, which I have just outlined, is to say that it is the result of the heresy of *Modernism*. As already mentioned, in *Pascendi* (1907), Pope St. Pius X, writing at the turn of the twentieth century, condemned Modernism in all its aspects. The many complexities of this heresy, which *Pascendi* calls "the synthesis of all heresies,"[67] are beyond the scope of this small book. Suffice it to say in general that a Modernist is someone who holds that both apostolic and ecclesiastical tradition are subject to substantial change over time: that dogmas and doctrines can "evolve" to acquire a different sense or even an entirely different meaning from what they had before, and that the received and approved liturgical rites of the Church and her other established observances can be altered or even entirely discarded whenever it seems convenient.

Quite simply, the **Modernist** sees *nothing* of unalterable permanence in the Church, and ultimately denies the very concept of objective truth itself. This is why St. Pius X said of the Modernists:

> there is no part of Catholic truth from which they hold their hand, none that they do not strive to corrupt. Further, none is more skillful, none more astute than they, in the employment of a thousand noxious arts; for they double the parts of rationalist and Catholic, and this so craftily that they easily lead the unwary into error...

Note well Pius X's phrase "they *double the parts of rationalist and Catholic...* to lead the unwary into error." That is, the Modernists pose as pious Catholics while they are busy undermining the Faith of the unwary. "Hence," St. Pius warned, "in their books you find some

---

[67]*Pascendi*, n. 39.

things which might well be expressed by a Catholic, but in the next page you find other things which might have been dictated by a rationalist..." The Modernists may seem Catholic one moment, but in the next they are attacking some aspect of the Faith. And they do this insidious work of combining truth with error by "the employment of a thousand noxious arts."

Because the threat of Modernism was so great—for Modernists were rearing their heads in many places in the Church at the time— St. Pius X commanded every member of the Catholic clergy and every theologian take the Oath Against Modernism that he promulgated. An extensive study of the Oath is not possible here, but two of its provisions are particularly pertinent to this discussion:

> I sincerely hold that the doctrine of faith was handed down to us from the apostles through the orthodox Fathers *in exactly the same meaning and always in the same purport*. Therefore, *I entirely reject the heretical misrepresentation* that dogmas evolve and change from one meaning *to another different from the one which the Church held previously*.

> I hold with certainty and sincerely confess that faith is not a blind sentiment of religion welling up from the depths of the subconscious under the impulse of the heart and the motion of a will trained to morality; but faith is a genuine assent of the intellect *to truth received by hearing from an external source*.

Part II will demonstrate that the New Church establishment, including such organizations as **EWTN**, at least implicitly claims that the Church's dogmas have somehow changed "from one meaning to another different from the one the Church held previously." This is what is implied when New Church spokesmen accuse wholly orthodox Catholics of "dissenting from Vatican II"—as if a Council held from 1962-1965 had somehow changed what Catholics were expected to believe during the previous nineteen centuries. This is what they imply, and even state explicitly, when they claim that since Vatican II the Church has achieved a "new and deeper understanding" of the spiritual condition of non-Catholics, such that the Church has "relaxed" or "broadened her interpretation" of the dogma that those outside of her cannot be saved.

As we shall also see, these same New Church spokesmen, including those who direct EWTN today, at least implicitly deny that true faith requires "a genuine assent of the intellect *to truth received by hearing from an external source.*" They do this by downplaying to the point of irrelevance the requirement that those who would be saved actually adhere to exactly what the Catholic Church—an "external source" founded by God Himself—specifically teaches for our salvation. Thanks to the "ecumenism" and "interreligious dialogue" that EWTN helps to promote, the false impression has arisen that an explicit profession of the *Catholic Faith* is no longer necessary for one's eternal salvation, but only for a certain "fullness" of the truth that is desirable, but not strictly necessary, to attain eternal beatitude.

In *Pascendi* St. Pius X also described "the Modernist as reformer"—that is, the Modernist in his subversive plan to innovate the liturgy, discipline and governance of the Church in order to bring it up to date with "modern times":

> From all that has preceded, it is abundantly clear how great and how eager is the passion of such men for innovation. *In all Catholicism there is absolutely nothing on which it does not fasten.*

> They wish philosophy to be reformed, especially in the ecclesiastical seminaries. They wish the scholastic philosophy to be relegated to the history of philosophy... and the young men to be taught modern philosophy which [they say] alone is true and suited to the times in which we live...

> Regarding worship, they say, the number of external devotions is to be reduced, and steps must be taken to prevent their further increase, though, indeed, some of the admirers of symbolism are disposed to be more indulgent on this subject.

> They cry out that ecclesiastical government requires to be reformed in all its branches, but especially in its disciplinary and dogmatic departments. They insist that both outwardly and inwardly it must be brought into harmony with *the modern conscience which now wholly tends towards democracy*; a share in ecclesiastical

government should therefore be given to the lower ranks of the clergy and even to the laity and authority which is too much concentrated should be decentralized.

The Roman Congregations and especially the Index [of forbidden books] and the Holy Office, must be likewise modified. *The ecclesiastical authority must alter its line of conduct in the social and political world*; while keeping outside political organizations it must adapt itself to them in order to penetrate them with its spirit... What is there left in the Church which is not to be reformed by them and according to their principles?

As we can see today, every one of these points in the program of "the Modernist as reformer" has been achieved since Vatican II: (a) the scholastic philosophy of St. Thomas Aquinas has been abandoned in the seminaries; (b) the liturgy has been "simplified" and radically altered; (c) the Church has been democratized under the vague notion of "collegiality"; (d) the Roman Congregations have not only been modified, but the Index was abolished by Paul VI and the Holy Office converted into the non-confrontational Congregation for the Doctrine of the Faith; and, (e) ecclesiastical authority has adapted itself to the modern social and political world—the very "opening to the world" which Paul VI himself came to regret, but too late. As Part II will demonstrate, EWTN either promotes or defends this entire program of the "Modernist as reformer."

How did this happen? Although St. Pius X succeeded in suppressing the Modernist uprising of his day, with all but a handful of rebellious clerics in Europe subscribing to the Oath Against Modernism, a new Modernist uprising succeeded in breaking through during and after Vatican II, almost exactly fifty years after Pius X's death in 1914.

As the previous discussion should make clear, it was precisely this Modernist breakthrough that the future Pius XII foresaw 31 years before the Council began, when he declared to his astonished companions that Our Lady of Fatima had issued "a divine warning against the suicide of altering the faith, in her liturgy, her theology and her soul...." and that "a day will come when the civilized world will deny its God, when the Church will doubt as Peter doubted. She will be tempted to believe that man has become God." What Pius XII described was the triumph of Modernism throughout the human element of the Church, producing what is undoubtedly the greatest crisis in Church history.

The aim of this discussion is to show, therefore, that it is not Catholics who uphold Tradition—the doctrine, dogma, liturgy and practice of the Faith in all its integrity—who are suspect, but rather the Modernist "innovators" foreseen by Pius XII, who have foisted all manner of unheard-of novelty upon the Church, and subjected the Church's very identity to attack.

With the post-conciliar crisis worsening with each passing day, the time for useless diplomacy and false charity is over. The time has come to put the matter clearly: Those who have held fast to the Faith of our fathers since Vatican II are Catholics. Those who in any way defend or promote the ecclesial "suicide" described by Pius XII in his prophecy linked to Fatima are not, objectively speaking, authentically Catholic. They are, more or less, Modernists infected by the Modernist heresy.

Having laid the groundwork for an understanding of the crisis in the Church as a Modernist resurgence provoking widespread apostasy, I will now set forth the evidence that EWTN is among the present-day Modernist innovators. The evidence shows that EWTN *does not present the authentic Catholic Faith*, but rather a counterfeit of our religion passed off as sound orthodoxy—a mixture of the orthodox and the heterodox, the sacred and the profane.

To repeat what I said in the Preface, in defending this claim there is no intention of assigning subjective guilt to any individual. It is not possible for one to judge another's internal subjective disposition, even if (as I will show) EWTN routinely accuses good Catholics of being "schismatic" merely for continuing to believe and worship as Catholics always believed and worshipped before 1965. Rather, I am speaking only of the plain import of objective words and deeds of a Modernist character that subvert or tend to subvert the integrity of the Faith.

# Part II

# EWTN's Role
# As Promoter of Modernism

# Chapter 6

# EWTN's "Moderate" Modernism

Within the four walls of the EWTN studios, it is as if the crisis in the Church just described did not exist. Quite the contrary, EWTN defends and promotes the very elements of the crisis as if they were Catholic verities. Heavily invested in the "renewal" of Vatican II and in maintaining close relations with the leading promoters of this disastrous "renewal," EWTN seems intent on protecting that investment from devaluation by the evidence of our senses. EWTN's supporters must not be reminded that there is a crisis, for then they might begin to wonder why EWTN (post-Mother Angelica) is not only failing to do a blessed thing to oppose it, but is also contributing substantially to its prolongation by actively promoting and defending the basic elements of ongoing ecclesial revolution.

As I stipulated in the Overview, EWTN's programming does include a considerable amount of solid Catholic material. But as Pope St. Pius X warned us in *Pascendi*, the danger of Modernism lies precisely in its combination of the orthodox with the heterodox. Anyone who monitors EWTN's programming for any length of time will see that it is saturated with the poison of theological and liturgical novelty, married to the crassness and vulgarity of popular culture, and especially rock and roll. The resulting potpourri can only be called a form of Modernism, seasoned with a few dashes of Tradition.

Perhaps one could call what EWTN presents a kind of "moderate" Modernism, but a moderate Modernist is a Modernist nonetheless. As the following examples will illustrate, there is no question that St. Pius X would be utterly horrified by much of what EWTN presents to the faithful as authentic Roman Catholicism. Never in the history of the Church have Catholics been presented with such an admixture of Catholicism and heterodox novelty under the guise of orthodoxy. As the experience of the past four decades should demonstrate to any Catholic in possession of his faculties, the same **Modernist** version of Catholicism has drastically eroded the integrity of the Faith, despite the pious wrapping in which it is so often presented.

In the following chapters I will examine the evidence of how EWTN supports the ruinous regime of New Church novelty that has emerged since Vatican II. The evidence will be augmented by the testimony of someone who knows EWTN from the inside: Dr. William J. Peterson. Dr. Peterson is a retired medical doctor who was employed in EWTN's Viewer Services Department from October 2001 until February 2004. During his employment, Peterson was asked to join EWTN's "theological committee," headed by the layman Colin B. Donovan, which met every two weeks to discuss EWTN's theological positions. The majority of the committee's members at the time, none of them priests, consisted of recently converted Protestants, two of whom were former Protestant ministers.

Like many Catholics, Dr. Peterson was encouraged by Mother Angelica's militancy and thought that her network could actually become a force for restoration in the Church: "Mother was there and she was preaching orthodoxy and there was hope," he told me in a recent interview. "She had broadcast one Tridentine Mass and it was hoped that maybe things might change and that she might get enough courage to become a traditionalist." As Peterson's own experience confirmed, however, after Mother's departure under episcopal pressure all hope of such a change in direction was dashed. Only two months after Peterson's hire in October 2001, Mother Angelica left the airwaves for good, her resignation from EWTN's board of directors having already taken place behind the scenes. To recall Raymond Arroyo's words: "By the end of 2001, Mother Angelica's detachment from EWTN was complete." The management of the network fell completely into the hands of its more liberal and "ecumenically"-minded lay directors, many of them ex-Protestants.

Dr. Peterson soon realized that he was a closet "traditionalist" — another word for simply a Catholic who has not changed his practice of the Faith over the past forty years—in an environment that was utterly hostile to any true restoration of Tradition. It became clear to Peterson that despite some traditional Catholic elements, EWTN would simply follow the prevailing winds of change wherever they led: "I had seen the watering down of the Faith... They were

defending the constant ecumenism, the lack of missionary zeal...
Before they stopped kneeling for Communion they supported that
diligently. As soon as the bishops stopped that, they supported
standing for Communion. Hypocrisy! I mean, they would support
one thing... then they suddenly changed their mind..." Peterson was
here referring specifically to EWTN's promotion of a Novus Ordo
liturgy with certain superficially "conservative" adaptations. This is
the same liturgy Msgr. Gamber, writing with Cardinal Ratzinger's
personal endorsement, called "the real destruction of the Roman
Rite" and "the wholesale destruction of the faith on which it was
based." It is with this liturgy that our examination of the case against
EWTN begins.

# Chapter 7

# EWTN's Promotion of Liturgical Destruction

As I mentioned in Part I, the Church teaches that the traditional Latin Mass is a bulwark against heresy in the realm of the liturgy, which is the very heart of our religion. The Mass is where Catholics encounter the central mysteries of the Faith and are reinforced in their fidelity. To tamper with the Mass is to tamper with the life of the Church itself and to risk mass apostasy—a turning away from the Faith. For this very reason Pius XII spoke of "the suicide" of altering the faith in the Church's liturgy, first of all. In 1969 Cardinal Ottaviani (who was no less than the former Prefect of the Holy Office) and Cardinal Bacci warned of precisely this danger in the letter introducing their famous *Critical Study* of Pope Paul's unprecedented New Mass (*Novus Ordo*), just before the *Novus Ordo* missal was promulgated:

> The innovations in the Novus Ordo and the fact that all that is of perennial value finds only a minor place, if it subsists at all, could well turn into a certainty the suspicions already prevalent, alas, in many circles, that truths which have always been believed by the Christian people, can be changed or ignored without infidelity to that sacred deposit of doctrine to which the Catholic Faith is bound for ever. Recent reforms have amply demonstrated that *fresh changes in the liturgy could lead to nothing but complete bewilderment on the part of the faithful, who are already showing signs of restiveness and of an indubitable lessening of faith.*[68]

---

[68]Alfredo Cardinal Ottaviani and Antonio Cardinal Bacci, *The Ottaviani Intervention* (Rockford, Illinois: TAN Books and Publishers, 1992), page 32.

As Pius XII and these two Cardinals understood, if the Mass were changed, then the faithful would be led to believe that the truths of the Faith the Mass is supposed to enshrine have also been changed. This is why the traditional Latin Mass—the received and approved rite of Mass in the Church—is a bulwark against heresy and apostasy. There are five basic reasons for this:

- First, the Latin language, which never changes, preserves the exact meaning and sense of the theological doctrine of the Mass as expressed in its text, principally the sacrosanct Roman Canon.

- Second, the Roman Canon, the very heart of the Mass in which the Consecration occurs, expresses perfectly the nature of the Mass as a Holy Sacrifice of the Son to the Father with the four-fold purpose of Adoration, Thanksgiving, Reparation and Petition. That is, the Mass (1) gives honor and glory to God, (2) offers thanks to God for His benefits—first and foremost the gift of His Son's sacrifice on the Cross; (3) makes reparation for and obtains the remission of sins; (4) obtains graces and favors, both spiritual and temporal.[69] The Roman Canon has existed in its present form since at least the fifth century, when "the Canon of the Mass had attained the form it has kept until now."[70]

- Third, the Offertory Prayers, which precede the Roman Canon, proclaim the Holy Sacrifice about to be offered during the Canon and affirm the sacrificial nature of the Mass in the minds of the faithful.

- Fourth, the orientation of the altar and the priest toward the East, from whence Our Lord will come again, rather than toward the people, reinforces the understanding of a Sacrifice being offered to God, not to "the community."

---

[69]*The New Roman Missal*, Rev. F.X. Lasance, (New York: 1945), Introduction, pages 16-22.
[70]Gamber, Klaus, *The Reform of the Roman Liturgy* (San Juan Capistrano, California: Una Voce Press, 1994), page 24.

- Fifth, the venerable and ancient practice of receiving Communion on the tongue from the hand of the priest while kneeling, *which is still the law of the Church,*[71] emphasizes the Divine Presence in the Blessed Sacrament, protects the Sacrament from profanation and sacrilege, or even the appearance thereof, and makes clear the radical distinction between the priesthood and the laity.

As Pope Leo XIII observed in declaring Anglican priestly orders absolutely invalid, the Protestant rebels of the sixteenth century understood as well as anyone the Catholic maxim *lex orandi, lex credendi.* Loosely translated, the maxim means that the law of prayer is the law of belief. That is, the way of worship reflects what one believes, so that if one prays in a certain way, over time he will come to believe *as* he prays. Hence, he who prays in the manner of heretics will himself become a heretic. That is precisely why the Protestant

---

[71]Most Catholics do not realize that Communion in the hand is actually a tolerated *exception* to Church law, but only if very precise and strict conditions are met. One has yet to see where those conditions have ever been met in any diocese.

The decree *Memoriale Domini*, issued by Pope Paul VI's Sacred Congregation for Divine Worship on May 28, 1969, decreed that the ancient law of the Church requiring Communion on the tongue must remain in force: "Therefore, taking into account the remarks and the advice of those whom 'the Holy Spirit has placed to rule over' the Churches, in view of the gravity of the matter and the force of the arguments put forward, the Holy Father has decided not to change the existing way of administering Holy Communion to the faithful. The Apostolic See therefore emphatically urges bishops, priests and laity to obey carefully the law which is still valid and which has again been confirmed."

*Memoriale Domini* had been issued precisely to address widespread disobedience to this law of the Church. Cardinal Suenens and other European prelates, aping Bucer and the other Protestant heresiarchs, had instituted the Protestant practice of Communion in the hand in open defiance of Church law, and then dared the Vatican to do something about it. But while *Memoriale Domini* upheld the law mandating Communion on the tongue, the same document fatally compromised with Suenens and the other liturgical rebels in Europe by agreeing that in any region where the abuse of Communion in the hand had already been established — the document uses the phrase "has already developed" — a two-thirds majority of the episcopal conference could petition the Holy See to ratify its disobedience and thus make it legal! This the European rebels promptly did. North America soon followed, even though the abuse had "not already developed" before *Memoriale Domini*.

rebels wanted to change the Catholic Mass: so that Catholics would pray according to their beliefs, rather than those of the Church, and thus be taught to accept Protestant errors. As Leo XIII wrote:

> They [Cranmer and the Anglican "reformers"] knew only too well the intimate bond which unites faith and worship, *lex orandi* and *lex supplicandi*; and so, under the pretext of restoring the liturgy to its primitive form, they corrupted it in many respects to bring it into accord with the errors of the innovators....

Luther, Calvin, Cranmer, Zwingli and the other Protestant rebels knew that to make the Catholic religion conform to their new heretical religions, all of which rejected the Mass as Sacrifice, they would first have to abolish the above-noted five elements of the Catholic liturgical bulwark: Latin, the Roman Canon, the Offertory, the Eastward-facing priest and altar, and Communion on the tongue. And that is exactly what they did.

The Overview notes how Mother Angelica had delivered a commentary, before she lost control of the EWTN network, in which she noted with great irony that the liturgical "reform" following Vatican II *removed the same five elements of the Catholic liturgical bulwark* that the Protestant rebels removed, thus accomplishing what has rightly been called a "liturgical revolution" in the Church. We have already seen how Cardinal Ratzinger and Msgr. Gamber concede that this liturgical revolution has been devastating to the Church. Even the Roman Canon has been reduced to the status of one of four "Eucharistic Prayers," and is now almost never used. ("Eucharistic Prayer II," which most closely resembles a Protestant communion service, is now the de facto universal substitute for the Roman Canon.)

Despite the encouraging signs we had from Mother Angelica before she relinquished control of EWTN under Vatican pressure, EWTN has failed to live up to its promise as a force for total liturgical restoration in the Church. Quite the contrary, the Novus Ordo Mass EWTN now televises around the world is missing the same five Catholic elements the Protestant rebels hated and the post-conciliar "reformers" removed from the Mass. And while at EWTN Communion on the tongue is "preferred," it is a mere option for those who "prefer" it.

Although EWTN's televised Novus Ordo Mass employs a few

Latin phrases, it uses the abominable ICEL English translation of "Eucharistic Prayer II" (not the Roman Canon). This "translation" — in all four "Eucharistic Prayers" — falsifies the very words of Our Lord by having the priest declare that the Blood of Christ was shed "for you and for *all*," when even the *Protestant "reformers" and Protestant Bible* retained "for you and for *many*."

Msgr. Gamber (again, with Cardinal Ratzinger's approval) called this mistranslation "Truly problematic, in fact truly scandalous" and "a translation inspired by modern theological thinking but not to be found in any historical liturgical text."[72] By this Gamber meant the Modernist attempt to deny the Catholic doctrine of divine election. In merit of the Sacrifice of the Mass, God does indeed bestow benefits upon the whole world: grace is made available to all men, the world is spared chastisements, temporal blessings of other kinds are received by men and nations, and it could even be said that the world itself is held in existence by the merits of the Mass. That is why Saint Padre Pio once observed that it would be easier for the world to exist without the sun than without the Mass. But, as the Church teaches in the Catechism of the Council of Trent (promulgated by Pope St. Pius V), when it comes to the fruit of eternal salvation *only the elect* benefit from the merits of the Mass as applied to them:

> The additional words for you and *for many*, are taken, some from Matthew, some from Luke, but were joined together by the Catholic Church *under the guidance of the Spirit of God.* They serve to declare the fruit and advantage of His Passion. For if we look to its value, we must confess that the Redeemer shed His blood for the salvation of all; but if we look to the fruit which mankind have received from it, we shall easily find that it pertains *not unto all*, but to *many* of the human race. When therefore (our Lord) said: 'For you,' He meant either those who were present, or those chosen from among the Jewish people, such as were, with the exception of Judas, the disciples with whom He was speaking. When He added, "and for many" He wished to be understood to mean *the remainder of the elect* from among the Jews or Gentiles.

---

[72]Gamber, *Reform of the Roman Liturgy*, pages 55-56.

> With reason, therefore, were the words "for all" not used, as in this place the fruits of the Passion are alone spoken of, and *to the elect only did His Passion* **bring the fruit of salvation**. And this is the purport of the Apostle when he says: Christ was offered once to exhaust the sins of many; and also of the words of Our Lord in John: I pray for them; *I pray not for the world, but for them whom thou hast given me*, because they are thine.[73]

Thus, to replace Our Lord's words "for many" with "for all" (again, not even the Protestant Bible dares to do this) is not only scandalous, but also a serious theological error, as it suggests universal salvation, which is heresy. As the Council of Trent infallibly declared, not all men are finally saved by the merits of Christ's Redemption, but only the elect who persevere unto death.[74] Yet EWTN slavishly adheres to the blatant error "for all," and presents its hybrid liturgy as solidly orthodox.

Moreover, while EWTN may have introduced a bit of Latin into its Novus Ordo Mass, it is fully prepared to adopt whatever liturgical innovation the bishops approve or Rome tolerates—even if these changes lead to or suggest heresy. Peterson's experience on the theological committee confirmed this. When the bishops decreed that after 2,000 years of kneeling Catholics must now stand to receive the Blessed Sacrament in America, Donovan's "position was to stand, and almost everyone started standing at Mass and bowing their heads," without even a genuflection when receiving the Sacrament. "There was one man that continued to kneel on both knees, but after awhile he started genuflecting and after a while he started bowing his head. I think they got to him." While Donovan allowed that people should be given the "option" of kneeling to receive Holy Communion, as the Vatican has indicated, he "strongly

---

[73]*The Catechism of the Council of Trent* (1564), Christian Book Club edition (Hawthorne, California: 1985), page 220.

[74]Council of Trent, Sixth Session, Chapter 13, *On the Gift of Perseverance*: "So also as regards the gift of perseverance, of which it is written, he that shall persevere to the end, he shall be saved: which gift cannot be derived from any other but Him, who is able to establish him who standeth that he stand perseveringly, and to restore him who falleth: let no one herein promise himself any thing as certain with an absolute certainty; though all ought to place and repose a most firm hope in God's help."

recommended the bowing of the head" while standing. Today, says Peterson, there are "zero" people who receive Communion while kneeling at Masses in EWTN's chapel or at the basilica EWTN built in Hanceville, Alabama with funds raised during Mother Angelica's tenure. This development, said Peterson, is typical of how EWTN "offers a little bit of traditionalism, but then it slowly disappears."

As EWTN's televised Mass demonstrates—and this is among the most "conservative" Novus Ordo Masses seen today—the post-conciliar liturgy has become a kind of an a la carte affair: a little of this, a little of that. Peterson noted the absurdity of creating a Mass full of such options:

> I mean it was almost ridiculous, it became almost humorous to me, that here was a Mass in quotation marks that was supposed to be simplified, and yet it turned out to be much more complicated than the Tridentine Mass ever was. I mean it was ridiculous... they fought over every little thing, whether you kneeled, whether you bowed your head, whether you genuflected before Communion, whether you kneeled during the Canon, whether you didn't kneel during the Canon—or whatever they call it, the Eucharistic Prayer—whether you received Communion in the hand, whether you received Communion on the tongue. *Think* of all these things—we never had that stuff.

And, as noted, Communion in the hand is always available at EWTN Masses for all who "prefer" it, even if most of the EWTN congregants "prefer" to receive Communion *sub lingua* (on the tongue). In fact, EWTN "experts" defend the practice of Communion in the hand against all objections, no matter how well founded. For example, one member of the faithful inquired on EWTN's Q & A forum concerning *Redemptionis Sacramentum*, the 2004 Vatican instruction on dangers to be avoided respecting the Sacrament of Holy Communion, which provides that "If there is a risk of profanation, then Holy Communion *should not be given in the hand* to the faithful."[75]

---

[75]*Redemptionis Sacramentum* (2004), n. 92, Congregation for Divine Worship and the Discipline of the Sacrament.

This admonition is in line with the above-noted *Memoriale Domini* (1969), issued during the pontificate of Paul VI. This document made the disastrous concession of allowing Communion in the hand as an *exception* to the universal law of the Church mandating Communion on the tongue, which law is still in force today. That exception, however, was limited to locales where the abuse had already become "established" by disobedience, and then *only* if "any danger is avoided of insufficient reverence or false opinions of the Holy Eucharist arising in the minds of the faithful and... any other improprieties be carefully removed."

Now, there is clearly always a danger of profanation or insufficient reverence when Communion is administered in the hand—the very reason it was prohibited in the first place. This is all the more true after forty years of liturgical destruction undermining belief in the Real Presence. Hence the Vatican's own instructions would require forbidding the practice. Accordingly, based on the quoted provision of *Redemptionis Sacramentum*, the inquirer posed the following question to EWTN: "Does this not mean that under certain conditions, i.e., if the priest discovers instances after Mass where the host was thrown away in the aisle, stuck under the pew with chewing gum etc. that he can refuse to give communion [sic] in the hand to prevent this?" Not on your life! says EWTN. Ignoring the clear import of both *Redemptionis Sacramentum* and *Memoriale Domini*, EWTN "expert" Mark J. Gantley, J.C.L., apparently a canon lawyer, gave the following answer: "The liturgical norm for the U.S. permits the faithful to choose whether to receive Holy Communion in the hand or on the tongue. Regardless of your opinion or my opinion, *this is the law*."[76]

So, EWTN favors the liberal American bishops even over the Vatican when it comes to liturgical innovation. What the bishops want is "the law," and no matter if the Blessed Sacrament is profaned. Gantley added that the problem of profanation of the Blessed Sacrament could be "solved" by "simply by following the law as it is written now—that anyone receiving Holy Communion in the hand MUST put the host into his or her mouth immediately in front of the priest (or other minister) giving out Holy Communion." But how is the priest to be certain that members of the congregation

---

[76]See EWTN Q&A Forum, advice by Rev. Gantley of May 27, 2005 on "Re Communion in the hand".

are not "palming" the host while appearing to put it in their mouths (as Satanists do when stealing hosts for their black masses) especially when administration of Holy Communion is now being entrusted to legions of lay "eucharistic ministers" who (by order of the same bishops) are routinely distributing the Blessed Sacrament with their *own* unconsecrated hands while the priest is elsewhere? (And notice how Gantley implicitly approves the use of these "ministers" other than priests.)

EWTN "expert" Fr. Vincent Serpa, O.P. (whose Modernist views are further discussed in Chapter 10) is another dogged defender of the abuse of Communion in the hand. Serpa received the following question from a justly angry member of the faithful: "In my Church [sic], Hosts have been found lying in church pews, on the stairs, and some people even put them in their pockets! Shouldn't Communion on the hand cease because of the large number of abuses?" Ignoring the thrust of the question, which concerned the wide-scale profanation of sacred Hosts due to Communion in the hand, Serpa offered the following irrelevant reply: "Our hands are not any less consecrated than our mouths. Most people sin more or at least as much with their tongues as with their hands."[77] This is a perfect example of how Modernists, like the liberals of secular politics, use empty slogans to distract people from the real issue, which they deftly avoid.

In the same vein is EWTN "expert" Robert Flummerfelt, J.C.L., a lay canon lawyer, who was presented with the question "Can a priest refuse to give communion [sic] in the hand to an individual or entire congregation in a diocese where the Archbishop and Vatican have permitted it? If so under what, if any, conditions can he refuse to give communion [sic] in the hand?" Flummerfelt replied: "No. A priest cannot violate universal law. People may receive Communion in the hand or on the tongue in the Latin Church…"[78]

Of course, as I have noted, "the universal law" cited by Flummerfelt actually *forbids* Communion in the hand, and the exception improvidently allowed by Paul VI does not operate if there is a risk of profanation, which there manifestly is. But EWTN, like the rest of the New Church innovators, is curiously unconcerned about

---

[77]See EWTN Q&A Forum, question from "Megan" on August 25, 2005, answer by Serpa on September 12, 2005.
[78]See EWTN Q&A Forum, advice by Robert J. Flummerfelt, J.C.L. of May 23, 2005 on "Communion in the Hand".

adherence to "the law" when it comes to *defending* the traditions of the Church, including due respect and reverence for Our Lord in the Blessed Sacrament. New Church always harps on "the law," however, when "the law" is being used to undermine or destroy some aspect of traditional Catholic belief or practice. Worse, this misstatement of "the law" comes from two *canon lawyers* on EWTN's roster of "experts". These supposed canonists clearly have no idea that the law of the Church still forbids Communion in the hand.

Thus, according to EWTN, the priest who is supposed to be (by God's own decree) the custodian of the Holy Eucharist he confects and administers to the faithful is nothing but the slave of the personal choice of the lay communicants—whatever they prefer the priest must do, even if he knows that profanation of the Host is occurring in his parish and even if the law, rightly construed, would give him the right to refuse Communion in the hand. Our Lord Himself is made the captive of a mere human *exception* to the law that imprudently opened the way to widespread abuse of Him in the consecrated Host, and all EWTN can say is: "That's the law." As with all other innovations in New Church, the exception becomes the rule and the rule becomes the exception—yet another example of the diabolical inversion that accompanies the diabolical disorientation of the Church.

In defense of Communion in the hand one EWTN "expert" went so far as to insist that we must suppress our own *sensus catholicus* that it is wrong to abuse the Blessed Sacrament by this practice, for after all "the law" allows it, so what appears to be an abuse must be good; and if we see an abuse, then the fault must lie with us, not the perpetrators of the abuse:

### Answer by Richard Geraghty on 11-23-2004:

... What has been approved by the Church is not an abuse. Thus the fact that the Church has approved communion [sic] in the hands makes it an acceptable practice.[79] Also acceptable is receiving communion on

---

[79]This is nonsense. The Church is infallible only in the universal laws she imposes upon the faithful in the practice of the Faith. The universal law mandating Communion on the tongue *is* such a law, but the occasional, if ever legitimately permitted, exception from that law is not. The infallible universal law of Communion on the tongue still remains in effect even to this day.

the tongue. Now we all may have our private opinions about each of these practices. But we cannot go by them. We should go by what the Church allows in order to preserve the unity which is so necessary to the Church. Personally speaking, *I must confess that sometimes the prevalence of communion in the hand depresses me. But that is a fault of mine.* I should not make my feelings of disapproval more important than the fact that the Church permits this while at the same time permitting communion on the tongue...[80]

In other words, ignore the profanation of the Blessed Sacrament and cling instead to "the law," which in truth is not "the law" but rather an exception to the law that still mandates Communion on the tongue. Better to have "unity" in sacrilege than to cause "disunity" by opposing sacrilege. Here we see the Protestant-style nominalism[81] of the New Church mentality: whatever "the law" permits must be good, even if the results are manifestly bad. Not even the testimony of Mother Teresa of Calcutta can sway this nominalist mentality. When asked what she considered to be the worst problem in the world today—I repeat, the worst problem in the world—she replied: "Wherever I go in the whole world, the thing that makes me the saddest is watching people receive Communion in the hand."[82]

EWTN, therefore, not only willingly accommodates, but affirmatively defends, the constantly changing liturgical "norms" of the post-conciliar Church and thus the state of liturgical confusion that grips the Church today. At EWTN any return to the traditional Latin Mass and rubrics is unthinkable, even though the late Pope himself mandated a "wide and generous application" of his permission (strictly speaking, unnecessary) for recourse to the 1962

---

[80]See EWTN Q&A Forum, advice by Richard Geraghty of November 23, 2004 on "RE: Communion in the hand and other 'abuses'".

[81]In law, "nominalism" is the idea that good is determined by what the law permits as opposed to the objective morality of a practice. Thus, nominalist theologians held that God, as sovereign lawmaker, could make any evil practice, even murder, a natural right by His simple decree. St. Thomas and the entire tradition of the Church reject this error. Not even God can make a wrong into a right, for it would be contrary to His very nature to do so.

[82]Eyewitness testimony of Fr. William Rutler, Good Friday, 1989, Sermon at St. Agnes Church, New York City. And yet Fr. Rutler, himself an EWTN celebrity, has not (so far as I know) called for an end to Communion in the hand.

Missal.[83] As Dr. Peterson observed, the consensus of EWTN's "theological" committee was that "the new Mass, even with its [defective] translation, was better" than the traditional Mass, and that a restoration of the traditional Mass at EWTN "was never going to happen."

And this is not even to mention EWTN's avid promotion of the "liturgies" at World Youth Days, during which scantily clad teens gyrate to rock music at so-called Pontifical Masses, which are conducted like Broadway-style rock musicals. John Vennari has documented these liturgical atrocities in great detail, and I need add nothing further.[84] Suffice it to mention here the unspeakable sacrileges that occur at these outdoor Masses, particularly because of Communion in the hand. As I noted in *The Great Façade*, the Catholic convert Gerry Matatics attended World Youth Day '93 in Denver. The enactment of the Stations of the Cross with a woman in the role of Jesus, already mentioned, was nothing compared to what he saw at the outdoor papal Mass:

> We had camped out the night before on the ground to be sure that we would have a place for the papal Mass. We all had grimy faces and "sleeping-bag" hair. The assisting priests who were to distribute Holy Communion, implementing inculturation, accommodated themselves to the heat and humidity by wearing tee shirts, shorts, flip-flops and baseball caps along with their stoles. Priests similarly attired were listening to confessions beforehand.

> The crowd had been roped off into quadrants, about a hundred of us in each one. When the time came for reception of Holy Communion I knelt at the front of my little quadrant in an attempt to receive the Sacred Host on my knees. Hosts were being distributed from big, shallow bowls that could have been used for punch or potato chips. People were reaching over each other's shoulders to grab the consecrated Hosts from the priests. I saw Hosts falling into the mud, where they were being

[83]Motu Proprio *Ecclesia Dei* (1988).

[84]"The World Youth Day Sleep-over," J. Vennari, *Catholic Family News*, October, 2002. See also *World Youth Day: From Catholicism to Counterchurch* (Toronto: Canisius Books, 2005).

trampled on. I reached down and rescued as many as I
could and consumed them.

I had been going to the Tridentine Mass since the fall of
1992 and the Novus Ordo on weekdays. At that moment
I realized that if this kind of sacrilege could occur at a
*papal Mass* because of the Novus Ordo rubrics, I could
no longer be a party to the new liturgy. It was the last
Novus Ordo Mass I ever attended.[85]

Michael Matt, Editor of *The Remnant*, offers testimony perhaps
even more horrific: "At the outdoor papal Mass in Des Moines
during the papal visit of 1980, consecrated Hosts were being
distributed from cardboard boxes. A group of Hell's Angels was
given Holy Communion in the hand. I saw them washing down the
Body of Christ with cans of beer. I was only a child then, but I will
never forget that awful sight as long as I live."

The practice of Communion in the hand ensures that even the
papal Masses in St. Peter's Square will result in sacrilege, including
the spiriting away of Hosts by Rome's many Satanists, who are now
*buying and selling the stolen Hosts in Italy*.[86] I repeat: Satanists are now
buying and selling stolen Hosts in Italy. On July 15, 2004 Catholic
News Agency reported that "Fr. Aldo Buonaiuto, director of an
'emergency help line' that assists young people wanting to get out of
satanic cults" is warning that the rapid growth of Satanism in Italy
"'has created a market' for consecrated hosts..." Buonaiuto told
*Famiglia Cristiana* magazine that "a proliferation of cults exists which
practice black masses, with the profanation of consecrated hosts, rape
and torture."[87] Father Buonaiuto also revealed the horrifying news
that consecrated Hosts "sell for 80-500 euros, depending on the size
of the Host, the prominence of the church from which they were
stolen, and who consecrated them..." Thanks to Communion in the
hand, non-Catholics can infiltrate Catholic congregations and
"harvest" consecrated Hosts by the hundreds or thousands in

---

[85]Christopher A. Ferrara and Thomas E. Woods, Jr., *The Great Façade* (Wyoming,
Minnesota: The Remnant Press, 2002), pages 227-228.
[86]"Alarm in Italy as growth of Satanism creates 'market' for consecrated hosts,"
CNA Report, July 15, 2004; online text available at: http://www.catholicnews
agency.com/new.php?n=1554.
[87]Ibid.

exchange for payments of up to 500 Euros (about $600 US dollars) for a single Host.

Sacrileges unimaginable in 1965 are now commonplace because of the liturgical degradation EWTN either practices itself, enthusiastically reports or refuses to oppose, even as it tries to make outcasts of those who rightly resist the liturgical revolution by calling for a total restoration of the traditional Latin Mass and refusing to participate in the Novus Ordo. Who will make reparation for these sacrileges, heaped upon all the others made possible by the post-conciliar "reforms"?

In sum, EWTN has become just another enemy of liturgical Tradition, hiding behind a false front of liturgical "conservatism" while continuing to capitalize on Mother Angelica's reputation for staunch defense of traditional Catholicism, long after she has been removed from the scene. In EWTN's presentation of the liturgy, *every single element of the post-conciliar liturgical revolution is preserved or defended and everything the Protestant "reformers" demanded is more or less present.* Where the liturgy is concerned, EWTN is precisely what St. Pius X called in *Pascendi* "the Modernist as reformer." But, exerting far more influence than any local Modernist bishop, EWTN's daily worldwide broadcast of its own Protestantized version of the Mass creates the false impression throughout the Church that what EWTN presents to the faithful is the Church's authentic Roman liturgy. While holding itself out as liturgically "conservative," EWTN is actually a major promoter of liturgical anarchy and thus a major impediment to the indispensable recovery of our Latin liturgical tradition — the Church's primary bulwark against heresy.

# Chapter 8

# Abandoning the Dogma
# "No Salvation Outside the Church"

God's mercy is as infinite as His justice. Thus it is a dogma of our Faith that "our Saviour... will have all men to be saved, and to come to the knowledge of the truth. For there is one God, and one mediator of God and men, the man Christ Jesus: Who gave Himself a redemption for all..." (1 Timothy 2:3-6) But while God would have all men be saved, not all men *are* saved, because in the exercise of their God-given free will many reject the narrow path of righteousness and choose the broader way of destruction: "Enter ye in at the narrow gate: for wide is the gate, and broad is the way that leadeth to destruction, and *many there are* who go in thereat." (Matt. 7:13) Hence, as the Council of Trent decreed: "But although Christ died for all, yet not all receive the benefit of His death, but those only to whom the merit of His Passion is communicated."[88]

This means that the notion of "universal salvation" is contrary to the Catholic Faith. It is a dogma of our Faith, defined at the Council of Florence and many other times, that "the souls of those who depart in actual mortal sin or in original sin only, *descend immediately into hell* but to undergo punishments of different kinds."[89] These punishments include the torment of "everlasting fire which was prepared for the devil and his angels."[90] The torments of hell are for all eternity: "if anyone without repentance dies in mortal sin, without a doubt he is tortured forever by the flames of eternal hell."[91] Whoever says that in the end all men will be saved and that hell will be "empty" is not a Catholic: "If anyone says or holds that the

---

[88]Council of Trent, *Decree on Justification*, Chapter 3; Dz. 795.
[89]Council of Florence, Dz. 694.
[90]Council of Florence, Dz. 714.
[91]Council of Lyons I, Dz. 457.

punishment of the demons and impious men is temporary, and that it will have an end at some time, that is to say, there will be a complete restoration of the demons or of impious men, let him be anathema."[92] Hell is forever, and men go there. There is no getting around this foundational truth of our religion. As even John Paul II (who was said to harbor liberal sentiments on this subject) declared in his *Crossing the Threshold of Hope*: "[T]he words of Christ are unequivocal. In Matthew's Gospel He speaks clearly of those who will go to eternal punishment."[93] This is not some sort of divine bluff, as the Modernist von Balthasar would have us believe. It is an inescapable fact of divine justice.

Given this fact of Revelation, it is of capital importance to hold fast to another dogma of our Faith: that in His Holy Catholic Church, Christ has established the exclusive means of our salvation, and that no one is saved outside of her. For why would Christ have founded a Church which He "hath purchased with His own blood" (Acts 20:28) if that Church were anything but indispensable? Hence, the Catholic Church has infallibly defined at least three times the dogma *extra ecclesiam nulla salus est* (outside the Church there is no salvation):

> There is but one universal Church of the faithful, outside which no one at all is saved. (Pope Innocent III, Fourth Lateran Council, 1215.)

> We declare, say, define, and pronounce that it is absolutely necessary for the salvation of every human creature to be subject to the Roman Pontiff. (Pope Boniface VIII, the Bull *Unam Sanctam*, 1302.)

> The most Holy Roman Church firmly believes, professes and preaches that none of those existing outside the Catholic Church, not only pagans, but also Jews and heretics and schismatics, can have a share in life eternal; but that they will go into the eternal fire which was prepared for the devil and his angels, unless before death they are joined with her; and that so important is the unity of this ecclesiastical body that only those

---

[92] Pope Vigilius, *Canons Against Origen*, n. 9; Dz. 211.
[93] Pope John Paul II, *Crossing the Threshold of Hope* (New York: Alfred A. Knopf, 1994), page 185.

remaining within this unity can profit by the sacraments of the Church unto salvation, and they alone can receive an eternal recompense for their fasts, their almsgivings, their other works of Christian piety and the duties of a Christian soldier. No one, let his almsgiving be as great as it may, no one, even if he pour out his blood for the Name of Christ, can be saved, unless he remain within the bosom and the unity of the Catholic Church. (Pope Eugene IV, the Bull *Cantate Domino*, 1442.)

In keeping with this infallible teaching, the Church has repeated again and again that outside of her no one may be saved:

**Pope Saint Gregory the Great** (590-604): "Now the holy Church universal proclaims that God cannot be truly worshipped, saving from within herself, asserting that all they that are without her shall never be saved."[94]

**Catechism of the Council of Trent** (1566): "infidels, heretics, schismatics and excommunicated persons" are "excluded from the Church's pale."[95]

**Pope Leo XII** (1823-1829): "… we profess that there is no salvation outside the Church… the Church is the pillar and firmament of truth, as the apostle Paul teaches. (1 Tim. 3) In reference to these words St. Augustine says: 'Whoever is without the Church will not be reckoned among the sons, and whoever does not want to have the Church as Mother will not have God as Father'."[96]

**Pope Pius VIII** (1829-1830): "… the people must be assured, Venerable Brethren, that the profession of the Catholic Faith is alone the true one, since the Apostle tells us that there is one Lord and one baptism. As Jerome says, the man who eats the lamb outside of this house is profane, and the man who is not in the ark of Noe is going to perish in the deluge. Neither is there any

---

[94]*Moralia*, XIV:5.

[95]*Catechism of the Council of Trent*, McHugh & Callan Translation, (Rockford, Illinois: TAN Books and Publishers, reprinted 1982), page 101.

[96]*Ubi Primum*, inaugural encyclical of Pope Leo XII, May 5, 1825.

other name apart from the name of Jesus Christ given to men by which we must be saved."[97]

**Pope Gregory XVI** (1831-1846): "The holy universal Church teaches that it is not possible to worship God truly except in her (the Catholic Church); all who are outside her will not be saved" (quoting Pope St. Gregory the Great).[98]

**Blessed Pope Pius IX** (1846-1878): "It must be held as a matter of faith that outside the Apostolic Roman Church, no one can be saved; that this is the only ark of salvation; that he who shall not have entered therein will perish in the flood." (*Singulari Quadem*)

**The Catechism of Pope St. Pius X** (1903-1914): "Outside the true Church are: Infidels, Jews, heretics, apostates, schismatics and excommunicated persons... No one can be saved outside the Catholic, Apostolic and Roman Church, just as no one could be saved from the flood outside the Ark of Noah, which was a figure of the Church."

Now, the Church allows for the possibility that certain souls who have not become formal members of the Church might in some way short of formal membership be incorporated into her before death. For example, one could, by a special grace, be enabled to make an act of faith together with salvific and sufficient repentance at the very moment of death. It is important to note that not just any weak act of faith or sentiment of repentance is enough to save one's soul, but only that which God deems sufficient in His reading of a man's heart. We cannot know our own hearts with certainty, for as Holy Scripture teaches: "The heart is perverse above all things, and unsearchable, who can know it?" (Jer. 17:9) Hence only God knows which, if any, are saved by incorporation into the Church short of formal membership, and we have no right to suppose that there is any great number of people in this category. For as Our Lord Himself has warned us, "few there are" who find their way through the narrow

---

[97]*Traditi Humilitati Nostrae*, May 24, 1829.
[98]*Summo Iugiter Studio* (1832), n. 5.

gate to Heaven. Every saint who has been favored with a vision or intuition in the matter confirms this admonition of divine Revelation. According to St. Jerome, the number of sinners saved by deathbed repentance is 1 in 200,000.

For this reason Blessed Pope Pius IX taught in his encyclical *Singulari Quadem*, quoted above, that the Catholic Church is "the only ark of salvation," and His Holiness condemned the error "that has taken up its abode in the souls of many Catholics": namely, that "one should have good hope of the eternal salvation of all those who have never lived in the true Church of Christ." He condemned as well the "impious and *equally fatal* opinion" that "the way of eternal salvation can be found in any religion whatsoever."

Blessed Pius IX warned that the faithful must not preoccupy themselves with speculation about "what will be the lot and condition after death of those who have never lived in the true Church of Christ," for it is not until the life hereafter that we will be able to see "by how close and beautiful a bond Divine Justice and Mercy are united." Until then, the Pope insisted, "it is *unlawful* to proceed further in inquiry." Rather, he declared, Catholics must hold fast to what we know with certainty and which "must be held by faith" because the Church has infallibly defined it as dogma — namely, that "outside the Roman Apostolic Church *no one can be saved*." Leaving no doubt of the matter, in his *Syllabus of Errors* (1864) Blessed Pius IX condemned (along with numerous other errors against the Faith) the proposition that "Good hope at least is to be entertained of the eternal salvation of all those who are not at all in the true Church of Christ." In other words, *Catholics are not permitted to entertain good hope* for the salvation of non-members of the Church, for if good hope were to be entertained in this regard, the dogma that there is no salvation outside the Church would be fatally undermined. Quite the contrary, as shown earlier, it is a dogma of our Faith that *not all men are saved*.

Moreover, God has positively revealed only one way to enter the Church outside of which no one is saved: baptism and (in adults who have reached the age of reason) profession of the Catholic Faith: "Amen, amen, I say to thee, unless a man be born again of water and the Holy Ghost, he cannot enter into the kingdom of God." (John 3:5) "He that believeth and is baptized shall be saved: but he that believeth not shall be condemned." (Mark 16:16) Even as to unbaptized infants, the Church did not hesitate to declare in the

Catechism of the Council of Trent, promulgated by Pope Saint Pius V, that they cannot be saved without the Sacrament:

> The faithful are earnestly to be exhorted to take care that their children be brought to the church, as soon as it can be done with safety, to receive solemn Baptism: infants, unless baptized, *cannot enter Heaven*, and hence we may well conceive how deep the enormity of their guilt, who, through negligence, suffer them to remain without the grace of the Sacrament longer than necessity may require, particularly at an age so tender as to be exposed to numberless dangers of death.

It is true that the same Catechism teaches that as to adult converts, who have already embraced the Faith as catechumens and are awaiting formal baptism, a delay in baptism "for a certain time" during their instruction is "not attended by the same danger," for even if some "unforeseen accident deprives adults of baptism, their intention of receiving it, and their repentance for past sins, will avail them of grace and righteousness." But notice how this "exception" to the revealed requirement of formal baptism is limited to adult catechumens who explicitly desire the sacrament, and who have, moreover, *repented of their sins* by the grace of God.

In any case, there is *nothing* in the constant teaching of the Catholic Church before Vatican II to suggest anything like optimism concerning the eternal salvation of those who are not formal members of the Catholic Church. This is because divine Revelation itself has given us no grounds for such confidence. As Ludwig Ott observed in his renowned compendium of Catholic dogma: "In view of the stress laid upon the necessity of membership in the Church for salvation, it is understandable that the possibility of salvation for those outside the Church is mentioned only hesitantly."[99] Blessed Pius IX knew that even to attempt to advance beyond such hesitancy would be to threaten the very mission of the Church and "the destruction of souls." For if the faithful were ever allowed to attain a false confidence in the salvation of non-Catholics, the Church's missionary impulse would begin to sputter and die. And that, indeed, is what we see today.

By 1950, however, only a few years before Vatican II began, the

---

[99]Ott, *Fundamentals of Catholic Dogma*, page 312.

dogma *nulla salus* was under direct attack by neo-Modernists who were trying to "interpret" it so broadly as to render it meaningless. Pope Pius XII (who, as noted, had foreseen the coming disaster in the Church some 20 years earlier) was compelled to combat the widely spreading error in his encyclical *Humani Generis*. In that encyclical Pius XII condemned the Modernists who "reduce to a meaningless formula the necessity of belonging to the true Church in order to gain eternal salvation" and who "say they are not bound by the doctrine, explained in Our Encyclical Letter of a few years ago, and based on the Sources of Revelation, which teaches that the Mystical Body of Christ and the Roman Catholic Church are one and the same thing."

Today, a meaningless formula is precisely what this dogma has become de facto in the course of the post-conciliar revolution in the Church. In the minds of many, the dogma has died the death of a thousand exceptions. Now we are told that the dogma is understood "more broadly" than before Vatican II, and EWTN slavishly promotes this grave error. For example, one of EWTN's theological "experts," on "Catholic Doctrine and catechetics," Fr. Robert Levis, gave this advice on the dogma:

> This ancient dogma remains the same, always true, but the Fathers of Vatican Council II interpret it in a much more generous way than their predecessors. And I think of this reason — of the 6,000,000,000 people on earth, only 1 billion are Christian of all sorts. Modern shepherds are concerned about their salvation *and so open up the more closed strictures to permit as many as possible to enter Paradise*, and of course, thru the good offices of the Church. God bless. Fr. Bob Levis[100]

According to Fr. Levis, Vatican II and "modern" shepherds "interpret" the dogma differently ("more generously") from the way the Church had always interpreted it for nearly 2,000 years. "Modern shepherds," says Levis, have decided to "open up the more closed strictures to permit as many as possible to enter Paradise" — as if "modern shepherds" personally controlled the gates of Heaven and could adjust the number of those who will be saved or damned!

Fr. Levis, it must be noted, also hosts the EWTN show "Voyage of

---

[100]See, EWTN Q&A Forum, advice by Fr. Levis of February 23, 2005 on "Change in Church Dogma?".

Faith," in which he dispenses spiritual advice to millions of Catholics on national television. His advice is thus EWTN's advice. So, EWTN's position is that for nearly her entire history the Catholic Church had erred by not "interpreting" the dogma broadly enough, by not opening the gates of Heaven widely enough. An EWTN supporter objected to this outrageous opinion as follows:

> Father, I'm asking about what it is that you call 'interpret', and that modern shepherds opened up the more closed strictures. You seem to be saying that (since it's bound on earth, it will be bound in Heaven) *Vatican II actually loosened the requirements for non-Catholics to attain Heaven.* That pre VII [sic] [pre-Vatican II], the requirements were more strict, but have been loosened, and that God has gone along with that loosening. Is that what you're saying? Thank you. Don

In his reply to this telling objection, Fr. Levis basically admits that this is exactly what he is saying:

> **Answer by Fr. Robert J. Levis on 02-25-2005:**
>
> Don, I don't know the mind of God about the salvation of Protestants. But we Catholics for centuries held pretty firmly that one has to be a full-fledged member of the Catholic Church in order to be saved. In more recent centuries, this Roman Catholic position has been lightened, softened so that others in good faith might be saved. Surely the documents of Vatican II are not as demanding as prior documents. And I think the main reason is charity and the tremendous number of souls who never even hear once the sweet name of Jesus...[101]

There we have it: while EWTN's theological "expert" admits that "we Catholics *for centuries* held pretty firmly that one has to be a full-fledged member of the Catholic Church in order to be saved"—i.e., that this is the only *known* way of salvation—Vatican II supposedly changed all that. The Church no longer holds "pretty firmly" that one

---

[101]See, EWTN Q&A Forum, advice by Fr. Levis of February 25, 2005 on "Re: Outside the Church ....".

must be a "full-fledged member" of the Church to be saved. The Church has now changed her "position"; she is "not as demanding as prior documents," her teaching has been "lightened and softened," and "the main reason is charity…" That is, according to Fr. Levis, the Church before Vatican II was *not charitable enough* and was *too demanding* regarding the salvation of non-Catholics. Perhaps Fr. Levis thinks the Church should apologize for all those centuries of pessimism about the eternal fate of non-Catholics, and the untold guilt the Church imposed on those who delayed baptism of their children for too long.

Notice, however, that Fr. Levis, as a kind of fig leaf to cover the nakedness of his "revision" of the dogma *nulla salus*, asserts that of the five billion non-Catholics in the world "as many as possible" enter the Church "thru [sic] the good offices of the Church." But if vast numbers of non-Catholics are saved by "the good offices of the Church" without baptism or any profession of faith, and without even any intention to join the Church, what becomes of the dogma that outside the Church there is no salvation? Why did the Church promulgate this dogma with such severity for so many centuries if non-Catholics are commonly saved without membership in the Church? What *difference* does the dogma make if people are saved "through the good offices of the Church" whether they join the Church or not?

It is not as if EWTN's denial of the dogma *nulla salus* were confined to the quirky advice of Fr. Levis, who thinks the Church has the power to "loosen the requirements for non-Catholics to attain heaven." As we will see in the next chapter, the idea that membership in the Catholic Church is desirable but not *necessary* for salvation is thematic to EWTN's presentation of its "moderately" Modernist version of Roman Catholicism. For our present purposes, however, suffice it to point to what is perhaps EWTN's leading theological "expert," Fr. Benedict Groeschel.

Fr. Groeschel is one of EWTN's "superstars," in fact its theological *eminence grise*, by virtue of his age. To listen to Fr. Groeschel for any length of time is to appreciate that this is a man who seems to think that Roman Catholicism consists of Catholic doctrines and dogmas as modified by his folksy "wisdom." If Catholic teaching just doesn't *seem* right to Fr. Groeschel based on his personal experience, he will simply "fix" it to suit his opinions — right on the air, if necessary.

A perfect example of this is Fr. Groeschel's recent appearance on *Sunday Night Live*, the live viewer call-in show that EWTN has built around his theological idiosyncrasies. The topic on this occasion was "Understanding People of Other Religious Faiths and Other Religious Denominations."[102] In the course of the one-hour show, Fr. Groeschel did all but announce that the dogma *nulla salus* had been repealed. A concerned Catholic, who alerted former EWTN personality Robert Sungenis[103] to the show, called it "one of the most destructive hours" he had ever seen on the network.

Groeschel began this destruction with a folksy anecdote from his childhood, the unmistakable import of which is that the practitioners of all religions are saved. The reader is invited to study the following passage carefully, bearing in mind that it was delivered in the haughty, know-it-all tone that is well familiar to Groeschel's just critics:

> Fifty years ago the understanding was very different because people were rather convinced — great numbers of people — that those who didn't belong to their denomination, or to their general group, like Protestants, didn't stand much of a chance of making it. *I never believed that — ever.*[104] When I was a little kid, a Lutheran pastor who lived next door to us used to take me for rides in his car. I had some German Lutheran relatives. I knew many very kindly Jewish people for whom I used to turn on the oven on the Sabbath day. I knew all kinds of people… I knew Orthodox boys whose fathers were priests of the Orthodox Church. And so, *I never bought the whole thing.* I do, did then, do now, believe that the Catholic Church is the Church

---

[102]*Sunday Night Live with Fr. Benedict Groeschel*, July 24, 2005. All of the following quotations are taken from a verbatim transcript based on the VHS videotape purchased from EWTN and the online audio file in EWTN's archives.

[103]Sungenis, a Catholic apologist and Scripture scholar, was once a fixture on EWTN, and his books on Sacred Scripture were avidly promoted by the network. Sungenis was "shown the door" when he found he could no longer remain silent about the direction of New Church and EWTN's role in it. Sungenis has since been shunned by the same New Church establishment that once lionized him, including such organizations as Catholic Answers. Sungenis has written extensively about the problems with EWTN in articles found at http://www.catholicintl.com.

[104]That is, Fr. Groeschel never assented to the teaching of the Catholic Church.

historically established by Jesus Christ... in order to
bring His sacraments... to the world... [and] to see that
the scriptures of the New Covenant were written,
published and recognized... But that doesn't mean that I
think that God in His providence and mercy is limited to
operating in the Catholic Church...

In other words, Groeschel thinks that Lutherans, Orthodox, Jews
and so forth are all saved *as such*, without need of joining the Catholic
Church. Yes, Christ established the Catholic Church, but that doesn't
mean (to Groeschel) that anyone *must* join her to be saved. He "never
bought" the infallible teaching of the Church that outside of her no
one can be saved, neither heretics, schismatics, Jews or pagans, unless
they are joined to her before death. That might have been believed
"fifty years ago" — that is, for the entire history of the Church before
1960! — but no one need believe it any longer, he suggested. He
assured EWTN's viewers that his opinion is correct, not by citing any
Church teaching to support his error (for there is no such teaching),
but by recalling that as a child he knew assorted members of other
religions who were nice people — including the "very kindly Jewish
people" who thought they were honoring the Sabbath by having the
young Gentile boy, little Benedict Groeschel, turn on their stoves for
them.

It is not as if Groeschel immediately qualified his remarks by
saying that God might save certain non-Catholics by granting them
the grace of a saving act of faith, a "baptism of desire," before death
by which they would be incorporated into the Church in a manner
known only to Him, and in the exceptional case that is not the
ordinary way of salvation. No, Groeschel wanted EWTN's audience
to understand that the members of *any and all religions* are saved *in
those religions* without the least need of conversion to Roman
Catholicism. His other remarks during the same show leave no
reasonable doubt of this:

Now do I think that you have to belong to the true
Church? You have to belong to the religion that you
*think* [his emphasis] is the true religion. God is true, and
if you want to follow God, you must follow Him by the
truth that *you* recognize.

This opinion, of course, flatly contradicts the teaching of Blessed

Pius IX, who, as already noted, condemned the "impious and *equally fatal* opinion" that "the way of eternal salvation can be found in any religion whatsoever." As Pius IX knew full well, this opinion destroys adherence to the dogma *nulla salus*.

Consider that Groeschel, wearing his Franciscan robes, made his remark as a purported representative of the Catholic Church to an audience that surely included non-Catholics. He was, in that capacity, advising these non-Catholics (along with all the Catholics in the audience) that one is obliged only to belong to that religion he *thinks* is true. He was telling these souls that they *did not need to convert to Catholicism* even though they were watching a Catholic show, supposedly concerning Catholic teaching, on an ostensibly Catholic network.

To drive his point home, Groeschel summoned another childhood memory, and offered this twisted interpretation of Our Lord's teaching in the Gospel of John (10:16) that there will be one fold and one Shepherd:

> And I think it's important to keep in mind this wonderful text of Jesus… "I am the good shepherd. I know my own and my own know me… and I have other sheep I have that are not of this fold, and I must bring them also. And they will heed my voice, and there will be one flock [fold!] and one shepherd." These are words worth meditating on: other sheep I have that are not of this fold. In our journey through life we meet many people who belong to other religions…. If you grew up in an American town you had *a Baptist Church, a Presbyterian Church, an Episcopal Church, a Congregational Church*, a Catholic Church, *a synagogue*. They were all there, and maybe some little churches on the side. And *all these people believed in the same Jesus Christ*. They all read *the same Bible*. They *all tried to please God in Christ as best they could*. And I think you wouldn't have to have a great imagination to realize that you should treat all of these people with courtesy and respect and with a special respect to *the way that God has called them*….

Thus, according to Groeschel, God has called the Protestants to be Protestants and the Jews to be Jews (although he failed to explain how the Jews "believed in the same Jesus Christ"). The Protestants, right alongside the Catholics, believe in the same Jesus, read the same Bible, and try to please Jesus "as best they could." No distinction whatever was drawn between Catholicism and other religions in terms of conformity to God's will and salvation. In addition to denying the dogma *nulla salus*, Groeschel blatantly advocated the very proposition infallibly condemned by Blessed Pius IX in the *Syllabus*: "Protestantism is nothing else than a different form of the same true Christian religion, in which it is possible to serve God as well as in the Catholic Church."[105]

In the way of all Modernists, Groeschel "interprets" out of existence the teaching of Our Lord that He will go out and "bring them also" *into the fold* of His Church, and that there will be *one* fold, not many, so that all of His sheep will be in the *same* fold, which is the Catholic Church. In Groeschel's Modernist rendering, the truth of the Gospel is totally inverted: those outside the fold are already *in* the fold, and we must "respect... the way that God has *called them*." This is simply monstrous—indeed, an insult to Our Lord Himself, who died for His Church, purchasing it "with His blood"[106] so that men might be saved within her and through her sacraments, whose very efficacy derives from the grace Our Lord won for us on the Cross.

But Groeschel will have none of the infallible dogma that he "never bought." Recalling yet another anecdote from his vast experience, Groeschel told EWTN's audience how during his early days in the monastery he was always "embarrassed to death" when he had to take his fellow monk, Fr. Innocent, to the doctor's office, because Fr. Innocent (being nearly deaf) would pray the Rosary loudly while "other people sat there reading *Better Homes and Gardens*." One day at the doctor's office they learned that one of the doctors, Dr. Clark, had passed away, causing Fr. Innocent to exclaim: "Ah, poor Clark. My dear friend, such a good man, I prayed for him for years, and he died a Protestant. I hope he didn't go to hell." This was all too much for the enlightened young Fr. Benedict: "It was one of the low moments of my life.... But that was what people thought, and quite honestly, I thought it was crazy."

So, Groeschel pronounces "crazy" the constant teaching of the Church that there is no salvation outside her. He calls "crazy" the Church's perennial concern for the eternal loss of souls deprived of

---

[105]*Syllabus of Errors*, condemned proposition n. 18; Dz. 1718.
[106]Acts 20:28.

her sacraments, a concern expressed by the clearly holy and pious priest who was his fellow monk.

What is crazy, however, is not what Catholics have always believed, but rather the teaching of EWTN and its "experts" on the crucial matter of salvation outside the Church—crazy, and potentially fatal to many souls. For there is no greater danger to souls than what Pope Gregory XVI condemned as "the deadly error of indifferentism"—an error His Holiness described as follows:

> This perverse opinion is spread on all sides by the fraud of the wicked who claim that it is possible to obtain the eternal salvation of the soul by the profession of any kind of religion, as long as morality is maintained. Surely, in so clear a matter, you will drive this deadly error far from the people committed to your care. With the admonition of the apostle that "there is one Lord, one faith, one baptism," may those fear who contrive the notion that the safe harbor of salvation is open to persons of any religion whatever. They should consider the testimony of Christ Himself that "those who are not with Christ are against Him," and that they disperse unhappily who do not gather with Him. Therefore "without a doubt, they will perish forever, unless they hold the Catholic Faith whole and inviolate."[107]

But the message that the practitioners of any kind of religion are saved so long as they are "good people" is precisely what Groeschel and EWTN are preaching.

As we can see, in the hands of "experts" like Levis and Groeschel, the dogma *nulla salus* becomes exactly what Pius XII feared it would become due to Modernist influence: a meaningless formula. The difference between the inside and the outside of the Church disappears in a haze of ambiguity, and the dogma is de facto given a meaning precisely the opposite of what the Church has always taught: "there *is no* salvation outside the Church" becomes "there *is* salvation outside the Church."

The implications of this line of thought for the Church's credibility are staggering. For if the Church can revise the interpretation of her own infallible dogma, what might she *not* revise

---

[107]*Mirari Vos* (1832), n. 13.

given sufficient time? What then becomes of her claim to teach the truth infallibly? If the Church was wrong to teach the dogma so strictly for so long, then why could she not be wrong about everything else she teaches? What, indeed, becomes of the very idea of objective truth itself if what the Church taught as true yesterday is no longer true today?

EWTN's position represents precisely that way of thinking condemned by the *First* Vatican Council, which declared: "that understanding of the sacred dogmas must be *perpetually retained,* which Holy Mother Church has once declared; and *there must never be recession from that meaning under the specious name of a deeper understanding...*" Rather, any development of the understanding of a dogma must be "solely in its own genus, namely in the same dogma, with the same sense, and *the same understanding.*"[108]

According to EWTN, however, the Church at Vatican II *has* receded from the original understanding of the dogma *nulla salus;* she no longer understands it in the same way she did before Vatican II. The old way of thinking is "crazy." So, as EWTN would have us believe, the Church has "loosened the requirements" for salvation. She is "not as demanding as prior documents." And by "documents" EWTN means the infallible pronouncements set forth above! What is this if not the very opinion the Oath Against Modernism required priests to reject before God: namely, "the heretical misrepresentation that dogmas evolve and change from one meaning to another different from the one which the Church held previously"?

---

[108]First Vatican Council, *Dogmatic Constitution Concerning the Catholic Faith,* Chapter 4; Dz. 1800.

# Chapter 9

# Abandoning the Return of the Dissidents to Rome

EWTN's heavily "ecumenical" New Church presentation necessarily undermines a constant teaching of the Roman Pontiffs closely related to the dogma *nulla salus*: that the only way to Christian unity — the *only* way — is what the Popes called "the return of the dissidents to the one true Church." As Pius XI declared in his encyclical *Mortalium Animos*, which condemned the Protestant-inspired "ecumenical movement" at its very beginnings: "And so, venerable brethren, it is clear why this Apostolic See has never allowed its subjects to take part in the assemblies of non-Catholics; for the union of Christians can *only* be promoted by promoting the *return to the one true Church* of those who are separated from it, for in the past they have unhappily left it…. Let them therefore *return* to their common Father, who, forgetting the insults heaped upon the Apostolic See, will receive them in most loving fashion…."[109]

This teaching was repeated emphatically in the 1949 Instruction of the Holy Office of Pius XII concerning the "ecumenical movement." The Instruction required of the bishops that in any "ecumenical" discussions they might authorize, the Protestant interlocutors must be presented with "the Catholic truth" and "the teaching of the Encyclicals of the Roman Pontiffs on *the return of the dissidents* to the Church."[110] The same Instruction declared: "The Catholic doctrine will have to be proposed and exposed totally and integrally: what the Catholic Church teaches about the true nature and means of justification, about the constitution of the Church, about the primacy of the jurisdiction of the Roman Pontiff, about the only true union which is accomplished with *the return of the dissidents*

---

[109]*Mirari Vos*, nn. 7, 10 and 11.
[110]*Acta Apostolicae Sedis* (AAS) 42-142.

to *the only true Church of Christ* will not at all be passed over in silence or covered over in ambiguous words."[111]

But covering over in silence and ambiguity the Catholic doctrine of the return of the dissidents is precisely what EWTN is doing. In EWTN's programming there is not (so far as I know) any mention of the return of the dissidents to the one true Church. There is, however, constant talk of many Christian churches or "ecclesial communities" of which the Catholic Church is merely the most excellent. EWTN's theological commentators, many of whom are recently converted Protestant ministers, habitually present the Catholic Church as merely possessing the "fullness" of the truth that other "Christian churches" also possess in lesser measure. There is not the least suggestion that the members of Protestant sects or schismatic Orthodox churches are in danger of damnation due to their separation from the Catholic Church, even if they are invited to "come home to Rome" for the "fullness" of Christianity.

To examine EWTN's content is to conclude that its position is that *no one* in the Protestant sects or schismatic Orthodox churches is in danger of damnation. "Coming home to Rome" is presented merely as one's arrival at the best-equipped vehicle for salvation, but by no means the only one. The Protestant denominations are no longer viewed as mere human associations whose doctrines are rife with heresy and immorality, from which one ought to depart for the spiritual safety of the Catholic Church, but rather as respectable (however imperfect) "ecclesial communities" whose ministers are bona fide (however mistaken) custodians of the Gospel.

We have seen evidence of this in the previous chapter, which mentioned Fr. Benedict Groeschel's televised attack on the integrity of the dogma *nulla salus*. But Groeschel also pontificates his Modernist views on specifically "ecumenical" issues. During the show discussed already, Groeschel, citing his personal experience as an ecumenist, painted the picture of a Catholic Church that has supposedly outgrown her narrow-minded view of the Protestant sects, which are now to be viewed as perfectly acceptable vehicles of salvation:

> When I was a young priest and the ecumenical movement was getting started, I preached in 200 Protestant churches and a hundred synagogues, and I

---

[111]Ibid.

> had a great time… In those old days, if I preached in a
> service, I was not permitted to participate in the service.
> This was by decree of Pope Pius XI—that we were not to
> pray at services with anybody but Catholics. Did I live to
> see that change? I sure did. I went to see the Pope pray
> in Canterbury Cathedral with the Archbishop of
> Canterbury… I saw photos of him praying in the
> synagogue in Rome, and I saw him praying in the
> mosque. *We came a long way on this one…*

So, as Fr. Groeschel would have it, the Catholic Church has come
a "long way" from the backward days of Pius XI (not to mention
every one of his predecessors), who wrongly forbade Catholics to
worship in common with objective heretics and schismatics because
of the danger to the Faith. The formal decrees of Pius XI, along with
the entire teaching of the Church on this subject before the
"springtime of Vatican II," are viewed as embarrassing relics of the
past merely because Pope John Paul II chose to engage in activities
any Catholic has the right to protest as scandalous.[112] But, after all,
Groeschel had "a great time" preaching in Protestant churches and
synagogues, so what could be wrong with common worship with
non-Catholics?

This hearty approval of the very thing the Church forbade for
centuries is part and parcel of Groeschel's promotion of EWTN's
basic "ecumenical" theme: that membership in the Catholic Church is
now to be seen as desirable, to be sure, but really not necessary for
salvation. On the same show Groeschel related that "One of the
questions I got this week was from a lady who said that her friends in
one church said you didn't have to have the Eucharist,
reconciliation—confession—or other sacraments to be saved." To this
question Groeschel replied: "*Indeed, you don't.*" "But," he continued,
"in the Gospel Jesus very clearly calls people to receive the Eucharist
and to confess their sins. And he says to the Apostles, 'Whose sins
you shall forgive they are forgiven.' It has to be fitted into a context."

Groeschel never qualified his remark that "Indeed you don't"
need the sacraments to be saved. Rather, he suggested that while
Jesus may have "called" us to receive the sacraments, and we should
receive them because He "called" us to do so, we don't actually *need*

---

[112]See Chapter 12 for a discussion of the Church's own teaching on the right and
duty of Catholics to protest the actions of even the Pope when he gives scandal to
the Church.

the sacraments to attain Heaven. But then, why would Jesus "call" us to receive the sacraments if we can be saved without them? Groeschel is here engaging in classic Modernist double-talk, appearing to affirm what he is actually denying. He does so by asserting that Christ calls us to receive that which it is *not necessary* to receive for salvation. The sacramental system established by God as the New Law for man is thus reduced to a mere option. This error against the Faith incurs the anathema of the Council of Trent:

> CANON IV.—If anyone shall say that the sacraments of the New Law *are not necessary for salvation*, but are superfluous, and that, although all (the sacraments) are not necessary for every individual, without them or without the desire for them through faith alone men obtain from God the grace of justification; *let him be anathema*.[113]

The Council of Trent was merely affirming the divinely revealed truth that, by the decree of God Himself, the sacraments are the *necessary* means of receiving salvific grace and reaching eternal beatitude: "Amen, amen, I say to thee, unless a man be born again of water and the Holy Ghost, he cannot enter into the kingdom of God....[114] Amen, amen, I say unto you: except you eat the flesh of the Son of man and drink His blood, you shall not have life in you."[115] By the Hebrew formula "Amen, amen," Our Lord introduced a teaching of utmost importance for the salvation of souls.

But according to Groeschel, "indeed you *don't*" need the sacraments, not even Baptism and Holy Communion, to be saved. Groeschel would not even admit that, as Trent taught, one needs (and this is the exceptional case) at least the desire for the sacraments to be saved—as, for example, in the case of catechumens who desire and intend to receive Baptism.

Lest the reader think I have placed an unfairly adverse interpretation on Groeschel's statements, his further remarks on the subject leave no doubt that in his view the sacraments are reduced to merely desirable superfluities. During the same show a caller (one "Hank" from Orlando) challenged Groeschel by observing that Jesus said to His disciples that if they did not eat His Body and drink His

---

[113]Council of Trent, *Canons on the Sacraments in General*; Denzinger, 847.
[114]John 3:5.
[115]John 6:54-55.

Blood "you have no life in you," whereupon many of His followers walked away. "And this is what has happened to some of the other religions," noted Hank concerning the Protestant denominations, "and I was wondering what kind of an answer you are going to give me on that…"

The answer Groeschel gave was *to deny that Our Lord ever taught this*! According to Groeschel, Our Lord's words "*except* you eat the flesh of the Son of man and drink His blood, you have no life in you" are a mere defect in translation!

> Part of the answer is a question of translation. If you look at the Greek—we don't have the original words of Jesus, we have a Greek edition of those words. And the statement, the statement reads better if you put it this way: "If you eat My flesh and drink My blood, you will have life within you." It's better in the positive. But because of linguistic difficulties they put it that way.[116]

Linguistic difficulties? *They* put it that way? "They" happens to be Saint John the Apostle, who wrote his Gospel *in Greek*, as any Catholic with the least knowledge of the New Testament would know.[117] To say that John the Apostle distorted the words of Our Lord Himself due to a translation problem in the "Greek edition," and that we don't have the "real words" of Jesus, is to attack the inerrancy of Sacred Scripture itself. Only a few years before Pope Saint Pius X stamped out the first Modernist uprising in the Church, Pope Leo XIII taught in *Providentissimus Deus* that "all the books which the Church receives as sacred and canonical, *are written wholly and entirely, with all their parts, at the dictation of the Holy Ghost*; and so far is it from being possible that any error can co-exist with inspiration, that inspiration not only is essentially incompatible with error, but excludes and rejects it as absolutely and necessarily as *it is impossible that God Himself, the supreme Truth, can utter that which is not true.*"

But it is precisely this error that Groeschel advocates. He would have us believe that despite what the Gospel of John says, it is *not true* that "*except* you eat the flesh of the Son of man and drink His blood you *shall not have life* in you." He would prefer that Our Lord

---

[116]*Sunday Night Live with Fr. Benedict Groeschel*, July 24, 2005. (See Footnote #102.)
[117]"The Fourth Gospel is written in Greek." *Gospel of John*, CATHOLIC ENCYCLOPEDIA (1907 Ed.).

teach that if you eat His flesh and drink His blood you will have life in you, but that you will *also* have life in you *without* eating His flesh and drinking His blood. That is, Groeschel would prefer a Gospel which teaches that Holy Communion is an optional means of obtaining divine grace. To drive home his error, Groeschel gave his viewers two irrelevant examples that are certainly gravely misleading:

> In fact, there are a number of people in the Bible, in the New Testament, who obviously get saved, who did not eat Christ's flesh and drink His blood. Right off the bat is the good thief. He was never baptized, but Jesus says to him "Today you will be with Me in paradise"....
>
> My friend Bishop Walsh couldn't go to Communion for 14 years because he was a prisoner in a Chinese communist cell. Was he lost? Of course not, he was a saint....[118]

Now of course the good thief was saved without Holy Communion or water Baptism because *the New Law had not yet come into effect.* The Church's mission did not even begin until Easter Sunday, when the Risen Lord entered the Upper Room, breathed upon His apostles and gave them the power to bind and loose sins.[119] Hence, as the Council of Florence declared infallibly, the necessity of the sacraments, and the duty to abandon the rituals of the Old Law, arose only "after promulgation of the Gospel" by the Apostles.[120]

As for the example of Bishop Walsh, this is pure sophistry: Bishop Walsh *had* received Holy Communion before his imprisonment, and he received it afterwards until his death. During his imprisonment the bishop's failure to receive the Sacrament at least once a year (as the law of the Church requires) was obviously excused by the circumstances.

Groeschel also stated: "I do think it [the Gospel] makes very clear that if a person understands the eating of Christ's flesh and blood as the Eucharist, they are very seriously obliged to receive the

---

[118]*Sunday Night Live with Fr. Benedict Groeschel*, July 24, 2005. (See Footnote #102.)
[119]John 20:22-23: "When He had said this, He breathed on them; and He said to them: Receive ye the Holy Ghost. Whose sins you shall forgive, they are forgiven them: and whose sins you shall retain, they are retained."
[120]Council of Florence, Dz. 712.

Eucharist..." This is another Modernist obfuscation of the truth, for it suggests that the sacrament of Holy Communion is necessary only for those who happen to believe in it, but not for those who do not believe. The truth, however, is that one who hears the Gospel's teaching on the Eucharist is *obliged to believe that teaching* as necessary for salvation. This is why, after many disciples abandoned Jesus when He revealed the command to eat His flesh and drink His blood, Peter, speaking for the faithful disciples who remained, told Jesus that they would not also go away, because "Lord, to whom shall we go? You have the words of *eternal life...*" (John 6:67-69) That is, Peter understood that the Eucharist is *objectively* necessary for the eternal salvation of all men *whether or not they believe*, since the Eucharist and the other sacraments are the ordinary means of salvation which God has entrusted to His Church. As Fr. Groeschel would apparently have it, however, the disciples who walked away because they did not "understand the eating of Christ's flesh and blood as the Eucharist" were in no need of the sacrament for salvation.

Yet Our Lord could not have been clearer: "Except you eat the flesh of the Son of man and drink His blood, you shall not have life in you. He that eateth My flesh and drinketh My blood hath everlasting life: and I will raise him up in the last day. For My flesh is meat indeed: and My blood is drink indeed. He that eateth My flesh and drinketh My blood abideth in Me: and I in him."[121] This does not mean that those who do not partake of the Sacrament of Holy Communion through no fault of their own are all lost. But it does mean that Holy Communion is the ordinary and necessary means by which God *feeds* His sheep so that they will not starve for lack of grace, and so that they will attain life everlasting.

And the other sacraments are, likewise, the ordinary and necessary means by which God grants saving grace, as the Council of Trent has infallibly declared. If it were not so—if God bestowed sanctifying grace and thus salvation equally on those who believe in the sacraments and those who do not believe in them—then, again, the sacraments would be rendered superfluous. In fact, the sacraments would be merely a burden imposed on Catholics only.

But Groeschel and EWTN, with their "ecumenical" agenda, cannot admit that the sacraments of the Catholic Church are objectively *necessary* for the salvation of all men. For if they were to admit this, they would also have to admit that *membership* in the

---

[121]John 6:54-57.

Catholic Church is not merely desirable, but a matter of eternal life and death, precisely as the Church has taught infallibly time after time. This is the very truth that New Church, and thus EWTN, finds intolerable and refuses to preach.

Indeed, New Church's fear and loathing of the dogma that outside the Catholic Church there is no salvation led Groeschel literally to turn away a convert at the door during his television show. A woman named Bertha from Rochester called and told Groeschel on the air a truly heart-rending story of a soul in search of the Catholic Church. The reader is invited to study the following words carefully for the obvious signs that this woman was being led by God to conversion in an extraordinary way:

> I'm not Catholic, although later in life I married a man who was Catholic. And I never went through the Church [to get married]. And how God works in infinite ways is that, you know, *I've always respected the Catholic Church*, and my husband was dying with cancer, and that's when the priest came over and said now your marriage has been recognized in the Church [an apparent reference to a solemnization of the marriage in view of the husband's nearness to death].

> And that was 25 years ago. And Father Groeschel, two years ago *I had a heart attack*, and I put on EWTN and listened to you... and I know I can't do the Mass (choking up). I don't know where I'm going with this, Father (choking up), but... I pray for each and every one of you.

> And Father, I want to let you know that years ago *I met Bishop Fulton Sheen*. And my nephew was in Vietnam, and he [Sheen] gave me a medallion, a medal, and said "See that your nephew gets that, and he'll come home safe." *And every day I lit candles at the Catholic church for him when he was in Vietnam.* And today he always says to me "Aunt Bert, all your prayers brought me home," and I said (choking up) "*It was the Catholic Faith that did it.*"

Groeschel, a Franciscan monk who is supposed to be a shepherd of souls, was here presented with a woman practically begging to be brought into the Church on national television. Her husband had already passed into eternity, and she herself had had a heart attack. She had even been graced by a personal encounter with the late, great Bishop Sheen, who had given her and her nephew spiritual assistance. She had prayed and lit candles in the local Catholic church and knew that *the Catholic Faith* had spared her nephew from death in Vietnam.

And what did Groeschel do for this poor, kindly soul who clearly wanted to come home to Rome before she dies? Here is what he said to Bertha — in tones of amusement, no less:

> Maybe you ought to think about talking to someone in your area. It sounds like (amused tone bordering on chuckle) you're awfully close to the Catholic Church. *I don't want to get accused by the Protestant clergy of Rochester of sheep stealing*, but sounds like you're practically at the edge of the door.

Yes, Bertha *was* practically at the edge of the door. But Groeschel did not want to "steal sheep" from the Protestant clergy of Rochester, with their "gospel" of divorce, contraception, abortion and innumerable heresies. Instead, Groeschel cut the conversation short and turned this potential convert away before millions of viewers:

> And you'll be interested to know that I had a Lutheran relative named Bertha when I was a boy. *And my Lutheran relatives were fine devout Christian people.* So God bless you and thank you for that witness, and please keep praying for me, that the Lord will let me get a little more use out of my left arm.

In perfect "ecumenical" fashion Groeschel assured Bertha that his Lutheran relative by the same name, indeed all his Lutheran relatives, were fine devout Christians, the implication being that Bertha herself, as another fine devout Christian, was in no need of the Catholic Church to save her soul. "Maybe" she should "think about talking to someone" about becoming a Catholic someday, but there was no great urgency — even if she had already had a heart attack! Groeschel did not even invite Bertha to call a private line for help in joining the Church, as even Protestant televangelists do in their "churches." Instead, he asked *Bertha* to pray for *him* so that his arm would get better, and told her goodbye.

This is the "ecumenical" attitude in all its evil: There is no longer any need for Protestants to return to the Catholic Church to save their souls. The truth that the Catholic Church is the ark of salvation for all mankind is hidden with embarrassment, and those outside the ark are assured that they are perfectly safe where they are. At most, the Catholic Church is presented as the best of the "Christian churches"—a cruise ship, as compared with the perfectly serviceable yachts and motor boats of the innumerable Protestant denominations.

The "moderately" Modernist theme that Catholicism is merely the best form of "Christianity," but by no means the only form pleasing to God, pervades EWTN's content. Another prominent example is the popular EWTN series *The Journey Home*, in which the ex-Protestant minister Marcus Grodi conducts cozy chats with former Protestants who uniformly describe their "faith journey" to the Catholic Church as essentially the perfection and fulfillment of their earlier Protestant Christianity. The truth that Protestantism is a human system fraught with error and immorality that is deadly to the soul, that its adherents are *dissidents* who must return to the one true Church, not merely for spiritual improvement but for the salvation of their souls, is never frankly discussed, not even in the most diplomatic terms. The show never even intimates that membership in the Catholic Church is, for anyone, a matter of spiritual life and death rather than "a closer walk with Jesus." Granted, prudence may preclude an overly aggressive approach to the subject of eternal damnation. But to *avoid it completely*, to refrain from providing even *a fraternal suggestion* that "life and salvation are here concerned," as Pius XI put it in *Mortalium Animos* when addressing the condition of the Protestants, is a grave disservice to Protestant viewers, if not in fact a sin of omission.

Typical of this approach to conversion as a kind of spiritual improvement program is Grodi's recent interview of a medical doctor who became a Catholic and now teaches RCIA (Rite of Christian Initiation for Adults) courses for potential converts at the local parish.[122] The guest described how he once led a "cell group" of Baptists as part of a large Baptist "community church." Grodi waxed enthusiastic about these Protestant cell groups: "they capture the enthusiasm that's there when you're starting a new church... Imagine a priest and some parishioners were starting a new church." Grodi

---

[122]Interview of Steve G. Milam, M.D. on *The Journey Home*, February 28, 2005.

thus implicitly validated Protestant cell groups as legitimate churches, not unlike Catholic parishes. These "cell groups," said Grodi, are "an important part of the growth of evangelicalism" — as if the growth of Protestant sects (many of whose members are ex-Catholics) were an auspicious social development that ought to be encouraged.

"Certainly as an evangelical [Protestant] I had the Gospel," said the doctor with complete confidence, as Grodi offered nothing to contradict this assertion. Of course, this man did not have "the Gospel" as a Protestant, but only a corrupted human version of it. As Pius XI observed in *Mortalium Animos*: "Everyone knows that John himself, the Apostle of love, who seems to reveal in his Gospel the secrets of the Sacred Heart of Jesus, and who never ceased to impress on the memories of his followers the new commandment 'Love one another,' altogether forbade any intercourse [close relations] with those who professed *a mutilated and corrupt version of Christ's teaching*: 'If any man come to you and bring not this doctrine, receive him not into the house nor say to him: God speed you.'" On EWTN's *The Journey Home*, as in New Church at large, one never sees anything like this kind of candor. Yet such candor is even more necessary today, when Protestants are drifting ever further from the truth and the Protestant sects are in vastly worse condition than when Pius XI was living.

Grodi's guest went on to say that "the addition of the sacraments to nourish my soul [was] wonderful" and that "my intimacy with my Lord and Savior is even greater" than it was when he was a Baptist. By implication, then, his Baptist friends are in no danger of damnation. They have the Gospel and they have intimacy with Our Lord, just as he did when he was a Baptist. But his Baptist friends could have *more* "intimacy," *more* "nourishment," if they were Catholics. This wrongly assumes, in the first place, that humanly-founded Protestant sects *as such* provide some degree of genuine spiritual nourishment, as opposed to the grace God may choose to bestow on certain individuals, *despite* their being members of a sect, in order to lead them toward the Catholic Church. Speaking of precisely such a grace, Pius XII declared in his encyclical letter *Mystici Corporis* that the members of Protestant sects must "correspond to the interior movements of grace, [and] seek to withdraw from that state in which they cannot be sure of their salvation" — i.e., they must enter the Catholic Church, which is the Mystical Body of Christ. As Pius XII observed elsewhere, the members of Protestant sects are "wandering sheep, *unknown to the Shepherd*, limbs who *are not part of a life-giving body*, but separated, arid and *deprived of spiritual nourishment*."[123] Objectively speaking, then, the members of Protestant sects are starving to death spiritually, and are facing eternal death in the life hereafter.

At any rate, this reduction of Catholicism to "Protestantism plus" (or greater "nourishment" than Protestantism) is implicit in the whole EWTN series and indeed the whole "ecumenical" approach to non-Catholics. But as noted earlier, the Council of Trent taught infallibly that the seven sacraments are necessary for our *salvation*, not merely for additional spiritual nourishment:

> CANON IV.—If anyone shall say that the sacraments of the New Law *are not necessary for salvation*, but are superfluous, and that, although all (the sacraments) are not necessary for every individual, without them or without the desire for them through faith alone men obtain from God the grace of justification: *let him be anathema*.[124]

And the Council of Trent specifically anathematized the idea that the sacraments were instituted merely to promote additional nourishment of faith alone.

> CANON V.—If anyone shall say that these sacraments have been instituted for the nourishing of faith alone: let him be anathema.[125]

EWTN's neglect of the infallible Catholic dogma that the sacraments—especially Holy Orders, the Holy Eucharist, Confession, Confirmation, and Extreme Unction, none of which the Protestants have—are necessary *to gain Heaven and to avoid hell* has resulted in de facto negation of the dogma. Neither Grodi nor his guest suggested *even to the ex-Catholics* who have defected into the Protestant sect to which his guest formerly belonged, that the adherents of that sect were in eternal jeopardy because of their defection from the Catholic Church and their abandonment of the sacraments. And this is not

---

[123]Pope Pius XII, *Sommamente Gradita*, September 20, 1942.
[124]Council of Trent, *Canons on the Sacraments in General*; Denzinger, 847.
[125]Ibid., Denzinger, 848.

even to mention millions of other ex-Catholics who have joined Protestant sects around the world.

And what sort of convert does the new "ecumenical" approach produce? One does not see any sign of the Church militant in the remark by Grodi's guest that he tells his RCIA students: "I can support the Church's teaching" against contraception, "but it's a whole lot easier for me" because he had had himself sterilized (an act he now admits was "a mistake"). The very phrase "I can support" reveals the persistence of a Protestant mentality rather than the obedient subjection of mind and will to an infallible teaching of the Magisterium. What one "can support" is irrelevant to what one must *believe* as a Catholic. What one "can support" is hardly the way to present an infallible Church teaching that condemns a mortal sin worthy of eternal damnation. What *does* matter is that adherence to the teaching of the Church on faith and morals is necessary for salvation. Our Lord could not have put the matter more clearly: "He who believes and is baptized shall be saved. He who believes not shall be condemned." Not only does the truth matter, it matters for salvation. It is only by living the truth, with the grace of the sacraments, that our souls can be made pleasing to God. As Our Lord admonished us: "*If* you keep My commandments, you shall abide in My love.... You are My friends, *if* you do the things that I command you." (John 15:10,14)

In fact, the notion that Protestants are committing mortal sins from which they need to be cleansed in the confessional for their salvation was never mentioned or even suggested by Grodi or his guest. (Nor is it suggested, to my knowledge, anywhere in EWTN's "ecumenical" content.) Concerning the Sacrament of Confession, Grodi's guest stated: "I actually don't mind confession." He doesn't *mind* it? This hardly reflects a Catholic understanding of how vital this Sacrament is to maintaining one's soul in a state of grace. A Catholic should be inclined to fall on his knees in gratitude for this wonderful sacrament, not receive it as a bleak exercise. The guest made a strange and heterodox distinction between confessing one's sins directly to the Lord and "sacramental confession." The guest contended that one must already have perfect contrition before he enters the confessional, and thus be forgiven by God, *before* "sacramental confession" allows one to "make peace with the Church." The suggestion that "sacramental confession" (unlike "direct" confession) is for "making peace with the Church" rather than reconciling oneself to God has no support in Catholic teaching.

This idea seems designed to create the impression in Protestants that Confession is "forgiveness plus" just as Catholicism is "Protestantism plus": i.e., that although one can readily be forgiven by God without the Sacrament of Confession, with the sacrament one receives the "plus" of "making peace with the Church," as if the Church were somehow entitled to a repentance distinct from that owed to God. From this heterodox idea logically follows the error that Protestants, who do not belong to the Church, do not need the Sacrament of Confession as such, since they do not have to "make peace with the Church."

More important, Grodi's guest seemed unfamiliar with the Catholic doctrine that outside of the Sacrament of Confession imperfect contrition—i.e., the mere fear of eternal punishment—cannot obtain God's forgiveness. Without *perfect* contrition—i.e., true and sincere sorrow for having offended God purely because He deserves all our love—one cannot be forgiven his mortal sins without absolution by a priest. The Catholic Church teaches, however, that with the Sacrament of Confession administered by a priest, imperfect contrition *does* suffice for the forgiveness of sins. As the Council of Trent declares, "*without the sacrament of penance* it [imperfect contrition] cannot per se lead the sinner to justification," but with the Sacrament it does.[126] This is the divine mercy inherent in the Sacrament of Confession, which enables even the weakest of sinners to be reconciled to God in the confessional, so long as they fear divine punishment.

Furthermore, the Council of Trent declared that even in the exceptional case where a sinner has perfect contrition for his sins and is thus forgiven before approaching the Sacrament—and who can be certain that his contrition is perfect?—the sinner's reconciliation with God cannot be separated *from his desire to receive the Sacrament*: "The Council further teaches that, though contrition may *sometimes* be made perfect by charity and *may* reconcile men to God before the actual reception of this sacrament, still the reconciliation is not to be ascribed to the contrition apart from the desire for the sacrament which it includes."[127] This means that even if there is an act of perfect contrition, one must still intend to receive the Sacrament of Confession at the first opportunity.

---

[126]Council of Trent, *Doctrine on the Sacrament of Penance*, Chapter 4; Denzinger, 898.
[127]Ibid.

Hence the Sacrament of Confession is not merely an optional mode of divine forgiveness. Without it, many souls would be damned for all eternity. Yet here again Catholic dogma—the general *necessity* of the Sacrament of Confession for the absolution from mortal sin—is implicitly denied by EWTN.

Bear in mind that the sentiments and faulty opinions expressed by Grodi's guest are those of *an RCIA instructor*—someone who is supposed to be forming potential new converts. I am not suggesting for a moment that this man is not sincere in his desire to be a Catholic and to live the Faith. I am suggesting that, due to the breakdown of sound catechesis in the Catholic Church since the Second Vatican Council, this man does not know the Faith as he should *because no one taught it to him* with the requisite thoroughness and accuracy. And yet EWTN holds this individual out as one who is competent to instruct others in the Faith, thereby compounding many times over the baneful effect of his dubious (if not outright heterodox) remarks.

At EWTN, and throughout the ecumenical landscape of New Church, the defined dogmas that outside the Church there is no salvation, and that the sacraments are *necessary* for salvation, have been replaced by the vague notion that outside the Catholic Church there is no *fullness* of spiritual life. This theme of a vague "fullness" as opposed to a concrete *salvation* being found in the Church pervades EWTN's programming.

One of many recent examples is an on-the-air Q & A session in which EWTN commentator Fr. John Trigilio remarked, in response to an emailed question, that a Protestant considering conversion is "being called into the fullness of Christianity"—not into the true Church, as in stepping over a threshold that separates human sects from the divine ark of salvation, but merely into the "fullness" of what a Protestant supposedly already possesses. As for a Jew who converts, said Trigilio, he is being called into "the fullness of the Covenant."[128] So even Jews, according to EWTN, merely need to acquire a "fullness" of what they already possess.

To suggest, however, that a Jew who converts is merely receiving the "fullness of the Covenant" is to imply that Jews outside the Church are still in a covenant relationship with God. This notion contradicts the defined dogma that the Old Covenant was abrogated by the New Covenant in Jesus Christ, leaving the

---

[128]*Open Line*, broadcast of March 10, 2005.

Jews who refused to recognize Jesus of Nazareth as the Christ and enter His Church in possession of no covenant at all. EWTN's avid promotion of this heresy (veiled in a certain ambiguity) is discussed further on.[129]

Given this kind of thinking, it is hardly surprising that since Vatican II the rate of conversions has plummeted: "fullness," as opposed to salvation, is not much of an incentive to leave a denomination whose teaching comfortably accommodates one's sins, while still allowing one to have "the Gospel" and "intimacy with Our Lord." Nor is it surprising that EWTN never issues any sort of plea to Protestants—or even to *ex-Catholics* in Protestant sects—that eternal salvation is at risk in their separation from the Church. One never hears this *because New Church really does not believe this.* Thus, the New Church mentality is at least suspect of heresy,[130] even if it is not possible for us to judge subjective intentions. (Nevertheless, Catholics have the right to demand that those whose words and deeds give rise to suspicion of heresy affirm their orthodoxy without equivocation. If they refuse, we are entitled to presume they are not orthodox Catholics.)

It must be said in all candor that the impression that the return of the Protestant dissidents to Rome is no longer necessary has been fostered by Pope John Paul II's own ecumenical gestures, such as bestowing pectoral crosses on pro-abortion and pro-"gay" Anglican "bishops" and celebrating joint Vespers services with pro-abortion Lutheran "bishops" (with *female* Lutheran "bishops" in attendance).[131] These "bishops" are really laymen, as Pope Leo XIII made clear in his infallible declaration on the invalidity of Anglican priestly orders, *Apostolicae Curae* (1893). According to Dr. Peterson, Donovan's position at the EWTN theological committee meetings

---

[129]See Chapter 10, "Promoting the Return of the Judaizers."

[130]A *material* heretic is one who does not think his erroneous belief is contrary to Catholic dogma, even though it is. A *formal* heretic, on the other hand, knows full well that he is contradicting Catholic dogma, but obstinately refuses to abandon his errors against the Catholic Faith. *See* Can. 751, CIC (1983).

[131]"Joint Catholic-Lutheran Vespers at Vatican," CWNews.com, November 15, 1999 (see http://cwnews.com/news/viewstory.cfm?recnum=11541): "Arch-bishops G.H. Hammar and Jukka Paarma—the Lutheran primates of Sweden and Finland, respectively—and Bishops Anders Arborelius of Stockholm and Czeslaw Kozon of Copenhagen joined with the Holy Father for the Vespers service. Several other Lutheran bishops from the Scandinavian countries were present for the ceremony, including two female bishops."

was that the Pope's gestures were "part of the overall ecumenical orientation of the Church, and that… the subject [of Anglican orders] was being discussed again and that we don't know the final story on that." That is, Donovan was prepared to question the permanent validity of Pope Leo XIII's infallible declaration. This, said Peterson, "was the general consensus of the theological committee." Yet even the former Cardinal Ratzinger, in his Doctrinal Commentary on the Concluding Formula of the *Professio Fidei* (1998) ranked Leo's declaration among those truths to be "definitively held" by Catholics because they are "truths connected to revelation by historical necessity" and therefore cannot be questioned.

The attitude taken by Donovan and EWTN seems to mirror that of Cardinal Walter Kasper, John Paul II's choice to head the Pontifical Council for the Promotion of Christian Unity, who has thus far been retained in office by Benedict XVI. Kasper openly declared within days of his elevation to the rank of Cardinal in 2001 that "The decision of Vatican II to which the Pope adheres is absolutely clear: Today we no longer understand ecumenism in the sense of a return, by which the others would 'be converted' and return to being 'catholics' [sic]. This was expressly abandoned by Vatican II."[132] In early 2003, Kasper called for a "re-evaluation" in the "new ecumenical context" of Pope Leo XIII's infallible declaration on the invalidity of Anglican orders.[133] The Vatican has done nothing to stop Kasper's bold injections of more ecumenical confusion into the

---

[132]*Adista*, February 26, 2001: "La decisione del Vaticano II alla quale il papa si attiene, è assolutamente chiara: noi intendiamo l'ecumenismo oggi non più nel senso dell'ecumenismo del ritorno, secondo il quale gli altri devono 'convertirsi' e diventare 'cattolici.' Questo è stato espressamente abbandonato dal Vaticano II."

[133]*The Tablet*, May 24: 2003. As Kasper said: "As I see the problem and its possible solution, it is not a question of apostolic succession in the sense of an historical chain of laying on of hands running back through the centuries to one of the apostles; this would be a very mechanical and individualistic vision, which by the way historically could hardly be proved and ascertained…. To stand in the apostolic succession is not a matter of an individual historical chain but of collegial membership in a collegium, which as a whole goes back to the apostles by sharing the same apostolic faith… It is beyond the scope of our present context to discuss what this means for a re-evaluation of *Apostolicae Curae* (1896) of Pope Leo XIII, who declared Anglican orders null and void, a decision which still stands between our Churches. Without doubt this decision, as Cardinal Willebrands had already affirmed, must be understood in our new ecumenical context in which our communion in faith and mission has considerably grown. A final solution can only be found in the larger context of full communion in faith, sacramental life and shared apostolic mission."

Church.[134] Perhaps that is because Kasper is hardly alone, but merely one of the more audacious mouthpieces for the currently prevailing attitude in the upper hierarchy. In early 2001, for example, Most Rev. Cormac Murphy-O'Connor, Archbishop of Westminster, declared that "if we look at all the Roman documents in recent years, it is clear that they do not spell a turning back to the 'ecumenism of return,' or 'you-come-inism.' The direction and dialogue of convergence were firmly set by the Second Vatican Council..."[135] In sum, forty years of ecumenism have practically destroyed recognition of the radical supernatural difference—a difference that could mean life or death for all eternity—between human organizations founded in rebellion and the one true Church founded by Christ, outside of which no one is saved and to which the dissidents ought to return. It is not that Grodi and his guests never mention that Protestants are mistaken in their doctrines. In fact, they do mention it, quite frequently. What is not mentioned, however, is that theological errors have eternal consequences, and that without the Catholic Church and her sacraments one cannot expect to be saved. Again, if it were otherwise, why would Our Lord have founded His Church at the cost of His own infinitely precious Blood?

EWTN's approach to the Orthodox schismatics is no better than its approach to the Protestants. During the aforementioned broadcast of *Sunday Night Live with Father Groeschel*, for example, Groeschel even went so far as to suggest that schismatic Orthodox worship is not only just as good as Catholic worship, but that it is just as good *for Catholics*. A woman caller asked Groeschel whether, if she attended a divine liturgy at an Orthodox church on Sunday, "do I have to go again to a Roman Catholic Church later on that day?" Here is Groeschel's astounding answer:

> Absolutely, you would *not* [have to go to a Catholic Mass] because *you've been to Mass*. However, if you

---

[134]This is not even to mention Kasper's public declaration that Vatican II repudiated any effort by the Catholic Church to convert the Jews: "[T]he old theory of substitution is gone since the Second Vatican Council. For us Christians today the covenant with the Jewish people is a living heritage, a living reality.... Therefore, the Church believes that Judaism, i.e. the faithful response of the Jewish people to God's irrevocable covenant, is salvific for them, because God is faithful to his promises." Address at the 17th meeting of the International Catholic-Jewish Liaison Committee, New York, May 1, 2001.

[135]De Lubac Lecture, Salford University, January 18, 2001.

wanted to be a *stickler to the law*, you're supposed to fulfill your Mass obligation in a Catholic Church. But let me tell ya, it's a cliffhanger.... You certainly would have gone, when you go to the Orthodox liturgy, you would have gone to what we call the Mass, and if you wanted to be *a canonical stickler* you could go to another Mass. But *you certainly have gone to Mass*. You've *fulfilled the commandment keep holy the Lord's day*. Whether you've fulfilled canon law, I really don't know.

So here we have EWTN's leading theological "light" telling millions of Catholics that attending Mass at a schismatic Orthodox church fulfills God's commandment and the Sunday obligation, and that only a "canonical stickler" would go to another Mass in a Catholic church. It seems the only "schism" that EWTN and the New Church establishment recognize is the "schism" of *Catholics* who hold fast to the traditional Latin Mass by attending it at "irregular" Catholic chapels.[136] This is a point to which I shall return presently.

Another example of EWTN's indifferentist "ecumenical" attitude toward schismatics is this advice on "non-Catholic salvation" by EWTN "expert" Richard Geraghty (whose actual field of expertise is philosophy, not theology). Geraghty was responding to a question posed by the Catholic wife of an Orthodox adherent:

**Non-Catholic Salvation**
**Question from S____**

Hi there, I am married to a wonderful, supportive, Orthodox Christian [sic] man. We have a good marriage,

---

[136]EWTN solemnly warns against anyone attending traditional Latin Masses offered by *the Catholic priests* of the Society of Saint Pius X, who are said to have "left the Church." For example, according to EWTN "expert" David Gregson, "Some groups (the largest being the Society of St. Pius X) have left the Catholic Church in order to celebrate the Tridentine rite without approval." EWTN Q&A Forum, advice of May 3, 2004 on "Catholic Rites". Irony of ironies, EWTN is even less tolerant of Roman Catholic Tradition than the Vatican apparatus, which advises that attendance at SSPX Masses *does* fulfill the Sunday obligation, even if the Vatican cannot recommend such attendance: "In the strict sense you may fulfill your Sunday obligation by attending a Mass celebrated by a priest of the Society of St. Pius X.... It would seem that a modest contribution to the collection at Mass could be justified." See, Letter from Pontifical Commission Ecclesia Dei, dated January 18, 2003, reproduced in full at: http://www.unavoce.org/articles/2003/perl-011803.htm.

although a part of me is very sad that he is not catholic [sic]. However, their service is extremely similar to ours. Except that it is much longer (3 hours as opposed to 1 hr in Catholic Mass). My question is this, since they are so close to Catholics in their beliefs and customs, except for not acknowledging the Pope as the supreme head of their church, is it not possible for them to attain everlasting life? *Surely Jesus didn't invent Catholicism, but rather, Christianity.* So, if we are all Christians and we follow his [sic] commandments, then shouldn't we be ok? Please advise. Thank you!

In reply, Geraghty stated:

**Answer by Richard Geraghty:**

Dear S____,
Certainly *it is very possible for your husband to attain everlasting life.* The requirement that God puts on any human being is that they live according to their conscience. Now the conscience of each man is not perfect. It may tell them different things because of their upbringing. But all in all, it will tell them to perform their duties to God and man *as they see those duties....* Dr. Geraghty[137]

Notice, first of all, that Geraghty does not take exception to the inquirer's objectively heretical statement that "Jesus didn't invent Catholicism, but rather, Christianity..." and that it suffices if one is a "Christian" and follows "his [sic] commandments." This opinion flirts with the very error condemned by Pope Gregory XVI in *Mirari Vos*: that all that matters for salvation is that one maintain morality, whether or not one embraces what has been revealed by Christ through His Church. As Gregory XVI declared:

Now We consider another abundant source of the evils with which the Church is afflicted at present: indifferentism. This perverse opinion is spread on all sides by the fraud of the wicked who claim that *it is*

---

[137]See EWTN Q&A Forum, advice by Richard Geraghty of February 19, 2005 on "Non-Catholic Salvation".

*possible to obtain the eternal salvation of the soul by the profession of any kind of religion, as long as morality is maintained.* Surely, in so clear a matter, you will drive this deadly error far from the people committed to your care.

Furthermore, the First Commandment is objectively violated by anyone, including members of the Orthodox churches, who refuses to worship God in the manner He ordains: in the Catholic Church according to Catholic dogma, including the papal primacy, which the Orthodox adamantly reject.

The inquirer expresses the errors of the "ecumenical" attitude in a nutshell, and EWTN does nothing to combat those errors. Rather, Geraghty *only confirms the inquirer in her indifferentism,* assuring her that it is "very possible for your husband to attain everlasting life" even though he persists in his membership in a schismatic Orthodox church despite his marriage to a Catholic, whose very marriage to him places him on notice of his duties to the Catholic Church. But according to Geraghty's version of Catholic teaching, "the requirement that God puts on any human being is that they live according to their conscience" which may "tell them different things because of their upbringing." All that matters, says he, is that people "perform their duties to God and man *as they see those duties...*" There is no discussion whatever of the husband's objectively culpable failure to embrace the Catholic religion, of whose claims he is fully aware by virtue of being married to a Catholic who *seeks his conversion.* Nor is there any discussion of culpability for the husband's promotion of religious division within his own household, where he gives scandal by refusing to submit to the same Roman Pontiff to whom his own wife submits. It is amazing that EWTN would dare to give such assurances concerning the eternal salvation of a man in this situation. But such is the "ecumenical" attitude EWTN promotes.

What EWTN promotes, however, is hardly the teaching of the Catholic Church. As Pope Gregory XVI (quoting St. Ignatius of Antioch) declared in his encyclical *Summo Iugiter Studio* (1832), concerning *the evil of mixed marriages* with schismatics: "Be not deceived, my brother; if anyone follows a schismatic, he will not attain the inheritance of the kingdom of God." As Pope Gregory later declared in *Mirari Vos:*

With the admonition of the apostle that "there is one Lord, one faith, one baptism" may those fear who contrive the notion that the safe harbor of salvation is open to persons of any religion whatever. They should consider the testimony of Christ Himself that "those who are not with Christ are against Him," and that they disperse unhappily who do not gather with Him. Therefore *"without a doubt, they will perish forever, unless they hold the Catholic Faith whole and inviolate."* Let them hear Jerome who, while the Church was torn into three parts by schism, tells us that whenever someone tried to persuade him to join his group he always exclaimed: "He who is for the See of Peter is for me." *A schismatic flatters himself falsely if he asserts that he, too, has been washed in the waters of regeneration.* Indeed Augustine would reply to such a man: "The branch has the same form when it has been cut off from the vine; but of what profit for it is the form, if it does not live from the root?"

Pope Leo XIII, in his apostolic exhortation *Præclara Gratulationis Publicæ* (1894) — only 68 years before Vatican II — reaffirmed the Church's perennial teaching on the spiritual necessity of the Orthodox reuniting themselves with Rome:

Therefore, Our mouth is open to you, to you all of Greek or other Oriental rites who are *separated from the Catholic Church.* We earnestly desire that each and every one of you should meditate upon the words, so full of gravity and love, addressed by Bessarion to your forefathers: *"What answer shall we give to God* when He comes to ask why we have separated from our brethren: to Him who, to unite us and bring us into one fold, came down from Heaven, was incarnate, and was crucified?... It is not for any human motive, but impelled by divine charity *and a desire for the salvation of all*, that We advise the reconciliation and union with the Church of Rome; and We mean a perfect and complete union, such as could not subsist in any way if nothing else was brought about but a certain kind of agreement in the tenets of belief and an intercourse [exchange] of fraternal love. The true union between Christians is that which Jesus Christ, the Author of the Church, instituted and desired, and *which consists in a unity of faith and a unity of government.*

In the same vein, St. Pius X, in his 1910 encyclical letter *Ex Quo* on the reunion of the Eastern churches, declared that any attempt at reunion with the Orthodox:

> will be in vain unless first, *and above all*, they hold *the true and whole Catholic Faith* as it has been handed down and consecrated in Holy Scripture, the tradition of the Fathers, the consent of the Church, the general councils and the decrees of the Supreme Pontiffs.... Let, then, all those who strive to defend the cause of unity go forth; let them go forth wearing the helmet of faith, holding to the anchor of hope, and inflamed with the fire of charity, to work unceasingly in this most heavenly enterprise; and God, the author and lover of peace, will hasten the day when the nations of the East shall *return* to Catholic unity, and, united to the Apostolic See, *after casting away their errors*, shall *enter the port of everlasting salvation*.

Notice how each of these Popes made it clear that *salvation* is at stake unless the schismatic Orthodox reunite with the See of Peter, and that reunion is not possible *unless and until the Orthodox accept the Catholic Faith whole and entire* and abandon their *theological errors*.

Contrary to what EWTN's "expert" advice would suggest, the errors of the Orthodox are not merely superficial differences with Roman Catholicism. As one Orthodox theologian has put it: "Most Orthodox, in attempting to distinguish between Orthodoxy and Roman Catholicism, usually mention the Pope or Purgatory, sometimes the *filioque*. Historically, the differences, however, are far more numerous and quite profound."[138] Indeed, the Orthodox reject not only the papal primacy, Purgatory (whose existence they deny) and the *filioque* (the Catholic dogma that the Holy Ghost proceeds from both the Father and the Son, and not the Father only as the Orthodox hold), but also the Catholic dogma on Original Sin (the Orthodox claim that we have inherited only the consequences of Adam's sin, but not the stain of his guilt). The Orthodox churches also more or less depart from the Catholic teaching on the indissolubility of marriage, as they allow divorce and remarriage in certain cases—as many as three times for one person, depending on

---

[138]"WHAT ARE THE DIFFERENCES BETWEEN ORTHODOXY AND ROMAN CATHOLICISM?" by Father Michael Azkoul at: http://www.ocf.org/Orthodox Page/reading/ortho_cath.html.

the Orthodox church in question.[139]

Moreover, doctrinal errors aside, no reunion with the Orthodox is even possible without their express submission to the Roman Pontiff, now and forever. Hence in the passage quoted above, Pope Leo XIII, contrary to today's "Catholic ecumenists," insisted that reunion with the Orthodox could not be achieved simply by "a certain kind of agreement in the tenets of belief and an intercourse of fraternal love." Only belief in *all* Catholic dogmas without exception *and* submission to the Pope can produce a true reunion and thus assure salvation for the Orthodox.

EWTN's "expert" advice to the Catholic woman with an Orthodox husband simply ignores these crucial matters of salvation. Yet the Catholic Church, speaking through her Popes and Councils, has not issued empty pronouncements, but rather vital truths actually applicable to real people living in schism. The Council of Florence in particular obviously had in view *the actual objective state* of the Orthodox schismatics then living when it declared that "those not living *within the Catholic Church*, not only pagans, but also Jews, heretics and *schismatics*, cannot become participants in eternal life, but will depart 'into everlasting fire which was prepared for the devil and his angels,' unless before the end of life the same have been added to the flock...." That is, the Council of Florence declared *infallibly* that schismatics are *outside* the Church, along with Jews, heretics and pagans.

Nor can it be argued that with the mere passage of time the Orthodox schism—or, for that matter, the Protestant rebellion—has somehow lost its objectively sinful character. The Council of Florence (1438 - 1445) condemned schism and warned of the prospect of eternal damnation for schismatics *four centuries* after the Greek schism started. (During the Council of Florence the Greek schism was actually healed, but only for just a few years.) The teaching of Pope

---

[139]See, e.g., the website of the Orthodox Church of America (OCA) an "autocephalous" (self-governing) Orthodox church that maintains ties with the Russian Orthodox patriarch in Moscow. Concerning divorce, the OCA declares: "While the Church stands opposed to divorce, the Church, in its concern for the salvation of its people, does permit divorced individuals to marry a second and even a third time. The Order of the Second or Third Marriage is somewhat different than that celebrated as a first marriage and it bears a penitential character. Second or third marriages are performed by 'economy' -- that is, out of concern for the spiritual well being of the parties involved and as an exception to the rule, so to speak." (http://www.oca.org/QA.asp?ID=139&SID=3)

St. Pius X in 1910, five centuries after the Council of Florence, does not in the least retreat from what Florence taught infallibly concerning the evil of schism.

Did the Orthodox somehow improve their standing before God between 1910 and 1962, when Vatican II began? Did they suddenly come inside the Church after having been infallibly declared to be outside her? This is impossible. Yet EWTN expresses no concern about the infallibly defined objective status of Orthodox schismatics,[140] but rather is now advising people—at the risk of their immortal souls—that it is "very possible to attain everlasting life" in one of the Orthodox churches cut off from Rome, so long as one follows whatever one's conscience tells him based on his "upbringing."

Thus, Donovan, his theological committee, and EWTN as a whole have followed the Modernist drift of the upper hierarchy, which has completely abandoned the constant teaching of the Roman Pontiffs before Vatican II: that the dissidents must return to the one true Church, outside of which there is no salvation. At EWTN the return of the dissidents to the one true Church is no longer necessary, it seems. Worse, EWTN's approach effectively dispenses not only with the doctrine of the return of dissidents, but also the dogma *nulla salus* itself.

It should be obvious that if the conversion of non-Catholics is no longer presented as necessary for their salvation, non-Catholics will be far less likely to convert and the number of conversions will, in consequence, plummet. That is exactly what has happened since the commencement of "the ecumenical venture" after Vatican II. As just one of innumerable indications, in 1965 there were 126,000 adult baptisms in the United States, but in 2002 there were only 80,000, even though the population of the United States has doubled over the past 40 years. Yet in the years before Vatican II, "the number of adult baptisms was skyrocketing: 38,232 in 1930, 73,677 in 1940, 84,908 in 1945, 119,173 in 1950, 137,310 in 1955, and 146,212 in 1960."[141]

Thanks to ecumenism and what EWTN's Fr. Levis calls the "more generous way" of "interpreting" the dogma that outside the Church

---

[140]We are not, obviously, speaking here of each and every particular soul that God will judge, but rather of the objectively observable condition of schismatics—i.e. that they are outside the Catholic Church, where none can be saved.

[141]Kenneth C. Jones, "The Vatican II Renewal: Myth or Reality?" at http://www.seattlecatholic.com/article_20031208.html.

there is no salvation, there has been a near-total collapse of missionary activity—just as Blessed Pius IX feared when he forbade all further speculation about "the lot and condition after death of those who have never lived in the true Church of Christ." Father Giovanbattista Mondin, the vice rector of the Pontifical Urban University, observed that "[w]hat is taking place today is actually a 'demissionization' of the Catholic Church."[142]

At EWTN's theological committee meetings Dr. Peterson tried to get the members to address the collapse of the Catholic missions due to the effects of ecumenism. "I was worried about the lack of missionary zeal. There were always Protestants pouring millions and millions of dollars into Guatemala, Honduras... It is a known fact that they have targeted several Central American countries. There was also Spain, and Italy now has 600,000 satanists. It seems to me like the whole thing [ecumenism] has backfired, and who is going to take responsibility for this, who is going to fix it? So basically, the issue presented to Donovan was, look, ecumenism is a disaster." Donovan's answer to these concerns was essentially a non-answer: "He has a way of not saying anything. He was always: 'Trust the Pope, he knows what he is doing'... This is nonsense. Wrong has got to be wrong."

Peterson's frustration is shared by many informed Catholics, who know that Pope Pius XI refused to allow Catholic participation in the fledgling "ecumenical movement" precisely because it would be wrong for Catholics to expose themselves to the temptation of indifferentism, to the risk that they would slowly but surely come to believe the deadly error that, as Pius XI put it in *Mortalium Animos*, "all religions are more or less good and praiseworthy." Pius XI understood that the Protestants who had originated the "ecumenical movement" were enticing Catholics to take part with the seductive plea "that all who invoke the name of Christ should abstain from mutual reproaches and at long last be united in mutual charity…. All Christians, they add, should be as 'one': for then they would be much more powerful in driving out the pest of irreligion, which like a serpent daily creeps further and becomes more widely spread, and prepares to rob the Gospel of its strength. These things and others that class of men who are known as *pan-Christians* continually repeat and amplify…"

---

[142]*The Fatima Crusader*, Issue #29, September-November 1989, pages 22ff (see also http://www.fatimacrusader.com/cr29/cr29pg22.asp).

In his wisdom Pius XI recognized that "beneath these enticing words and blandishments lies hid a most grave error, by which the foundations of the Catholic Faith are completely destroyed." We see that error at work today in the modern "ecumenical movement," which has practically destroyed belief in the status of the Holy Catholic Church as the sole ark of salvation. Thanks to ecumenism, we no longer hear the constant teaching of the Popes as repeated emphatically by Pius XI in *Mortalium Animos*:

> [I]n this one Church of Christ no man can be or remain who does not accept, recognize and obey the authority and supremacy of Peter and his legitimate successors. Did not the ancestors of those who are now entangled in the errors of Photius and the reformers, obey the Bishop of Rome, the chief shepherd of souls? Alas their children left the home of their fathers... Let them therefore return to their common Father, who, forgetting the insults previously heaped on the Apostolic See, will receive them in the most loving fashion. For if, as they continually state, they long to be united with Us and ours, why do they not hasten to enter the Church, "the Mother and mistress of all Christ's faithful"? Let them hear Lactantius crying out: "The Catholic Church is alone in keeping the true worship. This is the fount of truth, this the house of faith, this the temple of God: if any man enter not here, or if any man go forth from it, *he is a stranger to the hope of life and salvation*. Let none delude himself with obstinate wrangling. *For life and salvation are here concerned*, which will be lost and entirely destroyed..."

For EWTN, however, there seems to be no difficulty in ignoring the warning of Pius XI and all his predecessors by doing today precisely what was forbidden yesterday. Although current participation in the "ecumenical movement" rests upon nothing but a fallible prudential judgment on a particular plan of action, and although that plan has utterly failed to achieve Christian unity— indeed, after forty years of fruitless "ecumenical dialogue," the Protestants and Orthodox are more confirmed in their errors than ever—EWTN presents ecumenism as if it were a dogma of the Faith no one may question. Yet even John Paul II recognized the right of

Catholics to express their doubts about ecumenism. In his inaugural encyclical *Redemptor Hominis*, His Holiness wrote:

> There are people who in the face of the difficulties or because they consider that the first ecumenical endeavors have brought negative results would have liked to turn back. Some even express the opinion that these efforts are harmful to the cause of the Gospel, are leading to a further rupture in the Church, are causing confusion of ideas in questions of faith and morals and are ending up with a specific indifferentism. *It is perhaps a good thing that the spokesmen for these opinions should express their fears.*

Unlike John Paul II, however, EWTN refuses to acknowledge the liberty of the faithful to express their conscientious opposition to ecumenism. But while it refuses to question the wisdom of the "ecumenical venture," it acts as though an infallible dogma of the Faith—that outside the Catholic Church there is no salvation—were no longer applicable in the current "ecumenical context." This is how the Modernist "evolution" of dogma works. As we can see, EWTN has been a major accomplice in this "evolution." EWTN's entire presentation is tainted with the heresy of indifferentism—the inevitable result of aiding and abetting this heresy.

And yet, to return to the point I raised earlier, while bending over backwards to accommodate Protestants and schismatics, EWTN shows no tolerance for loyal Catholics who have refused to compromise with the post-conciliar revolution, but instead have sought refuge from Modernist bishops by repairing to Catholic chapels outside of the official diocesan structure. When it comes to these Catholics, who have never left the Catholic Church and who adhere to every one of her teachings, EWTN suddenly rediscovers the concept of schism and the need for submission to the Roman Pontiff (to whom, in fact, these Catholics do submit). Dr. Peterson noted that Donovan and the EWTN theological committee "were very much opposed to the Society of St. Pius X [SSPX] and independent priests hearing confessions, yet they would validate Orthodox priests hearing [Catholic] confessions. I couldn't quite understand that." The basic attitude at the theological committee meetings was that "anyone that participated with Father Gruner was schismatic, anyone that participated with [The Society of] St. Pius X was schismatic," whereas "outside the Church, if you were baptized in a Presbyterian or Methodist church, for some reason you were suddenly in the [Catholic] Church... It was ridiculous. It was totally ridiculous."

Indeed, it *is* ridiculous. And here, irony of ironies, EWTN is even less tolerant of the traditional Catholics of SSPX than the Vatican apparatus. In a recent interview with the prestigious *30 Days* magazine, Cardinal Dario Castrillon Hoyos, head of the Vatican's Congregation for the Clergy, reflected on the meeting in August 2005 between the head of SSPX, Bishop Bernard Fellay, and Pope Benedict XVI. Cardinal Castrillon Hoyos stated that SSPX's criticisms of the post-conciliar innovations "can be a treasure for the Church" and that "we are all free to formulate critical observations on what doesn't concern dogma and the essential discipline of the Church itself." The Cardinal even went so far as to state that SSPX's situation "was *not* a formal schism."[143]

At EWTN, however, the concept of schism now applies only to *Catholics* who are trying to preserve their faith in the midst of a failing ecclesial establishment in North America which even the Vatican's Cardinal Gagnon described (in 1987) as de facto schismatic. For EWTN, schism consists, therefore, solely in a Catholic's attempt to *escape* the veritable schism and heresy of neo-Modernist prelates such as Cardinal Mahony, who, as Mother Angelica herself courageously protested, are destroying the Faith in their dioceses. Such is the diabolical disorientation in the Church today.

As serious as all of this is, at EWTN the erosion of Catholic dogma on salvation apparently runs even deeper than I have suggested thus far, if that were possible. During a recent drive in California, where I was speaking at a Catholic conference, I heard an excellent discussion of the immorality of human cloning on EWTN's radio broadcast. During the same broadcast an EWTN personality did a promotional spot for his Catholic apologetics program on the network. He said that there are (according to him) three types of apologetics: natural, Christian and Catholic. Natural apologetics, he explained, seeks to make a case for the existence of God, natural law and morality based on reason alone—i.e., the case for natural religion. Christian apologetics seeks to make the case for Christianity based on the revealed truths in which "all Christians" believe.

---

[143] *30 Days*, No. 9, 2005, interview by Gianni Cardinale at www.30giorni.it/us/articolo_stampa.asp?id=9360.

Catholic apologetics, however, includes those revealed truths in which Catholics believe in the "fullness" of truth—another reference to the "fullness" theme that EWTN substitutes for the dogma of no *salvation* outside the Church. He concluded by saying that his apologetics program "concentrates" on Catholic apologetics.

This sort of thing is typical of EWTN's presentation of the Faith. There is not the least suggestion of any spiritually crucial difference, in terms of eternal salvation, between natural religion, the "Christian religion" and the Catholic religion. It is merely a question of specializing in one type of apologetic as a defense of what "Catholics believe" in the "fullness" of truth, but which no one else, apparently, need believe in order to save his soul. Yet, when it came to discussing the moral issue of human cloning, the speakers were unequivocal in their denunciation of it as immoral.

There is a rather subtle process of theological degradation at work here. At EWTN, as in the thinking of New Church in general, there is a staunch defense of morality when it comes to "pro-life" issues such as human cloning, but at the same time a retreat from the objective necessity of membership in the Catholic Church and adherence to her *specific theological doctrines* in order to be saved. But, as we have seen here, the specific truths of Revelation entrusted to the Catholic Church are no longer presented as making any real difference to one's salvation. Hence today's Catholic churchman might be staunchly "pro-life," but he is not staunchly *pro-Catholic* in the sense of advocating the necessity of adherence to the Catholic religion. In the New Church establishment, the Church Militant seeking to win souls has become, at best, a militant "pro-life" or a militant "social justice" organization, as liberalized New Church leaders content themselves with encountering non-Catholics only on the "common ground" of moral and social issues.

This is the very process of religious decay Pope Pius XI sought to avert when he condemned the "pan-Christian" congresses of the "ecumenical movement" of the 1920s:

> All Christians, they add, should be as "one": for then they would be much more powerful in driving out the pest of irreligion, which like a serpent daily creeps further and becomes more widely spread, and prepares to rob the Gospel of its strength. These things and others that class of men who are known as *pan-Christians* continually repeat and amplify…. Certainly such

attempts can nowise be approved by Catholics, founded
as they are on that false opinion which considers all
religions to be more or less good and praiseworthy,
since they all in different ways manifest and signify that
sense which is inborn in us all, and by which we are led
to God and to the obedient acknowledgment of His rule.
*Not only are those who hold this opinion in error and*
*deceived, but also in distorting the idea of true religion they*
*reject it,* and little by little turn aside to *naturalism* and
atheism, as it is called; from which it clearly follows that
one who supports those who hold these theories and
attempt to realize them, *is altogether abandoning the*
*divinely revealed religion.*

EWTN and the other ecumenically-oriented New Church
organizations have ignored the grave danger foreseen by Pius XI and
all his predecessors, who forbade interfaith religious activities
because they would in the end lead to a devaluation of the divinely
revealed religion. In consequence, after forty years of "ecumenical
activity" with non-Catholics, "pro-life" bishops and priests busy
themselves with moral and social issues in ecumenical alliances with
other religions on the purely natural level. They no longer engage in
the divine commission to "make disciples of all nations, baptizing
them in the name of the Father, and of the Son, and of the Holy
Ghost, teaching them to observe *all things whatsoever* I have
commanded thee". (Matt. 28:19-20) They no longer actively seek the
conversion of non-Catholics for the salvation of their souls. They no
longer believe that such conversions are necessary — or, if they do
believe it, they have been cowed into silence by the "ecumenical
movement" in which they participate with lemming-like conformity.

The end result is that in the "new ecumenical context" the
"fullness" of the theological truth of Roman Catholicism is presented
as merely desirable, perhaps even eminently desirable, but not really
necessary for the salvation of souls, and only basic morality is
defended with any degree of militancy. This can only mean the
effective death of the Church Militant and its replacement in practice
by a common denominator, vaguely Christian, but basically natural
religion that is little more than an adjunct of the "pro-life" and "social
justice" movements.

Whether or not its directors subjectively intend it, EWTN is
lending itself to widespread acceptance of the "deadly error"
condemned by Pope Gregory XVI in *Mirari Vos,* as noted earlier:

namely, that "it is possible to obtain the eternal salvation of the soul by the profession of any kind of religion, as long as *morality* is maintained." EWTN thus abandons the necessity of the return of the dissidents to Rome for the sake of their *salvation* through the sacraments and adherence to Catholic doctrine and dogma.

# Chapter 10

# Promoting the Return of the Judaizers

The constant and infallible teaching of the Catholic Church is that the New Covenant superseded the Old, and that the members of the Mystical Body of Christ, which is the Catholic Church, are the new chosen people, the new Israel. As even Vatican II declares: "Thus the apostles were the first budding-forth of the New Israel." (*Ad Gentes* 1, 5) Accordingly, a mere thirty-seven years before Vatican II, Pius XI directed the entire Church to pray publicly the following prayer for the Jews on the Feast of Christ the King: "Turn Thine eyes of mercy toward the children of that race, *once* Thy chosen people. Of old, they called down upon themselves the Blood of the Savior, may it now descend upon them a laver of redemption and life."[144]

The beginning of the New Covenant in the Blood of the Savior meant the end of the religion of the Old Covenant. At the moment of the Crucifixion, when the Temple veil was rent from top to bottom, God was making it known that "the ceremonies of the ancient law were to be abolished by Christ, and also that heaven should be open to all."[145] This is why Pius XI's *Act of Consecration* refers to the Jewish race as "*once* Thy chosen people." Only in the New Israel, in the Catholic Church, is the true worship of God now to be found. The rabbinical rituals and laws of the Old Covenant, being abolished, now count for nothing, confer no grace, and save no one. Worse, they bring a curse upon those who obstinately cling to them. Hence St. Paul warned the Jews: "for as many as are under the works of the law, are under a curse." (Gal. 3:10) In his Epistle to the Hebrews (7:18-19) St. Paul further declares: "there is *an abrogation* of the former

---

[144]From the Act of Consecration of the World to the Sacred Heart of Jesus, promulgated by Pope Pius XI in conjunction with his encyclical *Quas Primas* (1925), on the Social Kingship of Christ.

[145]Haydock Commentary, Douay-Rheims Bible, Matt. 27:51.

commandment, because of the weakness and unprofitableness thereof. For the law brought nothing to perfection." Thus, said St. Paul, "In saying a new, He [Christ] made the former old. And that which decayeth and groweth old, is near *its end.*" (Heb. 8:13)

As the Council of Florence infallibly declared, that definitive end to the Old Covenant religion came with the promulgation of the Gospel:

> It [the Catholic Church] firmly believes, professes and teaches that the matter pertaining to the law of the Old Testament, of the Mosaic law, which are divided into ceremonies, sacred rites, sacrifices, and sacraments, because they were established to signify something in the future, although they were suited to divine worship at the time, after Our Lord's coming had been signified by them, ceased, and the sacraments of the New Testament began.... [A]fter promulgation of the Gospel which it [the Church] asserts that they [the Old Testament sacraments] cannot be observed *without the loss of eternal salvation.* All, therefore, who after that time observe circumcision and the Sabbath and the other requirements of the law, it declares alien to the Christian faith and not in the least fit to participate in eternal salvation, unless someday they recover from these errors.[146]

The absolute continuity of the Church's infallible teaching on the supersession of the Old Covenant by the New is seen in the encyclical *Mystici Corporis* (1943) by Pope Pius XII. In two paragraphs, Pius XII provides a beautiful restatement of the Church's teaching, with references to both Pope Leo the Great and Saint Thomas Aquinas:

> And first of all, by the death of our Redeemer, the New Testament took the place of the Old Law, which *had been abolished*; then the Law of Christ together with its mysteries, enactments, institutions, and sacred rites was ratified for the whole world in the blood of Jesus Christ. For, while our Divine Savior was preaching in a restricted area—He was not sent but to the sheep that

---

[146]DS 712.

were lost of the House of Israel—the Law and the Gospel were together in force; but on the gibbet of His death Jesus *made void the Law with its decrees* and fastened the handwriting of the Old Testament to the Cross, establishing the New Testament in His blood shed for the whole human race. "To such an extent, then," says St. Leo the Great, speaking of the Cross of our Lord, "was there effected a transfer from the Law to the Gospel, from the Synagogue to the Church, from the many sacrifices to one Victim, that, as Our Lord expired, that mystical veil which shut off the innermost part of the temple and its sacred secret was rent violently from top to bottom."

On the Cross then *the Old Law died*, soon to be buried and to be *a bearer of death*, in order to give way to the New Testament of which Christ had chosen the Apostles as qualified ministers; and although He had been constituted the Head of the whole human family in the womb of the Blessed Virgin, it is by the power of the Cross that our Savior exercises fully the office itself of Head of His Church. "For it was through His triumph on the Cross," according to the teaching of the Angelic and Common Doctor, "that He won power and dominion over the gentiles"; by that same victory He increased the immense treasure of graces, which, as He reigns in glory in heaven, He lavishes continually on His mortal members; it was by His blood shed on the Cross that God's anger was averted and that all the heavenly gifts, especially the spiritual graces of the New and Eternal Testament, could then flow from the fountains of our Savior for the salvation of men, of the faithful above all; it was on the tree of the Cross, finally, that He entered into possession of His Church, that is, of all the members of His Mystical Body; for they would not have been united to this Mystical Body through the waters of Baptism except by the salutary virtue of the Cross, by which they had been already brought under the complete sway of Christ.[147]

---

[147]*Mystici corporis* (1943), nn. 29-30.

As we read in St. Paul's Epistle to the Galatians, however, the early Church had to struggle against "Judaizers" who thought they could combine the practices and rituals of the Mosaic Law under the Old Covenant with the religion of the New Covenant. This tendency had to be fought, because, as the above-quoted passage from the Council of Florence observes, the rituals of the Old Law only foreshadowed the coming of Christ and the Sacrifice of the Mass, and to persist in those rituals after His coming would be implicitly to deny that He *had* come. "O senseless, Galatians," thundered St. Paul, "who hath bewitched you, that you should not obey the truth, before whose eyes Jesus Christ has been set forth, crucified among you.... Did you receive the Spirit by the works of the law, or by the hearing of the faith?" (Gal. 3:1-2)

The supersession of the Old Covenant and its rituals by the New Covenant is another of the Catholic dogmas present-day Modernists are trying to "interpret" out of existence. Cardinal Walter Kasper, speaking as the papally-appointed President of the Pontifical Council for Religious Relations with the Jews, publicly declared that "*the old theory of substitution is gone since the Second Vatican Council.* For us Christians today the covenant with the Jewish people is a living heritage, a living reality.... Therefore, the Church believes that Judaism, i.e. the faithful response of the Jewish people to God's irrevocable covenant, *is salvific for them*, because God is faithful to his [sic] promises."[148] Once again we see in operation the condemned Modernist thesis that the Church can change her doctrines over time: what she used to believe about the status of the Old Covenant is merely an "old theory" that can be discarded "today."

Enter EWTN. Here, as elsewhere, EWTN lends itself to the Modernist "revision" of Catholic dogma. An EWTN supporter, rightly outraged by Kasper's remarks, asked EWTN's "expert" Fr. Levis about "notorious heretics like Cardinal Kasper, who [make] such a nonsensical statement as 'The old covenant was not revoked'... The Old covenant never saved anyone [after Christ's coming], and cannot be salvific for anyone. If it could, Christ's coming was meaningless, and the words of [the Council of Florence] would also be without meaning." As already noted, St. Paul himself declared that if justification came from the Old Law, "then Christ

---

148Address at the 17th meeting of the International Catholic-Jewish Liaison Committee, New York, May 1, 2001.

died in vain". (Gal. 2:21) Ducking the question, Fr. Levis replied: "Be very careful in calling Cardinal Kasper of Germany a heretic, a power none of us can boast. *Lumen Gentium* and other documents of Vatican II tried to see some small truths in Judaism, Islam, Hinduism, etc., real truths which we Catholics share."[149] What is that supposed to mean? Was the Old Covenant superseded or not? Levis refused to take issue with Kasper, and thus refused to defend the constant teaching of the Church against his objectively heretical statement.

EWTN only added to the confusion by posting this "expert" advice from Fr. Vincent Serpa, O.P., employed by Catholic Answers (another major New Church organization) in response to a question about Kasper's statement:

> Since Christianity is the fulfillment of Judaism, it has a relationship with Judaism unlike that with any other religion. As Rosalind Moss, a convert from Judaism and staff member here at Catholic Answers, says, one cannot be more Jewish than to be Catholic!

What is that supposed to mean? In what sense is, say, an Italian "Jewish" by virtue of being Catholic? Catholics are Catholics, not Jews. As the greatest Jewish convert of them all, Saint Paul of Tarsus, infallibly teaches us, in the Mystical Body of Christ "There is neither Jew nor Greek: there is neither bond nor free: there is neither male nor female. For you are all one in Christ Jesus." (Gal. 3:18)

Going on to address Cardinal Kasper's scandalous statement, Fr. Serpa wrote the following:

> In the recent past an unfortunate public statement was made, seemingly under official Catholic auspices, to the effect that Jews need not be evangelized since they are already in covenant with God. This is not what the Church teaches! Salvation for all people is only through Jesus Christ.

An "unfortunate statement"? The statement was heresy, pure and simple, and should have been condemned as such. The advice that salvation is only through Jesus Christ is certainly correct, but Fr.

---

[149]See, EWTN Q&A Forum, advice by Fr. Levis of November 11, 2004 on "The Council of Florence".

Serpa does not squarely address the question whether the Old Covenant remains in effect. And, in typical New Church fashion, Serpa undermines the truth he does present by seriously suggesting that there is nothing wrong with *Catholics celebrating Jewish holidays*:

> While we are not to supplant our Christian holy days by those of Judaism, there is no Church law preventing us from celebrating Jewish holidays in an effort to understand our Jewish roots.

Here we see how EWTN is contributing to a Judaizing tendency in the Church, a kind of return of the Judaizers, in the wake of Vatican II—another sign of "diabolical disorientation," to recall Sister Lucy's memorable phrase. As just one of innumerable examples of this reemerging Judaizing tendency, Bishop Bruskewitz of the Diocese of Lincoln, Nebraska conducted an interfaith Seder Supper with a group of rabbis in his own cathedral *during Holy Week*.[150] Yes, during the very week commemorating the Passion and Death of Our Lord at the instance of the Pharisees, a Catholic bishop celebrated a Seder Supper with descendants of the Pharisees. This, obviously, is madness; and it is spreading everywhere in the Church, as Seder suppers in Catholic parishes are becoming commonplace.[151]

As it does with all New Church trends, EWTN follows along, dutifully promoting the latest atrocities. For example, EWTN's programming includes televised segments on the Old Testament, conducted by a supposed convert *wearing a yarmulke and a rabbinical prayer shawl*. This "convert" begins his little discussions by intoning "Shalom." What kind of message does this send to already-confused Catholics?

Far worse than this, however, is EWTN's aggressive promotion of the organization called the Association of Hebrew Catholics (AHC). AHC advocates Judaization of Catholic worship, including "Catholic" Seder Suppers and the creation of a "Hebrew Catholic Community" within the Catholic Church—precisely what the Apostles themselves fought against. AHC has been endorsed

---

[150]John Vennari, *Catholic Family News*, January 1999. Mr. Vennari has shown me the original diocesan publications on which his report was based.

[151]See, e.g. http://www.staugustine-uf.org/holyday/Sedersupper.asp, where St. Augustine Church in Gainesville, Florida, has published photographs of its Holy Week Seder Supper in 2004.

enthusiastically by no fewer than *five* EWTN "experts,"[152] including Colin Donovan, who "heartily endorse[s]" AHC in his capacity as "Vice President of Theology."[153] EWTN "expert" William Carroll calls AHC a "great blessing."[154] AHC has also been featured twice on *The Journey Home* with Marcus Grodi.[155]

Let us examine briefly the program of the organization EWTN heartily endorses, calls a great blessing and features on its television broadcasts. As AHC's "Original Manifesto" declares:

> [A]t present the admission of the Jewish convert to the Church is governed by a regime of assimilation, which systematically ignores the specific elements of his identity… The ultimate effect of the regime is to alienate the convert from his people of origin and prepare the way for the total absorption of his descendants into *the Gentile community*…. [I]f all Jews were to be converted, only to be assimilated, the Jewish People would cease to exist: hence, their total opposition to the Christian Mission. The regime of assimilation has thus become the major obstacle to the admission of Jews to the Faith.[156]

That is, AHC apparently does not accept that in the Catholic Church "there is neither Jew nor Greek," as St. Paul wrote under divine inspiration. Nearly 2,000 years after St. Paul uttered those words, AHC now demands that "the Jewish People" not be "assimilated" into "the Gentile community" and that the Catholic Church abandon her "regime of assimilation." Instead, says the Manifesto, "the Association aims eventually at petitioning the Holy See to approve the erection *of a Hebrew Catholic Community, into which Jewish converts would be integrated at baptism and to which their*

---

[152]Colin Donovan, William Carroll (see also in the EWTN Q&A Forum his advice of March 29, 2002 on "Jews and Christians"), Rosalind Moss, Fr. Vincent Serpa, and Michelle Arnold (see also her advice of April 19, 2004 on "Messianic Judaism").

[153]See, EWTN Q&A Forum, advice by Colin B. Donovan of August 22, 2002 on "Jews no longer need to be converted? & Other questions".

[154]See, EWTN Q&A Forum, advice by Dr. William Carroll of June 15, 2001 on "Re: messianic jews".

[155]Episodes of January 14, 2000 ("Jews and Salvation History") and March 7, 2005 ("Jewish Convert"), available in EWTN's audio archives.

[156]http://hebrewcatholic.org/AbouttheAHC/AHCArticles/originalmanifest.html.

*descendants would belong.*" This incredible proposal would literally establish a "Hebrew" branch of Catholicism, whose potential members are already calling themselves "Hebrew Catholics." By this means, the Manifesto states, the Church "would correct the *grave deficiencies* [!] attendant on the admission of Jews to the Faith." This is now possible, says AHC, because "the Church, beginning with Vatican II, has been *revising its teachings* regarding Jews and Judaism."[157] New Church here proclaims another "revision" of Catholic teaching to "correct" "deficiencies" in the Church, according to the Modernist "evolution" of dogma. And EWTN is promoting it to the hilt.

AHC's current president is the Jewish convert David Moss, the brother of Rosalind Moss, a frequent EWTN guest and a New Church "apologist" employed by Catholic Answers, a New Church apologetics organization. David Moss himself has been featured twice on the EWTN series *The Journey Home*, as discussed further on. On the AHC website, David Moss declares that "For the last 1700-1800 years, the Church has become sociologically Gentile. In fact, the terms *Christian* or *Catholic* have become synonymous with the term *Gentile*. This development has obscured the Israelite origins and reality of the Church." Moss wishes to correct this "development" — i.e. the past 1800 years of Church history!—by "restoring" the Church's "Israelite origins" and Israelite "reality." This idea stands in direct contradiction of the revealed truth that there is no longer an Israelite nation constituting a distinct covenantal People of God, but only the new Israel of the Catholic Church to which all men embraced by the New Covenant belong, without distinction between Jew and Gentile.

In keeping with its Original Manifesto, the AHC under Moss "seeks to renew and preserve *the corporate identity and heritage of the People of Israel within the Church*, through a juridically-approved Hebrew Catholic Community. Through this community, the People will *once again be able to live out their collective vocation* and give corporate witness to Jesus, Messiah of Israel…" AHC, says Moss, has been "awakened by the same Spirit that animated the Second Vatican Council" and will, according to this "Spirit," pursue "the restoration and renewal within the Church of that from which the Church was born—a visible and dynamic Israelite community. In the restored

---

[157]From "About AHC", http://hebrewcatholic.org/AbouttheAHC/index.html.

community, the People of Israel will once again be able to live out their distinctive witness and their calling—to be a blessing—within the Church."

Note well: AHC, with EWTN's endorsement, contends that for the past 1800 years "the People of Israel" have been *denied their collective vocation in the Church founded by their own Jewish Savior.* A "juridically-approved community" of "Hebrew Catholics," says Moss, would allow "the People" to live their vocation "once again." In other words, for 1800 years Our Lord has failed to provide adequately for the Jews, but Moss and his organization will remedy this divine oversight. Yet again we are presented with a Modernist claim that the Catholic Church has gotten it wrong for practically her entire history and must now change her "position." With the aid of that all-purpose "Spirit of Vatican II," the Church is being called upon to correct the "deficiencies" in her perennial doctrine and practice concerning Jewish conversion. Moss, EWTN and other like-minded New Church innovators pay no heed to the fact that this sort of talk undermines all belief in the Church as an infallible teaching authority guided by the Holy Ghost. For if the Church has been wrong for so long in her constant theological and evangelical approach to the Jews, could she not be wrong about anything at all she has constantly taught to the world?[158] What Church teaching *isn't* subject to a change of "position" according to this way of thinking?

How does AHC's proposed Judaization project square with the Church's dogmatic teaching on the supersession of the Old Covenant by the New Covenant? Obviously, it doesn't. In Modernist fashion, Moss and AHC affirm that the Old Covenant was superseded, only to deny it implicitly by means of a novel and ambiguous "interpretation" of the supersession teaching. On AHC's website we find the following statement by Moss concerning "Jewish Catholic dialogue":

> The New Covenant in Jesus, therefore, *does not revoke the prior covenants* but, rather, fulfills and transforms them.... Therefore, it follows that the Jewish people

---

[158]I emphasize the word "constant" because the Catholic Church's charism of infallibility does not extend to some novelty that would be contrary to what the Catholic Church has always believed, such as the novelties advocated by Moss, AHC and EWTN. Nor, as already noted, can the Church proclaim new and previously unknown doctrines, such as a "new" doctrine concerning the Jews.

> today remain "most dear" to God and retain their gifts
> and calling. They continue to live, not in their own
> saving covenant, but alongside Christians in that
> primary covenant established with Abraham and
> fulfilled in Jesus—though they remain in an earlier stage
> of covenant development.

The New Testament does not speak of "one covenant" with two different stages of "development" in which Jews and Christians live side by side, but rather of the dramatic end of the Old Covenant and the beginning of the New and Eternal Covenant in the Blood of Jesus Christ. As the Jewish convert St. Paul teaches infallibly in the divinely inspired words of the New Testament, it is Christ who is the "seed" of Abraham, and thus whoever is incorporated into Him—that is, into His Mystical Body, the Catholic Church—by means of baptism, inherits the promise God made to Abraham and becomes a member of God's covenant people. *It is only the community of the baptized in the Church that comprises the covenant people descended from Abraham.* Let us examine the Scriptural text at Galatians 3:16-27:

> To Abraham were the promises made and to his seed.
> He saith not: And to his seeds as of many. But as of one:
> *And to thy seed, which is Christ.* Now this I say: that the
> testament which was confirmed by God, the law which
> was made after four hundred and thirty years [i.e. the
> covenant with Moses] doth not disannul, to make the
> promise of no effect. For if the inheritance be of the law,
> it is no more of promise. But God gave it to Abraham by
> promise.

That is, the fulfillment of the promise God made to Abraham is seen in Christ, who is Abraham's seed, not in the law of Moses. For if salvation were by operation of the Mosaic law, then it would not have come from God's promise to Abraham. St. Paul continues:

> Why then was the law? It was set because of
> transgressions, until the seed [Christ] should come to
> whom He made the promise, being ordained by angels
> in the hand of a mediator. Now a mediator is not of one:
> but God is one. Was the law then against the promises of
> God: God forbid! For if there had been a law given

which could give life, verily justice should have been by
the law. But the scripture hath concluded all under sin,
that the promise, by the faith of Jesus Christ, might be
given to them that believe. But before the faith came, we
were kept under the law shut up, unto that faith which
was to be revealed. Wherefore the law was our
pedagogue in Christ: that we might be justified by faith.

That is, the purpose of the law was to teach (to be a "pedagogue")
and to punish transgressions until Christ should come. The law could
not of itself give life, but it did prepare the way for the fulfillment of
the promise to Abraham and the giving of life (sanctifying grace) and
faith with the coming of Christ. St. Paul concludes:

But after the faith is come, we are no longer under a
pedagogue. *For you are all the children of God, by faith in
Christ Jesus.* For as many of you as have been *baptized in
Christ* have put on Christ.

That is, since Christ we are no longer under the Mosaic law, the
"pedagogue." For now faith has come, and the *baptized* who have
faith in Christ are the children of God and the heirs of the Abrahamic
covenant perfected in Christ. There is no separate group of
unbaptized Jewish children of God living "alongside" baptized
Christians within the same covenant people, as Moss would have us
believe. Again, this is why Pope Pius XI referred to the Jews as "*once
Thy chosen people*" in the aforementioned Act of Consecration of the
World to the Sacred Heart.

And while the Jewish people remain "most dear [to God] for the
sake of the fathers" — that is, because of the patriarchs, especially
Abraham and Moses — nevertheless, "because of unbelief they were
*broken off*" from the "olive tree," which is Christ.[159] But, "if they abide

---

[159]Cyril of Jerusalem: "Then, when ye were stripped, ye were anointed with
exorcised oil, from the very hairs of your head to your feet, and were made
partakers of *the good olive-tree, Jesus Christ.* For ye were cut off from the wild
olive-tree, and grafted into the good one, and were made to share the fatness
[abundance] of the true olive-tree. The exorcised oil therefore was a symbol of
the participation of the fatness of Christ, being a charm to drive away every trace
of hostile influence." (Catechetical Lectures, XX, 3) *Nicene and Post-Nicene Fathers*,
ed., Philip Schaff, (Hendrickson Publishers, 1994).

(This footnote continued on next page.)

not still in unbelief, shall be grafted in: for God is able to graft them in again". (Romans 11:20-23, 28) That is, by *conversion and baptism* the Jews can be *reincorporated* into the sole and exclusive covenant people of God, which is the Catholic Church, just as St. Paul himself was. Hence of the Jewish race "there is a remnant saved according to the election of grace" (Romans 11:5), and that remnant consists of those Jews who repent, are baptized and become members of the Catholic Church, following the example of St. Paul.

Moss cannot, therefore, avoid his contradiction of the Faith by arguing, as he does, that Jews and Christians exist alongside each other in the same Abrahamic covenant but at different "stages of development." It is utter nonsense to say that the Abrahamic covenant is both perfected *and* at an "earlier stage of development" at one and the same time. And it is equally nonsensical to say that God's covenant people could include both those who accept Christ and those who reject Him. But nonsense—Modernist nonsense—is what Moss must resort to in his attempt to reconcile the position of the Pharisees with the diametrically opposed dogmatic teaching of the Catholic Church.

---

(This footnote continued from previous page.)
Augustine: "Come, then, and be grafted into the root of the olive tree, in his return to which the apostle rejoices, after by unbelief he had been among the broken branches. He speaks of himself as set free, when he made the happy transition from Judaism to Christianity. *For Christ was always preached in the olive tree, and those who did not believe in Him when He came were broken off,* while those who believed were grafted in..." (Augustine to Faustus the Manichean, Bk. 9, 2) Ibid.

Ignatius: "These things I write to you, thou *new olive-tree of Christ,* not that I am aware you hold any such opinions, but that I may put you on your guard, as a father does his children. Beware, therefore, of those that hasten to work mischief, those 'enemies of the cross of Christ, whose end is destruction, whose glory is in their shame.'" (To the Antiochians, ch. VI). From *Ante-Nicene Fathers,* ed., Philip Schaff, (Hendrickson Publishers, 1994).

Irenaeus: "This truth, therefore, he [St. Paul] declares, in order that we may not reject the engrafting of the Spirit while pampering the flesh. 'But thou, being a wild olive-tree,' he [Paul] says, 'hast been grafted into the good olive-tree, and been made a partaker of the fatness [cf. Rom. 11:17] of the olive-tree.'" (*Against Heresies,* Bk. V, ch. X) Ibid.

So, contrary to what Moss suggests, the only "calling" the Jews have today is the same as that of all men: to recognize Christ as Messiah and to follow Him in His Church. When St. Paul speaks of "the gifts and calling" of the Jewish people in Romans 11:29, he does not mean a still-subsisting covenant with national Israel, but rather *the remnant of Jews* referred to in Romans 11:5, who will be saved by individual conversion to Christ. There is *nothing* in the New Testament or in the teaching of the Magisterium to support the perpetual existence of a national Israel that still has a collective "calling" whether or not its individual members accept the Messiah. *Only the Jew who converts to Christ can be grafted back into the olive tree.* The New Israel, the new chosen people, consists only of those who belong to the Mystical Body.

Now, there is certainly a valid theological opinion in the Church, based on an interpretation of the teaching of Saint Paul in Romans, that the conversion of the Jews as a people is inevitable. This opinion, never imposed by the Magisterium, is advanced by Saint Augustine, St. Thomas Aquinas and certain other Church Fathers (the Fathers by no means being unanimous on the point). The Fathers Lémann, two renowned Jewish convert priests, discuss the opinion in their *La Question du Messie et le Concile du Vatican* (The Question of the Messiah and the Vatican Council), written at the time of the First Vatican Council.[160] What they demonstrate, however, is that the postulated conversion of the Jews will not occur until the Last Days. As Suarez put it: "the conversion of the Jews will take place at the Last Judgment and at the height of the persecution which Antichrist will inflict on the Church."[161] In this sense only are members of the Jewish nation "called" by God. But they are *not* called to enter the Church as national Israel, occupying some special place in the Mystical Body with a special corporate "vocation" reserved for "Israelites." On this point the Fathers Lémann cite Saint Peter Damian, a Doctor of the Church, who wrote: "This obstinately unbelieving people, who now refuse to believe, will come back to the Faith and occupy *the lowest place in the Mystical Body of Christ*, that is to say, their conversion will take place in the last days of Holy Church, toward the end of the world."[162] Meanwhile, like every other

---

[160]*La Question du Messie et le Concile du Vatican* (Joseph Albanel, Paris and P.N. Josserand, Lyons: 1869).
[161]Fahey, op. cit., page 110.
[162]Op. cit., page 108.

race, the Jews are under an objective duty as *individuals* to acknowledge Jesus and to follow Him *today*. Jews who die without baptism or faith in Christ cannot offer God the excuse that they were entitled to shun conversion until the Church made a place for national Israel. The mass conversion of the Jews at the end of time— one by one, not as a "corporate entity"—does not excuse a Jew's refusal to convert today. Nor does it justify AHC's human project of creating a special "Hebrew Catholic" branch of the Church to serve national Israel.

Moss sails even further into heterodox waters when he argues that until the day when national Israel enters the Church, God has allowed an "adaptation" of the rabbinical religion of the Old Covenant to subsist *as a valid and effectual channel of grace* for Jews:

> [P]ost-biblical Rabbinic Judaism, *an adaptation of the Judaism of the Sinai Covenant*, can then be understood as the temporary provision allowed by God to preserve the Jewish people, *their faith in God, and their calling*. In the wisdom and timing of God, they will eventually be given the additional gifts of faith that will enable them to recognize their Messiah, Jesus. That recognition, in turn, will advance the Messiah's return (cf. CCC 674).[163]

This novel opinion contradicts the revealed truth of Holy Scripture declared by St. Paul and infallibly proclaimed by the Council of Florence, quoted above, that the rituals and observances of rabbinic Judaism now count for nothing and have no salvific power whatever, but that, on the contrary, any Catholic who practices them is guilty of mortal sin which, if unrepented, will lead to eternal damnation. The persistence of present-day Jews in their dead rituals and the intricacies of the hateful anti-Christian Jewish Talmud is the

---

[163]http://hebrewcatholic.org/AboutheAHC/ahcproposal.html; quoted from *Hebrew Catholic*, Issue #77 (Fall 2002). The section of the new Catechism cited by Moss gives no support whatever to his claim that at some point in time the Jews will be given "additional gifts of faith that will enable them to recognize the Messiah," as if they were unable to recognize Him now through no fault of their own. Rather, the Catechism states that the Messiah will not come until the total number of Jews who are to convert will have converted, after they have *repented and been baptized* for the forgiveness of their sins, as St. Peter exhorts his fellow Jews in Acts 3:19-21. Moss thus attempts to attribute his idiosyncratic "special gifts of grace" argument to the Catechism.

result of *willful spiritual blindness*. As the Church's perennial Good
Friday liturgy declared for century after century:

> Let us pray, also, for the faithless Jews, that our Lord
> and God may take away the veil from their hearts, so
> that they, too, may acknowledge Jesus Christ our Lord.
> Almighty, eternal God, Who repellest not even Jewish
> faithlessness from Thy mercy, hearken to our prayers
> which we make in behalf of *the blindness of that people*,
> that, recognizing the light of Thy truth, which is Christ,
> they may be delivered from their darkness. Through the
> same Lord Jesus Christ, Who livest and reignest, with
> God the Father, in the unity of the Holy Ghost, one God.

But according to Moss and AHC, whose views EWTN so avidly
promotes, the Jews are not in a condition of blindness, adhering to a
defunct religion superseded by the New Covenant. Rather, God has
allowed a "post-biblical" "adaptation" of the religion of the Old
Covenant to continue as a vehicle of grace, confirming the Jews in
their faith in God until such time as God gives them "additional gifts
of faith" that will "enable them to recognize their Messiah, Jesus."
Evidently, "Hebrew Catholics" believe that the graces already
available in merit of Christ's death on the Cross are not enough for
present-day Jews to recognize Him as Messiah, even though the
Apostles themselves and countless Jews during and since the
apostolic age (including Moss himself!) have recognized Him.
Today's Jews, says Moss, will be receiving "additional gifts of faith."
That is quite a presumption on Divine Mercy!

From this theory it follows that present-day Jews are in no danger
of damnation in failing to enter the Catholic Church. This, in fact, is
the explicit advice of EWTN "expert" Fr. Vincent Serpa, who, as
already noted, is also employed by the New Church apologetics
organization, Catholic Answers. In answer to a question posed by
none other than a Jewish inquirer, Serpa gave anything but a Catholic
answer:

> **Conversion of Jews, 'The Passion'**
> **Question from Jacob on 08-14-2003:**
>
> Must I, as a Jew, convert and believe that Jesus is the
> Messiah and is God, or does the current Catholic church

[sic] teach that I may be saved by my being a Jew? Also, isn't it a given that anti-Semitism will arise from Mel Gibson's movie?

**Answer by Catholic Answers on 08-14-2003:**

Dear Jacob,

Would that you were given the grace to recognize Jesus as the Son of God and could join the Catholic Church. But if you honestly cannot accept Him as such, by living a life as a devout Jew, you can reach heaven. This is what the Catholic Church teaches. AND Mel Gibson's movie, 'The Passion' does NOT contradict this.

Fr. Vincent Serpa, O.P.[164]

Fr. Serpa not only fails to present the Catholic Church's teaching on this subject, he directly contradicts it. According to Serpa's view of "the teaching of the Catholic Church", Jews have no obligation to convert if they "honestly" cannot bring themselves to believe that Christ is the Son of God and the Messiah foretold in the Old Testament. Of course, Serpa's heterodox notion would exempt virtually every Jew on earth from the duty to convert to Jesus Christ. Yet we know from Catholic dogma that God will condemn the Jews as much as anyone if they persist in their unbelief unto death.

Responding to a small storm of criticism from Catholics who remember what the Church teaches about Jewish conversion, Fr. Serpa "clarified" his answer by making it even worse. He stated: "[T]hose who honestly (the key word here is 'honestly') cannot see Jesus by means of *the light of faith*, can still be saved by that same Jesus Christ, even though they do not realize it—providing that they seek God and try in their actions to do His will, etc. as above."[165]

Here the "expert" Fr. Serpa hopelessly mangles the Church's teaching on invincible ignorance. He misapplies the concept of invincible *ignorance* of Christ and His Gospel to Jews who *know* of Him yet, according to Serpa, cannot "see" Jesus by "the light of

---

[164]See, EWTN Q&A Forum, advice by Fr. Serpa of August 14, 2003 on "Conversion of Jews, 'The Passion'".
[165]See, EWTN Q&A Forum, advice by Fr. Serpa of August 18, 2003 on "Heresy on EWTN?" (Answer to "Eric") and "Regarding the Jews" (Answer to "Jeff").

faith." But if they know of Jesus, then they cannot be invincibly ignorant, for the divinely imposed duty of every man to seek the truth would lead them, if honestly followed, to accept Jesus as God and Messiah. That is exactly what the Apostles did, and what every Jewish convert since their time has done. And God cannot fail to give present-day Jews the supernatural gift of faith in Christ if they are sincerely and diligently seeking to know the truth, because God wills the salvation of all men. (1 Tim. 2:4)

Our Lord Himself declares in Sacred Scripture: "[N]o one knoweth the Son but the Father: neither doth anyone know the Father, but the Son, and He to whom it shall please the Son to reveal *Him*." (Matt. 11:27) Yet Fr. Serpa would have us believe that present-day Jews can really know the Father, can really have the light of faith, while "honestly" rejecting the revelation of Christ—*even if they know full well of that revelation*. And if this were true of the Jews, then it would be true of anyone else in the world—all men could "honestly" reject the Gospel, even if they have heard it.

Fr. Serpa, like EWTN as a whole, thus dispenses with the entire mission of the Holy Catholic Church, whether he realizes it or not. For if even those who have heard the Gospel can be saved while "honestly" rejecting the Gospel, why preach the Gospel at all? All of these "honest" people can simply hear the Gospel after they have died and gone to Heaven. They have no need of the Gospel to be saved while in the wayfaring state on earth; the truth does not set them free, as Our Lord taught. No, they are free without the Gospel, according to Fr. Serpa.

But Our Lord could not have been clearer: "Go forth and preach the Gospel to all nations, baptizing them in the name of the Father and the Son and the Holy Ghost." (Matt. 28:19) "He who believes and is baptized shall be saved: but he who believes not shall be condemned." (Mark 16:16) Our Lord did *not* say what Fr. Serpa teaches: "He who honestly cannot believe shall be saved anyway." For God will give all truly honest men who know of His Son the grace to *believe* in Him. Fr. Serpa here implicitly denies the very efficacy of God's grace, reducing conversion to a heretical Pelagian exercise in human self-persuasion.

Serpa's errors are perfectly consistent with Moss's. For how can Jews be at fault for a failure to join the Church if, as Moss would have it, they have not yet been given "the additional gifts of faith" that will "enable" them to convert to Christ, and if God has in the meantime provided them a "post-biblical Rabbinic Judaism" that preserves "their faith in God, *and their calling*"? What all of this boils down to is that EWTN "affirms" in Modernist double-talk that the Old Covenant was superseded—but not really. And so, EWTN does with the Jews precisely what it does with the Protestants and the Orthodox, reducing conversion to the Catholic Faith to a desirable option, indeed very desirable, but not something objectively necessary for salvation. As previously demonstrated, EWTN, Fr. Serpa and Moss's false theses are extremely dangerous to Jews' eternal salvation for we have the infallible, irreformable definition of the Council of Florence:

> "The most Holy Roman Church firmly believes, professes and preaches that none of those existing outside the Catholic Church, not only pagans, *but also Jews* and heretics and schismatics, can have a share in life eternal; but that they will go into the eternal fire which was prepared for the devil and his angels, unless before death they are joined with her..."[166]

As I have mentioned, Moss was twice showcased (January 14, 2000 and March 7, 2005) on EWTN's *The Journey Home*, where the ex-Protestant minister Marcus Grodi lauded Moss (himself an ex-Protestant) and his organization.[167] During both shows Moss had good and pious things to say about Jesus, Mary and his own decision to become a Catholic, and I do not presume to judge the sincerity of his conversion. Quite the contrary, I presume that his erroneous opinions are the result of the near-total breakdown of the traditional catechesis and formation of Catholics since Vatican II.

Nevertheless, as always with New Church discussions of the Faith, there was a Modernist catch to Moss's rather moving conversion story: Moss used the forum to advance his rationale for a "Hebrew Catholic Community" in the Church. "Individual Jews have entered the Church," he said, "but the majority have not." The non-conversion of the Jews Moss attributed to a failure of *the Church* over the past 1700 years, rather than the Jews who have refused to join her. "If we failed over the past 1700 years" and if, thanks to the "fresh

---

[166]Bull *Cantate Domino* issued by Pope Eugene IV at the Council of Florence, February 4, 1442.
[167]All of the following quotations are from the January 14, 2000 show unless otherwise indicated.

breath of the Holy Spirit" at Vatican II, we "no longer have a program of direct evangelization," Moss argued, then a new approach is needed. According to Moss, when they come into the Church Jews must be allowed to pursue their "eternal election" and "vocation" in a way different from that of "Gentile" Catholics. "The problem is," he continued, "the only way they can remain faithful to their vocation is to stay out of the Church, because their vocation is to function as a people, a collective corporate entity." But, he continued, "they cannot exist as a corporate entity because they will be assimilated and cease to exist" if they convert to Catholicism. The Church, said Moss, had become "sociologically Gentile" over the past 1700-1800 years, and "the mission to Jews… has to be seen as a total failure." When Jews see the Catholic Church today, they will not enter because they see "a Gentile community, a Gentile religion."[168] Therefore, Moss concluded, "the Association [of Hebrew Catholics] exists to remove that obstacle" by advocating creation of a "Hebrew Catholic Community" that will not be "sociologically Gentile."

In other words, according to Moss, the Catholic religion founded by God Incarnate *is too Gentile for the Jews.* This objectively heretical opinion, a most terrible insult to Holy Church, passed without comment by host Grodi. Quite the contrary, EWTN seems determined to provide a forum for this blasphemous disparagement of the Church. So Catholics the world over were subjected to the televised spectacle of a mere layman—an employee of IBM, for goodness sake—belittling the divinely founded Catholic Church as a "Gentile" institution in need of improvements tailored to "Hebrew Catholics" which he and his man-made organization will supply. Whether or not Moss realizes it, his attitude cannot fail to remind one of the supreme haughtiness and pride of the Pharisees, who presumed to correct God Himself on matters of theology and morality.

Let us consider carefully what Moss is saying here: that Jews will not enter the Catholic Church unless the Church accommodates herself to the presence of a national Israel as a "corporate entity" within her. If this "vocation" is not recognized, the Jews will not convert. Moss thus concedes implicitly that for these Jews *national Israel is more important than salvation.* Or rather, for them national Israel *is* salvation; they think their *nation* will save them—and the

---

[168]Broadcast of March 7, 2005.

world. Moss, presumably in a good faith effort to attract Jews to the Church, is only catering to the same old heresy that has plagued the Jewish people since their willful separation from the Body of Christ in the Church's early days. Having rejected the Messiah, the Jewish people, in dispersion throughout the world, organized themselves around the power and influence of the Talmudic rabbis. The Talmudic formation inculcated the "nation of Israel" as an idolatrous substitute for the personal Messiah, Jesus Christ. This process was described by the Fathers Lémann in the aforementioned study. The historical analysis of the Fathers Lémann was summarized by Fr. Denis Fahey in his book *The Kingship of Christ and the Conversion of the Jewish Nation*:

> With the rise of the Catholic nations came a period of despair and silence [among the Jews] with regard to the Messiah. The Catholic Nations strove to organize themselves on the basis of membership in Christ. As the Jews rejected that sublime dignity and with it the Divine Plan for order, they sought to live apart in the Ghettos or Jewish quarters. All power was concentrated in the hands of the Rabbins, and these determined to forbid all discussion concerning the date of the coming Messiah and thus bury the question... It was not possible to alter all the [Old Testament] prophecies [of the coming of the Messiah] without running the risk of arousing suspicion, so it was decided [by the Rabbins] to make them refer either to David or to Solomon or to some other historical personage, and whenever possible, to *the Jewish nation itself*.... "The true interpretation of Psalm 22," writes Rabbi Kimchi, "is to understand it of *the people of Israel*." The Fathers Lémann sum up and conclude with the words: "Since this leaden book [the Talmud] presses down on Israel, there is no longer the question of the Messias among the Jews.... The Bible was too clear; the seventy weeks of Daniel were too clear; the twenty-second psalm of David was too clear; the fifty-third chapter of Isaias was too clear. Your Rabbins, o Israelites, have extinguished all these lights with the Talmud."[169]

---

[169]Father Denis Fahey, *The Kingship of Christ and the Conversion of the Jewish Nation*, (Palmdale, California: Christian Book Club of America, 1953), pages 93-96.

The insidiousness of Moss's views was revealed fully in his response to an emailed question about "Messianic Jews" during his appearance on *The Journey Home*. Messianic Judaism is a movement of Jews who become Protestants of a kind while following many of the observances and rituals of the Mosaic Law, including circumcision and the Kosher dietary laws. Many of their houses of worship resemble synagogues, and their Protestant pastors are often addressed as "rabbi."[170] Moss said that a Jew would enter Messianic Judaism "much faster" than he would enter the Catholic Church, "because they [Messianic Jews] can preserve who they are. They can be who God made them to be. And they can do that and believe in Jesus." But thanks to AHC, Moss claims, some Messianic Jews "have moved into the Catholic Church because they have someone here in the Church that understands their issues."

What Moss asserts here would be impossible to believe if it had not been uttered for all to hear on national television: He asserts that in the Holy Catholic Church founded by God Himself in the person of Jesus Christ, *Jews cannot be what God made them to be*, but that in Protestant sects founded by men they can be, because these sects allow them to follow Mosaic rituals and observances! To this he adds the amazingly impudent claim that his own man-made organization is the best vehicle for attracting Jews to the Catholic Church, because it alone understands their "issues." But Moss—again, I presume he speaks out of ignorance, not malice—only typifies the attitude so prevalent since Vatican II: that the Church is full of ancient defects which can now, at long last, be corrected by enlightened ecclesial technicians with the proper modern equipment.

In a classic example of Modernist double-talk, however, Moss himself observed on *The Journey Home* that "what is in the Church is the fulfillment of everything that is in Judaism."[171] If Moss really believes that the Church is the fulfillment of everything that is in Judaism—and, of course, she is—then how can he also say that Jews are not able to live their "vocation" in the Church, and why does he not abandon his entire project of a humanly-devised "Hebrew Catholic Community"? This is the Modernist way: to affirm the truth only to deny it in the next breath or on the next page.

---

[170]See, e.g. "MESSIANIC JUDAISM: BELIEFS, TERMINOLOGY & PRACTICE" at http://www.religioustolerance.org/mess_jud2.htm.
[171]Broadcast of March 7, 2005.

During his appearances on EWTN Moss further developed his view that Church teaching on the supersession of the Old Covenant was in need of revision. The belief that "the Church replaced the people of Israel... was an erroneous theology that was taught for many, many centuries..." Moss then ventured the heretical opinion that "[T]he Church *no longer teaches*... that the people of Israel, the Jewish people, are superseded... they are an eternal people... that have an irrevocable calling..."[172] According to Moss, "Old Israel included the people of the flesh... the root is Israel.... The people of the nations of the world are grafted onto the root, and the root is *Israel*."[173] More heretical nonsense. As the previous discussion shows, those who believe in Christ are not engrafted into "the people of the flesh" of the defunct nation of "Old Israel," but rather into Christ Himself, who is the seed of Abraham and the perfection of the Abrahamic covenant. This new covenant people, which is the Mystical Body of Christ, includes *all* nations that follow Him. Again, only by faith and baptism is one ingrafted into the Mystical Body of Jesus Christ.

Another featured EWTN guest, the "Hebrew Catholic" convert Roy H. Schoeman, is even more explicit than Moss in denying that the Old Covenant was superseded. In his book *Salvation is from the Jews* (also avidly promoted by EWTN) Schoeman writes: "We have seen how, at the very outset of Christianity, many held the mistaken belief that one must be a member of the Old Covenant (i.e., be a Jew) in order to be eligible for participation in the New." So far, so good. But while this error, says Schoeman, "was quickly corrected, [it] was soon followed by another known as supersessionism—that the Old Covenant was entirely replaced (or superseded, hence 'supersessionism'), made null and void, by the New. This view *dominated Christian theology for much of the past two thousand years*. It has only recently been rejected definitively by the Church"[174]

Objectively speaking, this "Hebrew Catholic" spokesman advances the heretical claim that the Church's teaching on abrogation of the Old Covenant *was in error*, and that after nearly 2,000 years of being in error the Church *definitively rejected* her own prior teaching. While Schoeman veils this outrageous claim by describing Church

---

[172]Broadcast of March 7, 2005.
[173]Ibid.
[174]Roy H. Schoeman, *Salvation is from the Jews* (San Francisco: Ignatius Press, 2003), page 352.

teaching as "Christian theology for much of the past two thousand years," he knows very well that he is referring to the Catholic Church, but clearly hesitates to say so explicitly. He identifies the teaching in question as "Christian *theology*" when it is really explicit Catholic *dogma*. In the objective moral order Schoeman is simply teaching heresy, and Catholics cannot lend an ear to his opinions.

Furthermore, Schoeman's claim of a "definitive rejection" of the doctrine of supersession is supported by nothing besides a reference to the conciliar document *Nostra Aetate*, and several addresses by Pope John Paul II to small groups. None of these documents even explicitly addresses the question of supersession, much less "definitively" rejects it. This, then, is another addition to the "great façade" of non-binding novelties discussed in Chapter 2—novelties New Church innovators try to pass off as new doctrines of the Church announced for the first time at Vatican II. But no such announcement was made, for such an announcement would be impossible.[175]

In contrast to Schoeman and his ilk, before Vatican II Jewish converts not only accepted the Church's infallible teaching, they staunchly defended it. For example, in the book *Campaigning for Christ*, the renowned Jewish convert David Goldstein observed that unbelieving Jews "suffer not for a defense of truth, but rather as a penalty for resistance to God's Revelation given into the keeping of the sons of Abraham, who were *once* God's chosen children. Their Own came unto them and they received Him not."[176] That is the mind of the Church based on her infallible teaching concerning the spiritual condition of unbelieving Jews. And nowhere has the Church "definitively rejected" this teaching.

On EWTN's *The Journey Home* Moss ventured another "Hebrew Catholic" error when he noted with satisfaction that thanks to the "fresh breath of the Holy Spirit" at Vatican II (apparently the Holy Spirit had grown stale as of 1962) the Church had "ceased from targeting peoples for conversion" and now practices "dialogue instead." That is, according to Moss, it was wrong for the Church to "target" specific peoples for conversion, but Vatican II put an end to

---

[175]I am not questioning the sincerity of Schoeman's conversion, any more than I would question the sincerity of David or Rosalind Moss. However, this affirmation by Schoeman is false and objectively contrary to the Catholic Faith.

[176]David Goldstein and Martha Moore Avery, *Campaigning for Christ* (Boston: Pilot Publishing Co., 1924), page 197.

this injustice. Moss's sister, the aforementioned EWTN personality and Catholic Answers staffer, Rosalind Moss, expressed the same opinion on AHC's website. While taking exception to Cardinal Keeler's infamous document "Reflections on Covenant and Mission" (which essentially declares the Old Covenant salvific and renounces any Jewish conversion) Rosalind agreed with Keeler's statement that "campaigns that target Jews for conversion to Christianity are no longer theologically acceptable in the Catholic Church." Of this statement Rosalind said: "*I could not agree more*. Nor should attempts to 'target' *any* people be the mode of operation in our missionary endeavors."[177]

So, EWTN celebrities are claiming still another "reversal" of Church teaching at Vatican II. But, contrary to what they suggest, "targeting peoples for conversion" *is the very purpose of the Church's existence.* The words of Our Lord's divine commission could not be clearer: "Go forth and make disciples of all *nations*, baptizing *them* in the name of the Father, and of the Son and of the Holy Ghost, teaching *them* to observe all things whatsoever I have commanded thee." Our Lord did not say: "Go forth and make disciples of one person at a time, but target no people for conversion." Nor did He say: "Go forth and dialogue with all nations." The "dialogue" that David Moss finds so praiseworthy appears nowhere in Scripture or in the teaching of any Pope or Council before 1962. "Dialogue" has no roots whatsoever in Tradition. "Dialogue" is a total novelty in the Church and thus cannot be part of her doctrine or dogma; for the Church had no power to invent new doctrines in the 1960s or at any other time.

It appears, then, that "Hebrew Catholics," EWTN and the rest of the New Church establishment now view the "targeted" evangelization of the Jews and other peoples as some kind of invidious racial discrimination rather than a work of mercy and salvation! Such is the condition of the "ecumenical" and "interreligious" mind. But what does it tell us about the state of the Faith in New Church that its spokesmen regard attempts to convert entire peoples, especially the Jews, as an offense?

In rejecting the "targeting" of the Jews for conversion, the "Hebrew Catholics" (and the so-called "Catholic" television network that promotes their views) reveal more about New Church theology

---

[177]http://hebrewcatholic.org/FaithandTheology/Reflections-Covenant-Mission/openlettertocard.html.

than perhaps even they might realize. Why would any *truly believing* Catholic *not* want to see the Church "targeting" the Jews and every other people of the world for conversion? What greater service could the Church perform for all peoples than to make them disciples and save their souls, precisely as Our Lord commanded? Was it wrong for St. Paul to "target" the Gentiles of Cyprus, Asia Minor, Macedonia, Corinth, Ephesus and elsewhere on his three missionary voyages? Was it wrong for Saint Patrick to "target" the pagans of ancient Ireland? Was it wrong for Saint Boniface to "target" the barbarians of Germany? Was it wrong for the Jesuits to "target" the peoples of Brazil, China, India and Japan, or for Isaac Jogues to "target" the Sioux and the Iroquois in America? Has the Church been wrong, then, throughout the entire history of her missionary expeditions to the peoples of the world in keeping with the divine commission? Has New Church decided to *repeal* the divine commission (as if that were possible)? One wonders whether people who think this way have not lost the Faith without even realizing it.

It is most telling that EWTN's "Hebrew Catholic" celebrities reject the "targeting" of the Jews for conversion *when they themselves profess to desire the corporate conversion of that entire people.* Here we encounter a revealing self-contradiction. Do the "Hebrew Catholics" really want to see all the Jews converted, or is it rather they wish to see *the Catholic Church* converted by a certain transformation and "perfection" of the Church through the incorporation of national Israel? That, amazingly enough, is what at least some "Hebrew Catholics" appear to believe. In *Salvation is from the Jews*, Roy Schoeman, as already noted, claims that the Church now rejects her own dogmatic teaching on the supersession of the Old Covenant. On the other hand, he argues, one cannot hold that membership in the Old Covenant is required for participation in the New Covenant. Therefore, Schoeman proposes what he calls a "third alternative":

> This book proposes a third alternative—that as the Old Covenant was brought to fruition by the New at the first coming (sic), *so will the New Covenant be brought to fruition by the Old*, by the return of the Jews at the Second Coming. Thus, the current wave of Jewish entry into the Church may be among the most important things going on today, or indeed, in the history of the world.[178]

---

[178]*Salvation is from the Jews*, page 353.

So, Schoeman suggests, the Old Covenant still subsists in order to bring the New and Eternal Covenant to fruition by the entry of Old Covenant practitioners into the Church. That this idea makes a shambles of the Church's defined dogma on the abrogation of the Old Covenant hardly needs to be demonstrated. But, even worse, Schoeman implicitly denies the infinite merit of the Redemption itself when he argues that the New and Eternal Covenant will be brought to "fruition" by the Old. The New and Eternal Covenant cannot possibly be lacking in fruition. Rather, it is a question of Jews and Gentiles alike availing themselves of the already fruitful New and Eternal Covenant by conversion, baptism and membership in the Catholic Church. Schoeman's opinion denies the very foundation of Christian faith, while implicitly endorsing the Talmudic notion that salvation will be effected (at least in part) not by the grace of Christ alone, but by national Israel as the survival of the Old Covenant. As St. Paul declared: "I cast not away the grace of God. For if justice be by the law [i.e. the Old Covenant] then Christ died in vain". (Gal. 2:21) I do *not* say that Schoeman subjectively intends this heresy, but this is the objective signification of his claim that the Old Covenant will bring the New Covenant to "fruition."[179]

One cannot help but notice how the entire "Hebrew Catholic" project of making way for national Israel in the Catholic Church savors of the Zionist agenda. On EWTN's *The Journey Home* Moss confirmed this impression by placing a Zionist "spin" on the conversion of Edith Stein, now known to the Church as Saint Teresa Benedicta of the Cross: Edith Stein, said Moss, is "a wonderful role model for Hebrew Catholics" because the graces obtained by her suffering and death in a Nazi concentration camp made possible "the rebirth of the state of Israel"! Likewise, in an interview with Zenit News that appears on AHC's website, Schoeman contended that "the re-establishment of a Jewish national homeland against all odds" is a

---

[179]I understand that Schoeman has since privately indicated that his formula "the New Covenant is brought to fruition by the Old" should be understood only to mean that the Messiah will come when the Jews convert at the end of history. But that is not what his words actually signify. The Old Covenant as such will have nothing to do with the hypothesized conversion of the Jews in the Last Days, for that conversion will involve simply and only a Jewish embrace of the *New* Covenant and the *abandonment* of the superseded Old Covenant religion. Schoeman's language is gravely misleading and objectively heterodox, no matter what his professed subjective intention may have been.

sign from God that "the Jews, as a people, have a major role in bringing about the Second Coming," and that the fulfillment of Old Testament prophecies concerning the End Times requires "the existence of a powerful Jewish nation-state with its capital in Jerusalem—a nation-state which only recently came back into existence after a hiatus of almost 2,000 years."[180]

That the creation of a man-made state by secular Jews who engaged in terrorism represents the fulfillment of God's prophecy and the Jewish "vocation," is an outrageous Zionist falsification of Scripture *even anti-Zionist Orthodox rabbis reject as unbiblical.* Consider, for example, an address delivered by Rabbi Yisroel Dovid Weiss at the United Association for Studies and Research (UASR), publishers of the *Middle East Affairs* Journal, on March 14, 2002.[181] Rabbi Weiss gave a theological critique of the Zionist agenda that is astonishingly consistent with the traditional Catholic view of the Jewish people and the Book of the Apocalypse, even if it fails to perceive that the exile of the Jews has resulted specifically from their rejection of their own Messiah. The Rabbi's remarkable observations (which reflect a substantial segment of Orthodox Jewish opinion) deserve to be quoted at length in answer to Moss, AHC and Schoeman:

> Through many of the Prophetic books in the Old Testament the Jewish people were warned that a serious rebellion against the Will of G-d would result in the most severe of punishments. Unchecked it could lead to the ruin of the Holy Temple in Jerusalem and the exile of the entirety of the Jewish nation.
>
> And, it is here, my friends, in those Old Testament prophecies, that the quarrel between Judaism and Zionism begins.
>
> Eventually the horrors foretold by the Prophets came to pass. Jewry was exiled from the Land. The first exile, also known as the Babylonian captivity, lasted only 70 years. By a series of miraculous events the people were returned to the land. This second entry into the land led

---

[180]"Jews' Role in Christ's First and Second Coming: Roy Schoeman on Salvation History," Zenit News interview, November 10, 2003.
[181]http://www.nkusa.org/activities/speeches/Boston061503.cfm.

to the rebuilding of the Temple. The Second Temple stood from about 2500 years ago until about 1900 years ago, then it too was destroyed. *This time the cause was once again the backsliding of the people who were, as always, held to a very demanding Divine standard....*

The exile would not be forever. There would be years of dispersion, many of them endured under persecution. Yet, there was the promise that the people would yet return to the Land. *But this return was not to be under human control.* It would be heralded by the advent of Elijah the Prophet and accompanied with many miracles. *And, this time, the redemption would not just be for the Jewish people but rather for all men....*

Thus, at the burning of the Second Temple, the Jewish people were sent into an exile *which extends till today.* For two thousand years Jews have prayed for the end of their exile and the accompanying redemption of the entire world....

*To suggest that one could use political or military means to escape the Creator's decree was seen as heresy*, as a denial of the Divine stewardship over sin and forgiveness.... [N]o Jew anywhere suggested—and this among a people that studied its sacred texts constantly and wrote about them voluminously—that exile could be ended by human means.

It was only towards the end of the nineteenth century, among Jews far estranged from their faith, that the notion began to be put forth that exile was the result of Jewish weakness. Theodore Herzl and a handful of others, all ignorant or non-observant of Torah, began to set the process in motion that by the end of the next century would have produced untold suffering for Jews and Palestinians.

Rabbi Weiss went on to observe that: "The very concept of Zionism was a refutation of the traditional Torah belief in exile as punishment and redemption and as dependent on penitence and Divine intervention." The Rabbi then uttered a conclusion that should be self-evident to anyone who calls himself a Catholic: "*Friends, there will be no peace in the Middle East until there is no state of Israel.* The Torah cannot be violated. Our task in exile cannot be fulfilled by trying to end exile *by human agitations.* Nor can our hopes for redemption be realized in the Israeli state."

Hence even Orthodox rabbis can see that the state of Israel is not part of God's plan, but a rebellion against God by Jews who will not accept the divine punishment for their faithlessness: the Jewish dispersion. As Rabbi Weiss rightly notes, because it is contrary to God's will, the very existence of an Israeli state has brought untold suffering to Jews as well as Arabs. Yet, amazingly enough, EWTN lends itself to quasi-Zionist theories advanced by "Hebrew Catholics." As Moss and his fellow "Hebrew Catholics" would have it, Saint Teresa Benedicta is the "patron saint" of the state of Israel founded by secular Jews such as Menachem Begin, whose terrorist activities were denounced by his own fellow Jews![182] Whether or not they understand the implications of their program, the "Hebrew Catholics" are actually advocating the ecclesial equivalent *of an Israeli state within the Catholic Church* that would parallel the creation of the Israeli nation-state in Palestine.

Enough! Edith Stein's death had nothing to do with the founding of the merely human nation-state of Israel. Nor is she a role model for "Hebrew Catholics." She is a role model for *all humanity* because she submitted herself in total humility to Christ without seeking to alter His Church to accommodate any sort of Jewish racial demand. When Edith Stein became a Catholic she did not agitate for a "Hebrew Catholic Community" in the Church. Naming herself after a Spanish nun, Saint Teresa of Avila, she became Sister Teresa Benedicta, a cloistered Carmelite like any other cloistered Carmelite. St. Teresa Benedicta of the Cross did not complain that Catholicism is a "Gentile religion" which needs to make a special place for "Israelites," because the Church is "sociologically Gentile." While Sister Teresa Benedicta never repudiated her Jewish ancestry—in fact, she rejoiced that as a daughter of Israel she had been united at

---

[182]As noted in the Wikipedia: "In 1948 Begin was at the center of the shipping of Irgun arms to Israel, ending in the sinking of the *Altalena* by gunfire ordered by [later made Israeli Prime Minister] David Ben-Gurion... The *Irgun*, together with the underground *Lehi* militia (also known as "The Stern Gang"), were widely denounced by left-wing Israelis, particularly Ben-Gurion, as 'terrorist' organisations...." (http://en.wikipedia.org/wiki/Menachem_Begin)

last with the Jewish Messiah—she recognized that Catholicism is *already* the perfection and fulfillment of the religion of the abrogated Old Covenant, and that it always has been.

Putting aside the heresies that underlie the "Hebrew Catholic" Judaization project, what would AHC's Hebrew Catholic Community look like if, God forbid, the Church ever approved it? On EWTN's *The Journey Home,* Moss gave a good indication of AHC's plans in response to a question by email about why Catholics do not celebrate the Jewish holidays "like Jesus and Mary did." Ignoring the Church's teaching that the rituals and observances of the Mosaic law have been abolished with the New Covenant and that it is mortally sinful to observe them, Moss recommended that the Catholic inquirer "go to a local synagogue and watch what they do and listen to it. You can *take part in a Seder,*" he added. Moss was even more explicit in answering another viewer question about the Protestant "Messianic Jews" who celebrate the Jewish feasts. Moss noted uncritically that the Messianic Jews "are Jews who have come to faith in Jesus under the Reformation umbrella" (as if a heretical human version of Christianity were perfectly acceptable) and that "most of the Messianic Jews do celebrate most of the Jewish feasts..." Moss then recommended that *Catholics follow suit* by celebrating Passover and Rosh haShanah:

> Passover of course is fulfilled in the Mass and so it's a recent set of events that Catholics are beginning to celebrate the Passover in one sense or another. I think that this exercise is helping many, many Catholics appreciate the Mass better because they're getting a firsthand experience of the Passover. But there are people in the Church who are celebrating the [Jewish] feasts. In fact my pastor at my Catholic church said "Why do we celebrate January 1st as New Year's? We should be celebrating Rosh haShanah." *There's nothing in the Catholic Faith that would work against that,* and he [the pastor] wants to do *a Hebrew Mass* on Rosh haShanah. *And so the future holds a lot of potential...*[183]

Notice the Modernist double-talk in this quotation: The Passover was fulfilled in the Mass, but Catholics should celebrate the Passover.

---

[183]Broadcast of March 7, 2005.

If the Passover was fulfilled in the Mass, then the way to appreciate the Mass better is to study *the Mass*, not return to the practice of a defunct Jewish supper ritual that merely prefigured the true worship God enjoins upon His Church. As for the "potential" Moss has in mind for "the future," one can only contemplate it with dread. Meanwhile, Moss revealed, "we [AHC] hope to be able to provide published literature that would take what was prevalent at the time of Jesus and bring it up to today and *into the Catholic Faith*." In other words, Moss and AHC, with EWTN's hearty endorsement, plan to introduce texts for the Judaization of Catholic worship *throughout the Church* by some sort of return to Jewish observances in effect before the New Covenant.

This conclusion is supported by an item on AHC's website entitled: "Through the Hebrew Catholic Year: A Collection of Traditions and Prayers for the Jewish Holidays for Catholics." Here AHC advocates a "Catholic" celebration of Rosh haShanah, Yom Kippur, Succoth, Purim, Passover, Shavuoth, and Hanukkah, using prayers "adapted from traditional Jewish prayer books."[184] While affirming that Catholics celebrate the Sabbath on Sunday, AHC— again, in typical Modernist fashion—undermines what it affirms by commending the following Jewish Sabbath ceremony for Saturday night: "On Saturday evening, I light the Sabbath candles as I remember my [non-converted] mother doing. My head covered and my hands over my eyes, I recite the blessing, adding a prayer of thanksgiving for Yeshua (Jesus) the Light who has come into the world."[185] When using the special "Hebrew Catholic" prayers to celebrate the Jewish holidays, the text advises that "you may [may!] want to begin and end each service with the sign of the Cross in Hebrew." Here is the English translation of the recommended "Hebrew Catholic" version of the Sign of the Cross:

> *In the name of the Father*
> *and of the Son*
> *and of the Holy Spirit*
> *one God, Amen*

---

[184]http://www.hebrewcatholic.org/HCLiturgicalYear/ThruHebrewCatholicYear/throughthehebrew.html
[185]http://www.hebrewcatholic.org/HCLiturgicalYear/ThruHebrewCatholicYear/sabbath.html

What sort of arrogance gives rise to the idea that "Hebrew Catholics" are free to add "one God" to a formula that goes back to the very beginning of the Church—as if the Church had, for twenty centuries, been insufficiently mindful that the Triune God is One? Or is this an attempt to deemphasize the Trinity? On *The Journey Home*, Moss intoned this "modified" version of the Sign of the Cross in Hebrew, adding: "the emphasis always being that the Trinity is still only one God." *Still* "only" one God? When have Catholics ever believed otherwise? And by what right does the Association of Hebrew Catholics decide what the "emphasis" should be in the Church's Trinitarian formula of apostolic origin?

Will this Judaization plan include even a return to circumcision for "Hebrew Catholics" a la the Protestant Messianic Jews, despite the Church's rejection of that ritual as vain, useless and even cause for damnation, as the Council of Florence taught? Just how far will this Judaizing project proceed? Neither Moss nor any of the other "Hebrew Catholic" leaders EWTN promotes have addressed this question. In fact, Moss is a bit mysterious about what exactly he and AHC have in mind for the worship of their "Hebrew Catholic Community." On *The Journey Home* Moss criticized the Messianic Jews who seek to follow *all 613* of the Mosaic commandments, because that would cause a strict "separatism" between Jews and Gentiles, given such requirements as not eating with Gentiles or entering their homes. The practice of *all* of the Mosaic rituals, said Moss, is not "a valid way of interpreting the Scriptures... the Church does not teach that..." Moss failed to mention that not only does the Church "not teach that," she positively forbids and anathematizes *any adherence at all* to any of the Mosaic rituals.

Yet Moss clearly advocates a significant return to Mosaic rituals, even if it falls short of all 613 Mosaic commandments. On the AHC website Moss states: "I do not yet know what ecclesiastical format the Hebrew Catholic Community will take." But, he adds ominously, "There is much work that has to be done by theologians and those involved with canon law." Who these theologians and canonists are is anyone's guess. If the material on the AHC website is any indication, however, while "Gentile" Catholics are being introduced to the celebration of Seder Suppers, Jewish feast days and "Hebrew Masses" on Rosh haShanah, the Hebrew Catholic community will have its own "Hebrew Catholic paraliturgy now being developed," and a Hebrew calendar, including "saints of the Old Testament, whose sanctity is *not recognized by the generality of Catholics."*[186]

Moss is hardly alone in promoting "Catholic" Seder suppers and other "Hebrew Catholic" observances that the "Gentiles" in the Church would be expected to practice. On his "Second Exodus" website, EWTN celebrity Marty Barrack, another Jewish convert who identifies himself as a "Hebrew Catholic," outlines his own plans for Judaizing Catholic worship in every parish:

> Many Catholic parishes [since when?] would like to have a Passover Seder to learn much more about Christ's Last Supper. The Daughter of Zion Havurah, my little Hebrew Catholic team, is working on *a Seder package that we believe will be ideal for most parishes*. However, it will not be ready for the year 2005 celebrations. For now, I recommend Roy Schoeman's excellent "A Passover Seder in the Light of Christ". This is the complete *haggadah* (script) for a parish Passover Seder.[187]

Barrack here mentions that Roy Schoeman's version of a Catholic Passover Seder is already available for use in parishes and can be downloaded from AHC's website.

In summary, whatever their subjective intentions—and, once again, I do not judge those intentions here—there is abundant objective evidence that "Hebrew Catholic" leaders, all of them EWTN celebrities, are planning at least in part precisely what the Council of Florence condemned as a mortal sin when it declared that the practice of the Mosaic religion "cannot be observed *without the loss of eternal salvation*" and that those who continue Mosaic practices "are alien to the Christian faith and not in the least fit to participate in eternal salvation, unless someday they recover from these errors."

As we can see most clearly with this veritable return of the Judaizers, the Church has become a plaything in the hands of Modernist New Church innovators, as the exercise of authority in the Church collapses from the top down (except, of course, when it comes to punishing Catholics who defend the traditional Faith in all its integrity). In the resulting vacuum of authority, ex-Protestant

---

[186]See, http://www.hebrewcatholic.org/currentevents.html.

[187]See http://www.secondexodus.com/html/education/catholicparishpassover seder.htm. For "A Passover Seder in the Light of Christ", see http://www .hebrewcatholic.org/HCLiturgicalYear/SederinChrist/passoversederint.html.

converts are Protestantizing the Church, turning it into "Protestantism plus," while converted Jews are trying to Judaize the Church—with the approval of the ex-Protestants! According to the celebrities and "experts" of EWTN, as we wait for the Jews to catch up on their "covenant development" we are free to don yarmulkes and prayer shawls, intone "Shalom," celebrate Seder suppers on Passover, observe the Jewish feast days, participate in a "Hebrew Mass" on Rosh haShanah, and attend synagogue services to appreciate "our Jewish roots," while ostensible Jewish converts can erect an entire "Hebrew Catholic Community" within the Church, replete with its own Hebrew Catholic "para-liturgy" and Hebrew calendar.

For the first time since the Apostles overcame the early Judaizing heretics, "Hebrew Catholics" are agitating for the right to create a Jewish branch of Catholicism distinct from that practiced by "the Gentiles." And EWTN is only too happy to assist in this endeavor. EWTN thus opens up another avenue to confusion and apostasy in the Church under the guise of "traditional" Catholicism.

# Chapter 11

# Promoting Paganism and Sacrilege

Thus far we have seen that EWTN is promoting liturgical destruction, creating "ecumenical" obfuscation of the crucial difference between the inside and the outside of the Catholic Church, implicitly negating the dogma that outside the Church there is no salvation, abandoning the return of the dissidents to Rome, retreating on the necessity of Jewish conversion for salvation, and encouraging Judaization of Catholic worship. If only the damage ended there.

But EWTN goes even further down the path of ruinous innovation by providing adulatory coverage of a whole host of "officially approved" New Church fads that have drastically compromised the dignity and very integrity of the Faith. No matter how unprecedented, bizarre and shocking to the Catholic conscience, EWTN reports all of these events as if they were the most solemn of Catholic ceremonies, even though the very sight of these doings would have reduced any of the pre-conciliar Popes (not excluding John XXIII) to a state of apoplexy.

Perhaps the most telling example of this is EWTN's coverage of Pope John Paul II's trip to Mexico City in the summer of 2002. Here we see how EWTN tries to pass off the most abominable novelties of the post-conciliar epoch as if they were perfectly Catholic. The papal Mass to celebrate the beatification of Juan Diego, which began with great dignity, soon descended to sacrilege with the appearance of a band of "indigenous people" (we must not call them Indians) who danced before the altar in the garb of Aztec warriors, replete with headdresses and breast plates that left their midriffs exposed. As the choristers sang some hymn I do not recall, the Aztec dancers did their own thing with the snake-like hiss of rattles and the beating of tom-toms.

Confronted by this outrage, EWTN's Raymond Arroyo, who serves as a sort of Dan Rather for the New Church establishment—

the talking head of post-conciliar correctness—offered the following EWTN analysis: "I love the way they balance the reverence with the indigenous [sic]." Here we see how the New Church has replaced a once-untouchable form of divine worship, the sublime result of the influence of the Holy Ghost over centuries, with the ecclesial equivalent of a Broadway show, in which the players strive for the proper "balance" in their mounting of the piece and are rewarded for their efforts by favorable reviews by New Church commentators.

For Catholics who can still recognize a scandal when they see one, however, a question presents itself: Why in Heaven's name was there a commemoration of the diabolical Aztec culture, which murdered in ritual sacrifice 20,000 humans in a day, during a Mass for the canonization of the very saint chosen by God to herald the disappearance of that culture through the miraculous conversion of nine million Aztecs within a few years? Juan Diego was a humble Indian who did not belong to any of the upper social classes of the Aztec empire, such as the dreaded warrior priests whose vainglorious headdresses and breastplates were paraded so proudly at the papal Mass. Juan Diego wore the simple tunic of an Indian peasant, the very tunic on which Our Lady's miraculous image would be imprinted. It was a tunic not unlike that worn by Our Lord Himself, or by the Franciscan missionary, Fray Toribio, who received Juan Diego into the Church. In its own small way Juan Diego's tunic, which remains miraculously intact to this day, is a sign of the divine constancy of the Church, just as the liturgy that nurtured the Catholic faith of the tunic's original owner was, and is, the greatest sign of that same constancy.

After Juan Diego became a Catholic in 1524, he worshipped the true God at the traditional Latin Mass; the Mass that had been brought to Mexico by the Spanish missionaries; the Mass that would soon be defended by the Council of Trent against the furious attacks of Luther and his fellow Protestant rebels. By the time the Mother of God appeared to Juan Diego on the hill at Tepeyac in the year 1531 (only fourteen years before the Council of Trent), the former pagan was already receiving Holy Communion—on his knees, on the tongue—at least three times a week. When he attended Mass at his Franciscan parish, Juan Diego did not encounter there any dancing "indigenous people" in headdresses and breastplates, shaking rattles and beating tom-toms. He encountered only the timeless peace and dignity of the perennial Roman Rite.

Arroyo and his EWTN co-commentator dutifully defended the indefensible as a legitimate example of liturgical "inculturation." But Arroyo was not about to address the obvious objection: If the Mass was not "inculturated" in Juan Diego's own time, what possible justification is there for such absurd cultural regression during a papal Mass five centuries later? Why in the name of God did we see at a Pontifical Mass in the year 2002 pagan excrescences that would have horrified Juan Diego in the year 1531?

The day after the canonization of Juan Diego, the Pope returned to the Basilica of the Virgin of Guadalupe to conduct the beatification of the martyrs Juan Bautista and Jacinto de Los Angeles. Of course, there would be more "inculturation" of the liturgy. During the "Liturgy of the Word," four women in Indian garb approached the altar with smoking bowls in one hand and bunches of herbs in the other. One of the women doused her bunch of herbs in the smoke emanating from another's bowl, and then walked over to the papal throne, where she proceeded to perform a pre-Christian Indian "purification" ritual on the Vicar of Christ. The UPI report described this ritual as "a traditional practice originally meant to cleanse people of illness and evil spirits." As the Pope grew visibly discomfited, the woman rubbed her bunch of herbs up and down his arms and across his shoulders, over and over again. For an exquisitely painful moment, it seemed the woman would not quit unless someone dragged her away, but she finally finished her "purification" of the Pope.

Arroyo and his EWTN co-commentator on this occasion, Msgr. Michael Heras of the diocese of Corpus Christi, Texas, immediately leapt into action. "Some people," said Arroyo, might think that what they had just witnessed was the introduction of pagan superstition into Catholic worship. Well, if that is not what it was, why would "some people" think so—and why would Arroyo feel compelled to raise the issue on the spot? According to Arroyo, however, this pagan purification ritual was merely an example of how the Church follows the teaching of Saint Pius X that, in the liturgy, the Church "takes what is pagan and makes it holy." Arroyo would have us believe that Saint Pius X would heartily approve of being rubbed down with "holy" herbs by an Indian woman in the sanctuary. I cannot think of a more apt example of how EWTN aids and abets the destruction of the liturgy, extending even to its outright paganization, under the guise of solid Catholic orthodoxy.

Arroyo (or was it Heras?) added that the ritual was nothing more than a legitimate way to express the Catholic petition *parce nobis, Domine* (Spare us, O Lord). So, according to EWTN, this pre-Christian pagan superstition is really quite in harmony with Catholic tradition—if only EWTN can find a way to *pretend* that it is. Msgr. Heras chimed in that, of course, there was no suggestion here that the herbs or the smoking bowls had any power in themselves. No, the women were merely "cooperating with God" in this ancient Indian form of "exorcism"—yes, he called it precisely that—to rid someone of "sickness and evil spirits." The power came only from the Holy Ghost, said Heras, not any false god of the Aztecs.

Putting aside Heras' surely unintended implication that John Paul II could have benefited from an exorcism, neither he nor Arroyo even attempted to explain how the elements of a useless—if not diabolically dangerous—pre-Christian purification ceremony could now serve as channels of divine grace when neither Christ nor the Magisterium has established this ceremony as part of Catholic ritual. On the other hand, if the smoking bowls and herbs of pagan ritual are not channels of grace—and, obviously, they are not—then the whole spectacle was as gratuitous and ridiculous as it was scandalous. But far worse than this, such pagan practices, like the use of Ouija boards, could actually be the cause of vexation by the devil, given that "the gods of the Gentiles are devils". (Psalm 95) The subjection of the Pope to pagan rituals might even have required him to receive a special blessing to remove the vexation. Diabolical vexations are known to be the cause of physical as well as spiritual ailments—a thought that could not have been comforting to Catholics who witnessed the Pope's ever-increasing physical suffering before his death.

Irony of ironies, this pagan ritual from pre-Christian Mexico was made part of a ceremony to beatify two Catholic martyrs, both attorneys general, who were tortured and killed in 1700 because they had alerted local authorities to the clandestine practice of pagan rituals by Indians in the Catholic vicariate of San Francisco Cajonos. The irony was not lost on the press. As UPI noted: "Ironically, Thursday's ceremony was filled with rituals reminiscent of the pagan ceremonies about which the men had warned authorities." But EWTN's commentators somehow failed to notice what even secular news reporters could see: that today's Churchmen are paganizing the Catholic liturgy.

During the "Liturgy of the Word" in Mexico City, Msgr. Heras committed a slip that could not be more telling. After the Pope had been "purified" by the Indian woman, he said: "We are now continuing with the liturgy of the *world*," when he meant to say "Liturgy of the Word". Arroyo attempted to repair the damage by adding that, yes, "it's the liturgy of the world as well." But Arroyo only dug a deeper hole for his co-commentator, for a "liturgy of the world" is a contradiction in terms. It is just such contradictions which lie at the heart of the current confusion in the Church—the very confusion in evidence when dead pagan rituals are revived during a liturgy to commemorate the beatification of two Catholics who were martyred for their role in helping Church authorities stamp out pagan rituals.

But EWTN dearly wants its viewers to believe that nothing is amiss. EWTN's basic approach to the emergence of one scandalizing novelty after another since Vatican II can be summed up with one of Groucho Marx's best lines: "Who are you going to believe, me or your own eyes?" In the face of these scandals, EWTN is dedicated to suppressing the *sensus catholicus* and stilling the troubled consciences of Catholics who have not yet been fully lobotomized by the post-conciliar regime of novelty, assuring them that what they think they see is not really there.

But it *is* there. Much of the hierarchy of the Catholic Church is now in the grip of the lunacy that Sister Lucy called "diabolical disorientation." It is lunacy to commemorate the canonization of Juan Diego with a regression to the diabolical Aztec culture in the midst of a Pontifical Mass. It is lunacy to allow an Indian woman to rub down the Vicar of Christ with smoked herbs in a pagan ritual, during a ceremony to beatify two Indians who were martyred for reporting pagan rituals. It is lunacy to paganize Catholic worship at the very moment the Aztec cult is rising again in Mexico and Mexico's "indigenous people" are abandoning the Church in large numbers to join the Jehovah's Witnesses and fundamentalist Protestant sects.

And if there is any doubt that this is lunacy, consider that while the Novus Ordo liturgy is now subject to a rampant "inculturation" in order to introduce pagan rituals abandoned centuries ago by Indian converts, the traditional Roman rite of Mass—the very heart of Catholic culture for more than 1500 years—is kept under lock and key and its use de facto strictly forbidden without special permission. This cannot be anything other than a diabolical inversion of the good order of the Church, the very depth of lunacy. Yet EWTN does not wish us to notice that the Church has been turned upside down. Mother Angelica did, but, alas, that feisty nun no longer speaks for the network. She was manlier in her opposition to error and harmful novelty than any of the men who speak for that organization now. Such is the condition of EWTN today.

Another major example of how EWTN turns a blind eye to paganism and sacrilege is its coverage of the World Day of Prayer for Peace in January 2002, which I attended as a Vatican-accredited journalist. The event featured such shocking spectacles as the appearance of Chief Amadou Gasseto of Benin, a Voodoo practitioner (i.e., a witch doctor) who was allowed to sermonize on world peace from a high wooden pulpit suitable for a cathedral, set up in the lower plaza outside the Basilica of Saint Francis. The Chief declared to the Vicar of Christ and the assembled Cardinals and Catholic guests that "The invitation to take part in the Prayer for Peace at Assisi is a great honour for me, and it is an honour for all the followers of Avelekete Vodou *whose high priest I am.*" The high priest of Avelekete Vodou then gave the Pope and all the Catholic faithful the Vodou prescription for world peace, which included "asking forgiveness of the protecting spirits of regions affected by violence" and "carrying out sacrifices of reparation and purification, and thus restoring peace."[188]

The faithful Catholic cannot fail to be outraged at the sight of such things, but EWTN resolutely refuses to see anything wrong with them. Dr. Peterson recalls that the committee meetings, which consisted largely of lectures by EWTN's own Donovan, avoided any criticism of the papal prayer meetings at Assisi in 1986 and 2000—events which have been widely criticized by many loyal Catholics, including Vittorio Messori, the Italian journalist whose interview of Pope John Paul II became the bestseller *Crossing the Threshold of Hope.* The issue "was almost completely disregarded," said Peterson. "Every time it would come to the Pope and the Faith, it would always be the Pope as opposed to the Faith." Peterson recounted how all viewer objections to Assisi and other ecumenical and interreligious gestures were met with the same response: "The Pope

---

[188]I attended the Assisi event as a reporter with a Vatican press credential. The voodoo chieftain's remarks are taken verbatim from the Vatican's official booklet for the 2002 Assisi event, entitled "Together for Peace," and can be found at pages 50, 51 and 52.

knows what he is doing and we are to support him and follow him in this situation. I could not believe that I had been raised where I was not even to attend a Protestant church and suddenly that this was now okay."

There seems to be no limit to EWTN's willingness to justify scandal and sacrilege in the post-conciliar climate of "creeping apostasy." As discussed in Chapter 16, EWTN even defended (or tried to cover up) the worldwide scandal of the Hindu desecration of the Fatima Shrine in May of 2004, which it has tried to pass off as a "prayer for peace." Not even John Paul II's well-documented kissing of the Koran[189] was viewed critically in the committee meetings Dr. Peterson attended. "We were told it was just part of the overall plan to get closer to the Moslems and hopefully convert Moslems. That was about all we could say [to EWTN supporters]."

Peterson observed how ironic it was that Donovan and the other committee members were prepared to defend actions "that they would never do" themselves, but which they try to justify merely because the Pope or some other Church authority has done them. The general attitude Peterson observed during his tenure "was almost worship or idolatry of the Pope as opposed to the traditional Faith. That's the thing that really bothered me."

---

[189]Fides news agency reported this eyewitness testimony of Catholic Patriarch Bidawid of Iraq: "On May 14th I was received by the Pope, together with a delegation composed of the Shiite imam of Khadum mosque and the Sunni President of the council of administration of the Iraqi Islamic Bank. At the end of the audience the Pope bowed to the Muslim holy book the Koran presented to him by the delegation and he kissed it as a sign of respect. The photo of that gesture has been shown repeatedly on Iraqi television and it demonstrates that the Pope is not only aware of the suffering of the Iraqi people, he has also great respect for Islam." (Fides news agency, Rome, June 4, 1999; see also CWNews report of June 1, 1999 at: http://www.cwnews.com/news/viewstory.cfm?rec num=10415) Some New Church apologists obstinately deny that the incident occurred, while others explain it away. Photographs of the event abound. See, e.g. http://www.traditioninaction.org/RevolutionPhotos/A055rc Koran.htm.

# Chapter 12

# Quasi-Idolatry of the Pope's Person

By "almost worship or idolatry of the Pope" Peterson meant EWTN's blind, unquestioning acceptance of every papal word and deed during the recently-concluded reign of John Paul II, no matter how scandalous or deserving of correction: e.g. kissing the Koran; holding prayer meetings with witch doctors at Assisi; staging Vespers and other joint liturgical services with pro-abortion Protestant "bishops;" opening the Holy Door at St. Paul's basilica in Rome with the pro-contraception, pro-divorce, and (at least in some cases) pro-abortion Anglican "Archbishop" of Canterbury and a schismatic Greek Orthodox prelate;[190] bestowing pectoral crosses, the symbol of episcopal authority, on Anglican "bishops" who are mere laymen;[191] turning over Catholic churches in Rome to Orthodox congregations;[192] donating $100,000 to build an Orthodox cathedral in

---

[190]As the Vatican website reported concerning this event, which took place on January 18, 2001: "Joining the Pope in opening the Holy Door were Metropolitan Athanasios of Heliopolis and Thera, representing the Ecumenical Patriarch, and Dr George Carey, Archbishop of Canterbury and spiritual leader of the Anglican Communion...." See, http://www.EWTN.com/library/PAPALDOC/JP2JA18A .HTM. An earlier press account noted that "a spokesperson for Carey said, 'He believes that the case for terminating a pregnancy depends substantially on the particular circumstances—and that is fully in line with the teaching of the [Anglican] Church.'" See, http://www.theinterim.com/1999/nov/05morning after.html.

[191]As just one of many examples of this, Zenit News reported (August 26, 2004) that a Protestant evangelical "bishop" named Huber received a pectoral cross from the Pope: "Not only did the Pope give me his words," said Huber, "he gave me a real gift: a pectoral cross, made for the 25th anniversary of his pontificate. This has impressed me profoundly."

[192]See, e.g., *The Tablet*, July 10, 2004: "In a token of friendship, the Pope turned over to Bartholomew I the church of San Teodoro on the Palatine Hill for the liturgical use of the Greek Orthodox community of Rome. The church predates the schism of 1054, when Eastern and Western Churches split."

Bucharest;[193] attending a Mass in Papua New Guinea at which the Epistle was read by a bare-breasted woman and another bare-breasted woman presented the "Offertory Gifts" to the Pope;[194] attending a Bob Dylan concert;[195] and so on.

*The Fatima Crusader* has demonstrated abundantly with citations to Doctors of the Church that nothing could be more un-Catholic than the attitude that the Pope may never be opposed or even criticized in anything he says or does.[196] This attitude makes of the Pope precisely the Protestant caricature of an absolute dictator. Here too, Cardinal Ratzinger, now Benedict XVI, has conceded a key point: that even the Pope must be faithful to Tradition as its servant, not its master. Speaking of the liturgy in particular, Ratzinger observed that

> In fact, the First Vatican Council had in no way defined the Pope as an absolute monarch. On the contrary, it presented him as the guarantor of obedience to the revealed Word. The Pope's authority is bound to the Tradition of faith, and that also applies to the liturgy. It is not "manufactured" by the authorities. Even the Pope can only be a humble servant of its lawful development and abiding integrity and identity.

---

[193]ZENIT.org, November 2, 2000: "Romanian Orthodox clergy said today that John Paul II has donated $100,000 toward the construction of an Orthodox cathedral here that will accommodate up to 2,000 people, Agence France-Presse reported."

[194]See, photo of event at http://www.traditioninaction.org/RevolutionPhotos/A028rcReceivingCommunion1.htm.

[195]One Protestant website, citing Associated Press, reported: "A crowd of 300,000 young people attended the festival. The 56-year-old Dylan, who has performed for more than 30 years, sang two songs directly to the pope... The Associated Press exclaimed: 'It's the stuff of which legends are made: the rebel who's been knock, knock, knocking on heaven's door meeting the man with the keys to the kingdom.'" The Protestant website concludes: "Wicked music cannot be used to glorify Jesus Christ." (http://www.wayoflife.org/fbns/bobdylan.htm).

[196]See "In Defense of All Catholics Who Defend the Church", *The Fatima Crusader*, Issue #74, Summer 2003, pages 19-20 (http://www.fatimacrusader.com/cr74/cr74pg19.asp). See also John Malloy, "Can There Be Any Public Criticism Of Bishops?", *The Fatima Crusader*, Issue #35, Winter 1990-91, pages 35-37 (http://www.fatimacrusader.com/cr35/cr35pg35.asp); and Jonathan Tuttle, "Mission Infallible: When is he? When is he not?", *The Fatima Crusader*, Issue #66, Winter 2001, pages 23-31 (http://www.fatimacrusader.com/cr66/cr66pg23.asp).

In sum, Ratzinger concluded, the authority of the Pope *"is not unlimited; it is at the service of Sacred Tradition."*[197]

Scripture itself teaches that there are times when the Pope's subjects have not only the right, but the duty, to speak out against papal actions which cause scandal and endanger the Faith. We see this in St. Paul's rebuke of Peter, the first Pope, for his refusal to eat with the Gentiles, thus endangering the very mission of the Church to make converts among them: "But when Cephas [Peter] was come to Antioch, *I withstood him to the face*, because he was to be blamed. For before that some came from James, he did eat with the Gentiles: but when they were come, he withdrew and separated himself, fearing [the opinion of] them who were of the circumcision. And to his dissimulation the rest of the Jews consented: so that Barnabas also was led by them into that dissimulation." (Galatians 2:11-14)

That is, Paul stood up to the first Pope and rebuked him because Peter was misleading the Church by his bad example. Explaining the moral duty this passage of Scripture teaches us, St. Thomas Aquinas wrote: "It must be observed, however, that if the Faith were endangered, a subject *ought* to rebuke his prelate even publicly. *Hence Paul, who was Peter's subject, rebuked him in public, on account of the imminent danger of scandal concerning faith....*" St. Thomas here observes that the public rebuke of a prelate "would seem to savor of presumptuous pride; but *there is no presumption in thinking oneself better in some respect*, because, in this life, *no man is without some fault*. We must also remember that when a man reproves his prelate charitably, it does not follow that he thinks himself any better, but merely that he offers his help to one who, 'being in the higher position among you, *is therefore in greater danger*,' as Augustine observes in his Rule quoted above."[198]

Thus, not to correct the Pope when such correction is necessary in charity is a disservice to the Pope, not an expression of "loyalty" to him, because the Pope, as our superior, is in far greater danger than we.

Moreover, a craven or sycophantic refusal to criticize the Pope when the good of the Church requires it actually undermines the Pope's high office. The words of the Dominican theologian Melchior Cano, a leading theologian at the Council of Trent, could have been written for the current directors of EWTN, who confuse slavish

---

[197]Ratzinger, *The Spirit of the Liturgy*, pages 165-166.
[198]*Summa Theologica*, IIa-IIae, Q. 33, Art. 4.

adherence with true loyalty to the Vicar of Christ: "Peter has no need of our lies or flattery. Those who blindly and indiscriminately defend every decision of the supreme Pontiff are the very ones who do most to undermine the authority of the Holy See—they destroy instead of strengthening its foundations."[199]

But a bouquet of lies and flattery is what EWTN bestowed without ceasing on Pope John Paul II, no matter how scandalized the faithful were by certain papal actions. The false principle that The Pope Can Do No Wrong has done incalculable harm to the Church over the past forty years, because it requires Catholics to defend the indefensible and thus causes in many a crisis of faith in the papacy itself.

The homosexual priest scandal that erupted around the world in 2002 is a prime example of the consequences of cowardly silence in the face of papal malfeasance. Speaking at the American bishops' conference in Dallas concerning the scandal, even Bishop Fabian Bruskewitz of Nebraska condemned the entire American episcopate as "this hapless bench of bishops" for failing to follow the example of the St. Catherine of Siena, a Doctor of the Church, who "was brave enough to tell the pope off when he needed telling off" just before the Great Western Schism in the fourteenth century. "She did her duty. We must too," added Bruskewitz. Bruskewitz revealed that he had passed on to John Paul II "a letter that the medieval St. Bernard of Clairvaux wrote to a pope of his day, warning the pontiff that if he (the pope) was going to be sent to hell, it would be because he failed to get rid of bad bishops."[200] As the Catholic columnist Rod Dreher recounted, Bruskewitz "went on to praise the Holy Father for coming up with beautiful words and noble sentiments, but to fault him for failing to implement them through responsible governing of the Church."[201] That, of course, was the Catholic thing to do.

Precisely because the Pope is capable of erring and giving scandal in his prudential judgments, gestures and policy decisions, Vatican I defined strict limits on the dogma of papal infallibility

[W]hen he speaks *ex cathedra*, that is, when carrying out

---

[199]Cited in John Jay Hughes, *Pontiffs Who Shaped History* (Huntington, Indiana: Our Sunday Visitor Publishing Division, 1996), page 11.
[200]Rod Dreher, "Done in Dallas: The Problems that Persist," National Review Online, June 17, 2002.
[201]Ibid.

the duty of the pastor and teacher of all Christians in accord with his supreme apostolic authority, *he explains a doctrine of faith or morals to be held by the universal Church*, through the divine assistance promised him in blessed Peter, operates with that infallibility with which the divine Redeemer wished that His Church be instructed in defining doctrine on faith and morals; and so such definitions by the Roman Pontiff *of themselves*, but not from the consensus of the Church, are unalterable. (Cf. Dz. 1839-1840.)

As Cardinal Newman noted in his discussion of the definition, "these conditions of course contract [restrict] the range of infallibility most materially."[202]

Indeed, the Pope is subject to the possibility of error, and thus the need for correction, whenever he is not properly exercising his God-given authority to promulgate doctrine or discipline to be imposed on the universal Church. A classic historical example is Pope John XXII, who was denounced as a heretic when, in 1331, he preached and developed in a series of sermons the thesis that the beatific vision of the saved awaited the final judgment of God on the Last Day. Cardinal Orsini even called for a council to pronounce the Pope a heretic. When John XXII was opposed in his erroneous teaching, he declared that he had not meant to bind the whole Church and he impaneled a commission of theologians to consider the question. The commission *informed the Pope that he was in error*. John XXII retracted the error on his deathbed.[203]

Thus, the dictum that to err is human applies even to a Pope acting outside the narrow scope of an infallible pronouncement (always accompanied by such formal language as "we declare, define and pronounce"), a universal disciplinary command binding on the entire Church, or the repetition of something the Church has always taught and which is thus infallible doctrine (e.g. the constant teaching, never formally defined as dogma, that the Blessed Virgin Mary is Mediatrix of All Graces). To hold otherwise is to say that every word and deed of the Pope must be treated as if it were

---

[202]John Henry Newman, *Certain Difficulties Felt by Anglicans in Catholic Teaching* (London, 1876), cited in Michael Davies, *Lead Kindly Light: The Life of John Henry Newman* (Long Prairie, Minnesota: Neumann Press, 2001), page 179.
[203]Eric John, *The Popes: A Concise Biographical History* (1964; reprinted, Harrison, New York: Roman Catholic Books, 1994), page 253.

infallible. This would effectively equate obviously fallible statements (such as those of John XXII, already mentioned) or prudential judgments with infallible pronouncements and thereby make a mockery of the Catholic teaching on papal infallibility. It would also require us to ignore reason itself, which Vatican I defined as being in no way opposed to the Catholic Faith.[204] When John Paul II kissed the Koran, for example, not only our faith but our reason should have told us that a scandal had occurred, for even unaided reason recognizes that a book which blasphemes Christ ought not to be venerated by the Vicar of Christ. As St. Thomas Aquinas teaches, against a fact there is no argument. A scandal is a scandal no matter who perpetrates it; an error is an error no matter who commits it.

By wrongly elevating the Pope to the status of an utterly inerrant and impeccable demigod, EWTN and other New Church "papalators" placed upon John Paul II a burden he could never carry, a burden no Pope could carry. Such papalatry sets the faithful up for confusion and disillusionment when a Pope errs, as any human can, in a matter of prudential judgment or in some non-binding statement. Some misguided Catholics, following this false notion of an inerrant papacy, conclude that any Pope who does err in some word or deed affecting the Catholic Church has ceased to be the Pope; they become *sedevacantists*—Latin for "empty seat." To recall the words of Melchior Cano, this is how papalators "destroy instead of strengthening" the foundations of the papacy.

---

[204]"But although faith is above reason, nevertheless, between faith and reason *no true dissension can ever exist....* [F]aith and reason *can never be at variance with one another...*" First Vatican Council, *Dogmatic Constitution Concerning Faith*, Chapter 4; Dz. 1797, 1799.

# Chapter 13

# Promoting Destruction
# of the Traditional Rosary

One matter of papal prudential judgment that in no way binds the universal Church was Pope John Paul II's idea, introduced in his encyclical *Rosarium Virginis Mariae* (*RVM*), of adding five new "luminous mysteries" to the Rosary. For the first time in the history of this signal devotion of the Catholic Faith, the Rosary would be expanded to twenty mysteries divided into four parts instead of the traditional fifteen mysteries divided into three parts. Confronted with this innovation, one thinks immediately of Our Lady of Fatima's prescription for the First Saturday observance:

> I promise to assist at the moment of death, with all the graces necessary for salvation, all those who, on the first Saturday of five consecutive months shall go to Confession, receive Holy Communion, recite five decades of the Rosary, and keep Me company for fifteen minutes while meditating on *the fifteen mysteries of the Rosary*, with the intention of making reparation to Me.[205]

One certainly does not see Heaven's approval of *twenty* mysteries of the Rosary in these words of Our Lady, who stands outside of time and certainly foresaw John Paul's proposal. Quite the contrary, Heaven's prescription for the First Saturdays, which is tied to nothing less than God's promise of eternal salvation, conspicuously fails to endorse an innovation Heaven certainly foresaw.

Now, *RVM* makes it clear that the new mysteries are merely "a proposed addition to the traditional pattern" to be "left to the freedom of individuals and communities." But as we know from

---

[205]Our Lady of Fatima to Sister Lucy on December 10, 1925.

bitter experience, in New Church newly introduced "options" become mandatory while ancient traditional observances become optional, if they are not forbidden outright. And, sure enough, in its section on how to pray the Rosary, EWTN's website presents the traditional Rosary of fifteen mysteries as a mere option "for those who prefer the traditional order."[206] Once again in New Church a key element of traditional Catholic faith and devotion is overturned by being reduced to a "preference" that one can take or leave. But the process does not end there. In its television programming EWTN is now promoting the innovation as if it were the only form of the Rosary. As one longtime EWTN viewer reports: "At first the 6:30 a.m. televised Rosary followed the traditional pattern of the Fifteen Mysteries, while the afternoon and evening broadcasts, when far more people are watching, followed the 'new' Rosary of twenty mysteries. By late summer of 2005, however, the traditional pattern was completely abandoned and all televised Rosary recitations now include the 'luminous' mysteries. The traditional Rosary has disappeared from EWTN."[207] As always in New Church, the optional innovation becomes the norm, and then the traditional practice is finally eliminated completely.

No one denies that the Pope had the right to propose some additional mysteries to contemplate while praying the Rosary, if it pleases him to do so. Nor does anyone deny that the faithful themselves are free to adopt their own local customs and preferences in praying the Rosary, such as the preference many people develop for the Sorrowful mysteries. In fact, certain religious orders have developed their own variants of the Rosary, such as the Franciscan Rosary (which arose in the early fifteenth century), with its meditations on the Seven Joys of Mary, employing a Rosary of seventy beads divided into seven groups of ten.

What *is* objectionable, however—and John Paul II left us free to make the objection—is any attempt to abolish *a universal and ancient tradition of the Catholic Church* by replacing the traditional form of the Rosary with a new version. This kind of innovation is unheard-of in the Church. As St. Thomas Aquinas observed in his *Summa Theologica*, speaking of merely human traditions: "It is absurd, and a detestable shame, that we should suffer those traditions to be

[206]http://www.ewtn.com/Devotionals/prayers/rosary/how_to.htm.
[207]Personal testimony of EWTN viewer M.A.M., given to author on November 2, 2005.

changed which we have received from the fathers of old."[208]

St. Thomas's dictum is all the more true of traditions in the Church, and especially traditions the Church believes to have had a directly supernatural origin. As the Catholic Church teaches, Saint Dominic instituted the Rosary around 1206, under a divine inspiration in response to his supplications to the Blessed Virgin Mary for aid in combating the Albigensian heresy.[209] A long line of Popes has affirmed the supernatural origin of the Rosary, including Leo X (1521), St. Pius V (1572), Gregory XIII (1585), Sixtus V (1590), Clement VIII (1605), Alexander VII (1667), Blessed Innocent XI (1689), Clement XI (1721), Innocent XIII (1724), Benedict XIV (1740-58) and Leo XIII (1878-1903).[210] As Pope Leo XIII declared in his encyclical *Supremi Apostolatus Officio* (quoting Gregory XIII): "[T]he Rosary had been instituted by St. Dominic to appease the anger of God and to implore the intercession of the Blessed Virgin Mary."

Even in the time of Saint Dominic, the 150 Hail Marys were divided into *three* groups of 50, accompanied by meditations on *three* groups of mysteries: Joyful, Sorrowful and Glorious. Around 1500, for the sake of a simpler recitation by the faithful, the 150 separate meditations (one for each bead) began to be supplanted by the fifteen mysteries in use at the time Saint Pius V canonized the Rosary in its traditional form. As if to give the stamp of approval of Heaven itself, *these are the same fifteen mysteries mentioned by the Virgin of Fatima.* When Our Lady of Fatima announced the First Saturday devotion to Sister Lucy, the Virgin referred not only to "the *fifteen* mysteries of the Rosary" and to "keeping Me company for *fifteen* minutes," as already noted, but also to reciting "um Terco" — the Portuguese term for five decades, or *one-third* of the Rosary. (In Portugal, when one says, "Let's pray the Rosary," one means the whole Rosary of fifteen decades. One says "um Terco" — one-third — to mean only five decades.) Thus, the Mother of God, in whose honor the Rosary is recited, clearly did not endorse a Rosary in four parts (a clear break with the Trinitarian form of the Rosary), even though She foresaw

---

[208]*Summa Theologica*, II-I, Q. 97, Art. 2, citing The Decretals (Dist. xii, 5).

[209]See, *Supremi Apostolatus Officio*, nn. 2, 3, 4, Leo XIII.

[210]Cf. "In Defense Of A Tradition," Father Paul A. Duffner, O.P., *The Rosary Light & Life* – Vol. 49, No. 5, September-October 1996.

this innovation and could have allowed for it in Her requests to the Fatima seers.

Just how serious abandoning the traditional form of the Rosary would be is perhaps best appreciated by reference to the teaching of none other than Pope Paul VI in his encyclical *Marialis Cultus* (1974). In this encyclical Paul VI strongly affirmed the teaching of St. Pius V, in his Apostolic Letter *Consueverunt Romani Pontifices* (1569), canonizing the traditional form of the Rosary. As Pope Paul VI declared:

> We, too, from the first general audience of our pontificate on July 13, 1963, have shown our great esteem for the pious practice of the Rosary. Since that time we have underlined its value on many different occasions, some ordinary, some grave.... We renewed this appeal in our Apostolic Exhortation *Recurrens Mensis October* (October 7, 1969), in which we also commemorated the fourth centenary of the Apostolic Letter *Consueverunt Romani Pontifices* of our predecessor Saint Pius V, who in that document explained and in a certain sense *established the traditional form of the Rosary.*

Having rooted himself in the teaching of St. Pius V, Pope Paul introduced that teaching with the following explanation:

> It has also been more easily seen how the orderly and gradual unfolding of the Rosary reflects the very way in which the Word of God, mercifully entering into human affairs, brought about the Redemption. The Rosary considers in harmonious succession the principal salvific events accomplished in Christ, from His virginal conception and the mysteries of His childhood to the culminating moments of the Passover—the blessed Passion and the glorious Resurrection—and to the effects of this on the infant Church on the day of Pentecost, and on the Virgin Mary when at the end of Her earthly life She was assumed body and soul into Her heavenly home. *It has also been observed that the division of the mysteries of the Rosary into three parts* not only adheres strictly to the chronological order of the facts *but above all reflects the plan of the original*

*proclamation of the Faith* and sets forth once more the mystery of Christ *in the very way in which it is seen by Saint Paul* in the celebrated "hymn" of the Letter to the Philippians—kenosis, death and exaltation (cf. 2:6-11).

Pope Paul then presented as authoritative and binding the teaching of St. Pius V on the elements of the Rosary:

The Rosary of the Blessed Virgin Mary, according to the tradition accepted by our predecessor St. Pius V and *authoritatively taught by him*, consists of various elements disposed *in an organic fashion*:

a) Contemplation in communion with Mary, of a series of mysteries of salvation, *wisely distributed into three cycles*. These mysteries express the joy of the messianic times, the salvific suffering of Christ and the glory of the Risen Lord which fills the Church....

b) The Lord's Prayer, or Our Father...

c) The litany-like succession of the Hail Mary, which is made up of the angel's greeting to the Virgin (cf. Luke 1:28), and of Elizabeth's greeting (cf. Luke 1:42), followed by the ecclesial supplication, Holy Mary. The continued series of Hail Marys is the special characteristic of the Rosary, and their number, in the full and typical number of *one hundred and fifty*, presents a certain analogy with the Psalter and is *an element that goes back to the very origin of the exercise of piety*. But this number, divided, according to a well-tried custom, into decades attached to the individual mysteries, is distributed in the *three cycles* already mentioned, thus giving rise to the Rosary of fifty Hail Marys as we know it. This latter has entered into use as *the normal measure of the pious exercise* and as such has been *adopted by popular piety and approved by papal authority*, which also enriched it with numerous indulgences.

d) The doxology Glory be to the Father which, in conformity with an orientation common to Christian piety, concludes the prayer with the glorifying of God

who is one and three, from whom, through whom and
in whom all things have their being (cf. Rom. 11:36).

*These are the elements of the Rosary.* Each has its own
particular character which, *wisely understood and
appreciated*, should be reflected in the recitation in order
that the Rosary may express all its richness and
variety....

Thus, Paul VI, in union with all his predecessors, including Leo
XIII (cf. *Iucunda Semper Expectatione*) and in conformity with the
definitive teaching of Saint Pius V, affirmed that the elements of the
Rosary, "disposed in *organic fashion*" over centuries of development,
consist of:

- *three* cycles of mysteries, corresponding to the mystery of
  Christ as taught by St. Paul;

- 150 Hail Marys prayed in *three* groups of fifty, corresponding
  to the Psalter, which is as old as Catholic piety itself;

- the Our Father and the Glory Be.

Paul VI made it clear, then, that the Rosary is not some
changeable arrangement of prayers that can be altered whenever it
seems a good idea, but a *triune pattern* of prayer, "disposed in an
*organic fashion*," that constitutes an ancient foundation stone of
popular Catholic piety, long approved by the Magisterium. But if the
new "luminous mysteries" were made a permanent and universal
part of the Rosary, the three-part traditional Rosary, corresponding to
the Triune God, would become a four-part Rosary, and the 150
salutations of the Virgin, corresponding to the 150 Psalms of praise to
God in the Psalter, would become 200 salutations, corresponding to
nothing. The innovators of New Church, however, led by such
organizations as EWTN, would now abandon even the teaching of
the "liberal" Paul VI *only 30 years ago*, so rapid is their advance in the
ceaseless pursuit of innovation.

Even more damage to the Rosary tradition would result if the
optional innovation of *RVM* became the universal norm. *RVM*
proposes that the new "luminous mysteries" be inserted into the

traditional Rosary cycle on Thursdays. In order to make room for this "insertion," the traditional Joyful Mysteries would be moved to Saturday—where, in turn, they would displace the traditional Glorious Mysteries, which are now contemplated on Wednesdays, Saturdays and Sundays. This one change alone would shatter the symphonic progression of the Rosary from Birth to Passion to Resurrection. Consider that the traditional Rosary cycle proceeds as follows:

Monday—Birth

Tuesday—Passion

Wednesday—Resurrection

Thursday—Birth

Friday—Passion

Saturday/Sunday—Resurrection

With this change, the Rosary cycle would collapse into a jumble of disconnected events as the liturgical week progresses:

Monday—Birth

Tuesday—Passion

Wednesday—Resurrection

Thursday—Public life ("luminous" mysteries)

Friday—Passion

Saturday—Birth (!)

Sunday—Resurrection

Notice that under the "proposed addition to the traditional pattern" the entire Church is asked to move in prayer from the

Resurrection on Wednesday to the public life of Christ on Thursday, skipping over His Birth. Worse, the Church would move in prayer from the Passion on Friday *back to the Birth* on Saturday, skipping over the Resurrection, and then from the Birth on Saturday to the *Resurrection* on Sunday, skipping over the Passion. As one very learned priest I know has observed, the effect is rather like some present-day composer inserting a new movement into a Brahms symphony, while rearranging the existing movements to accommodate the new one. Only in this case, the symphony being tampered with was written by the Holy Ghost over centuries of development, based on the staff (150 Hail Mary's corresponding to the 150 Psalms in the Psalter) provided by the Mother of God.

It is no wonder Paul VI observed that the Rosary is "wisely distributed into *three* cycles" and that this arrangement "above all reflects the plan of the original proclamation of the Faith and sets forth once more the mystery of Christ *in the very way in which it is seen by Saint Paul* in the celebrated 'hymn' of the Letter to the Philippians—kenosis, death and exaltation (cf. 2:6-11)." Under the new form of the Rosary being promoted by EWTN as if it were already the norm, the Scriptural consonance between the Joyful, Sorrowful and Glorious mysteries and the kenosis, death and exaltation of Christ would be ended forever.

Not content with his central role in the disastrous "liturgical renewal" of Pope Paul VI, Annibale Bugnini also proposed a "renewal" of Marian devotional practices. In September of 1972 he drafted a schema in this regard and submitted it to the Congregation for Divine Worship (CDW). In this schema, Bugnini proposed to rearrange the Rosary so that the Our Father would be recited only once at the beginning, and the Hail Mary edited to include only "the biblical portion of the prayer." The "Holy Mary, Mother of God" would be said "only at the end of each *tenth* Hail Mary." There would also be a new "public" version of the Rosary, consisting of readings, songs, homilies, and "a series of Hail Marys, but limited to one decade."[211]

Paul VI responded to this ridiculous proposal through the Vatican Secretary of State: "[T]he faithful would conclude that 'the Pope has changed the Rosary,' and the psychological effect would be

---

[211] Annibale Bugnini, *The Reform of the Liturgy* (Collegeville, Minnesota: Liturgical Press, 1990), page 876.

disastrous.... Any change in it cannot but lessen the confidence of the simple and the poor."[212] Undeterred by this rejection, Bugnini obstinately presented two more schemas calling for revisions in various practices of Marian devotion. In each schema, Bugnini smuggled in more paragraphs calling for revisions to the Rosary. His third schema, submitted in April 1973, elicited a specific request by Pope Paul VI for "deletion of some paragraphs on the rosary and the removal also of a reference to *a different order of the mysteries.*" The Pope admonished Bugnini that: "The rosary is to remain single in form and *unchanged* from what it now is. Let any new forms of Marian devotion take their place *alongside* the Rosary." Recognizing his defeat, Bugnini noted that "in the fourth schema all references to a revision of the rosary have disappeared..."[213] Two years later, Bugnini was sacked and sent off to Iran, after Paul VI read a dossier documenting Bugnini's Masonic affiliation—a dossier whose existence Bugnini himself admitted in his autobiography.[214] The traditional Rosary had been spared the fate of the traditional Mass.

It is supremely ironic that even as Pope Paul approved Bugnini's plan to destroy the Roman Rite de facto by suppressing the form of Mass canonized by St. Pius V in his Bull *Quo Primum*, he nonetheless felt obliged to reject Bugnini's advice and follow the teaching of the same Pius V when it came to the Rosary. Nearly forty years have passed since then, but the heirs of Bugnini have finally come to do their best to bury the traditional Rosary. And EWTN is quite willing to help shovel dirt into the grave by abandoning the traditional Rosary and promoting "the new Rosary" in its worldwide daily television broadcasts. At EWTN, as in the rest of New Church, we see at work the destructive Modernist spirit of endless innovation remarked by St. Pius X in *Pascendi*: "In all Catholicism there is

---

[212]Ibid.

[213]Ibid., page 877.

[214]Ibid., page 91: "Toward the end of the summer a cardinal who was usually no enthusiast for the liturgical reform told me of the existence of a 'dossier' which he had seen (or brought to?) the Pope's desk and which proved that Archbishop Bugnini was a Freemason." Bugnini here referred to himself in the third person. Bugnini denied any Masonic affiliation, but one can hardly be convinced by such a denial when the very aims of Masonry, denounced in dozens of papal pronouncements, would require concealment of its highest-ranking members— especially when destruction of the traditional Latin Mass was one of their prime objectives. One would like to see the contents of the admitted dossier on Paul VI's desk, which evidently provoked Bugnini's immediate sacking.

absolutely nothing on which it does not fasten." Not even the Holy
Rosary will they leave untouched.

# Chapter 14

# Promoting Sexual Gnosticism
## and the NFP Cult

As if all this were not bad enough, we also see in EWTN's theological presentation an increasingly bizarre and offensive sexual gnosticism, presented by various self-appointed experts as an explication of Pope John Paul II's "theology of the body." Despite John Paul's 130 audience addresses on the subject, after his death it remains so obscure that, as neo-Catholic commentator and papal biographer George Weigel has written, "a secondary literature capable of 'translating' John Paul's thought into more accessible categories is badly needed."[215] And who will now provide this "translation" of the late Pope's teaching, since no one in the Vatican has seen fit to undertake the task? According to New Church luminary George Sim Johnston, "Right now, those in the Church who are shaping its future are busy unpacking [John Paul's] teachings."[216]

Just who are these Church-shaping people busily unpacking the papal teaching that we ourselves, apparently, could not understand without their assistance? These quasi-gnostic exegetes, says Johnston, include "Christopher West, Janet Smith, Mary Beth Bonacci, John Haas, and others [who] are out there explaining to audiences the beauty of the pope's theology of the body." Not surprisingly, we find that all of those named are EWTN celebrities who have appeared on EWTN multiple times. In their completely non-authoritative interpretation of the "theology of the body," these lay exegetes extol the marital act not as the passing earthly good which it is, but as a kind of quasi-sacrament only those initiated into "the theology of the

---

[215]Weigel, *Witness to Hope*, page 343.
[216]"After the Council: Living Vatican II," *Crisis*, July 8, 2004.

body" can appreciate in all its mystagogical[217] significance.

The proponents of "the theology of the body" uniformly present it as a great advance over the Church's former teaching, which they portray as lacking in theological "richness" and sophistication. For example, during a recent EWTN appearance Christopher West said that while he was "raised in a Catholic home in the seventies and eighties as I was coming of age, the message I got in my Catholic schools and in my own family was okay [skeptical tone of voice], but it didn't present this glorious vision that the Pope presented to me when I was in my early twenties, when I discovered it [the "theology of the body"]. So when the Church herself *is not giving an effective vision of an alternative* the media is screaming at us with how to indulge our sexuality..."[218] Without the "theology of the body," then, the Church is "ineffective" in her preaching against sexual license. Fellow "theology of the body" promoter and EWTN celebrity Janet Smith speaks in the same vein: "The faithful Catholics of my generation have rushed to the intellectual ramparts. We have been determined to do so not in any *pre-Vatican II formulaic fashion*, but to do so by *reformulating the basics in terminology more accessible to our times* and to draw upon the best of modern thought (especially that of John Paul II) to deepen our understanding and the understanding of others."[219] The casual denigration of the teaching of the Church before Vatican II as "formulaic" is a staple of New Church thinking. As for Smith's grand project of "reformulating" Catholic teaching to make it "more accessible to our times," there has never been a time in which Catholic truth, obscured by a cloud of neologisms ("theology of the body," "civilization of love," "ecumenism," "dialogue," "ecumenical dialogue," "collegiality," "inculturation" and so forth), has been *less* accessible, and less heeded, than our own.

It seems not to have occurred to West, Smith and their EWTN collaborators in novelty that all that needs to be done to help Catholics resist modern hedonism is to rediscover and promote throughout the Church the teaching of the great pre-conciliar Popes in such monumental encyclicals as Pius XI's *Casti Connubii*, or Leo XIII's *Arcanum Divinae Sapientiae*, both of which state with clarity, precision and dignity the Church's indispensable doctrine on

---

[217]Mystagogy is the study of spiritual mysteries, particularly those evidenced by physical signs.

[218]*Life on the Rock*, broadcast of October 6, 2005.

[219]*Catholic Dossier*, November-December 1997, page 60.

marriage and procreation. Completely lost on these innovators is the fact that after some twenty-five years of the "theology of the body" and other forms of theological "renewal," the overwhelming majority of those who call themselves Catholics openly reject the Church's infallible teaching against contraception, along with any other Catholic doctrine they find disagreeable. And, as already noted, John Paul II himself lamented not long before his death "the diminishing number of births, the decline in the number of vocations to the priesthood and religious life, and the difficulty, if not the outright refusal, to make lifelong commitments, including marriage."[220] With all due respect to the late Pope, what is urgently needed today is not some "glorious vision" supposedly contained in an obscure and novel theology that a few lay people have taken it upon themselves to "unpack" for the rest of us, but rather a return to the basics of Catholic morality, beginning with a healthy fear of damnation for sins of the flesh. As Our Lady told Blessed Jacinta of Fatima: "The sins which hurl most souls into hell, are the sins of impurity." It is precisely this forthright proclamation of the truth that has been lost over the past forty years of theological innovation and obscurity.

EWTN's priestly "experts" contribute mightily to the network's promotion of sexual gnosticism with their own elaborations on the never-quite defined "theology of the body." In my article "The Mysticism of Charting"[221] I showed how Fr. Stephen F. Torraco, one of EWTN's clerical exponents of the "theology of the body," attributed profound mystical significance to the practice of natural family planning (NFP), which requires the use of thermometers and charts to plot the wife's body-temperature in order to determine when it is "safe" to engage in marital relations—i.e., the best time *not* to conceive a child.[222] Without any discussion of the Church's teaching that recourse to infertile periods can be moral only for grave reasons,[223] Torraco declared: "It is not wrong to regulate the number of births in your family. But there is a right way and there are wrong ways of doing so." NFP, he assured the questioner "is as effective in

---

[220]*Ecclesia in Europa*, June 28, 2003.

[221]"NFP and the Mysticism of Charting," available from *The Remnant* reprint service (see http://www.remnantnewspaper.com).

[222]The text of Fr. Torraco's advice, quoted here, can still be found in EWTN's database at EWTN Q&A Forum, advice of October 17, 2005 on "Family size".

[223]Pope Paul VI used this term in *Humanae Vitae* (HV) in describing the grounds for moral use of NFP: "grave motives" (HV, 10), "serious motives…" (HV, 16).

avoiding pregnancy as contraception, if not more so."

So, EWTN advocates the New Church idea that Catholics ought to "regulate" the size of their families by human decisions and techniques. During the conciliar debates on the morality of birth regulation, Cardinal Ottaviani expressed horror over this innovation:

> I am not pleased with the statement in the text that married couples may determine the number of children they are to have. *Never has this been heard of in the Church.* My father was a laborer, and the fear of having many children never entered my parents' minds, because they trusted in Providence. [I am amazed] that yesterday in the Council it should have been said that there was doubt whether a correct stand had been taken hitherto on the principles governing marriage. Does this not mean that the inerrancy of the Church will be called into question? Or was not the Holy Spirit with His Church in past centuries to illuminate minds on this point of doctrine?[224]

Cardinal Ottaviani had touched upon the problem that confronts us today at the height of the post-conciliar crisis: the way in which utterly novel changes of attitude and the relaxation of teaching have called into question the very credibility of the Church.

Happily adopting the novelty of Catholic "birth regulation," EWTN is promoting a veritable cult of NFP. Torraco actually claimed that the practice of charting wifely body temperature creates a mystical link to God as seen through the "theology of the body":

> [T]he daily charting called for by natural fertility care holds up a tremendous spiritual benefit in what I call *the mysticism of charting*, a complement to Pope John Paul II's new way of handing on the Gospel of Life, namely his theology of the body. The definition of mysticism is "the knowledge of God arrived at through the embrace of unifying love." Isn't this what husband and wife are doing when they chart? *Like mystical knowledge, the mysticism of charting has the same object as the knowledge of faith and theology,* but its method is more intuitive and

---

[224]Father R. M. Wiltgen, *The Rhine Flows Into the Tiber*, TAN Books and Publishers (1967), page 299.

direct than discursive and scientific. *Like mysticism, the discipline of charting involves contemplation and sets the stage for an intimate knowledge and experience of God that* God bestows through a special grace.[225]

According to Torraco, then, the charts and thermometers employed in NFP are veritable sacramentals by which a couple can obtain special graces from God and ascend to higher levels of mystical knowledge as they "regulate" family size. Is this the sort of thing Catholics need to hear at a time when, as John Paul II himself lamented, former Christendom is being decimated by declining birth rates in once-Catholic nations?[226] That EWTN presents Torraco's loony advice as Catholic orthodoxy is reason enough to question EWTN's entire theological enterprise. Just who *is* exercising theological oversight down in Irondale, Alabama? As we have seen throughout this book, *no one* is. EWTN's theological positions are determined entirely by Mr. Donovan and his theological committee of laymen, the majority of whom are ex-Protestants.

Another, even more outrageous, example of EWTN's Modernist "sexual theology" and its NFP cult is the network's resident "marriage counselor," one Gregory Popcak, who hosted (together with his wife Lisa) the EWTN television series "Marriage: for Better, Forever," based on his book by the same title, which EWTN markets.[227] Popcak bills himself as a "nationally recognized Catholic psychotherapist," based on his B.A. from the University of Steubenville (the flagship university of New Church) and a Masters in social work from the University of Pittsburgh.[228] His marital and family "advice" is peppered with vulgar, blasphemous and even obscene material he evidently views as a clever "updating" of Catholic teaching.

Popcak is a "specialist" in the New Church project of attempting to sexualize Roman Catholicism by elevating the physical aspect of marital relations to the level of a quasi-sacrament. As Popcak declares

---

[225]See, EWTN Q&A Forum, advice by Fr. Torraco of March 10, 2002, "Contraception: Question from Stephanie on 03-10-2002".

[226]In the context of lamenting Europe's "silent apostasy," His Holiness also noted that "The signs and fruits of this existential anguish include, in particular, the diminishing number of births..." *Ecclesia in Europa*, n. 8.

[227]The book is item #6887 in EWTN's religious catalogue.

[228]http://www.exceptionalmarriages.com/about.htm.

in *For Better... Forever!*: "Sex is holy because it is the most profound way one's 'divinized nature' can give itself to another. Sex is holy because *you are holy* [Popcak's emphasis]... Sexual intercourse is holy because it is the most complete way to share the gift that you are with another person."[229] This would be surprising news indeed to the Church's vast communion of celibate saints, who shunned all carnal relations precisely in order to perfect their gift of self in the love of God.

For Popcak, as with other New Church sexualizers, "sexuality" is a master concept of theology. Man and his relation to God are depicted in revolting sexual terms, as if the goodness of the marital union were such an overwhelmingly profound insight that it must be allowed to permeate all subjects theological. Speaking on EWTN's *The Abundant Life* series, Popcak, when asked by host Johnnette Benkovic to define "sexuality," declared:

> Sexuality is really who I am and how I relate to those around me. It's the power to unite and the power to create. And people have sexuality even if they are not being sexual. *You know, so, for example, with priests and religious, always, they talk about their sexuality. They have a very life-giving sexuality as well*, but they exercise it in a different way than a person who is married, in the married state, who is actually engaging in sexual intercourse. So sexuality is who am I as a person, and how I communicate that personhood to another person.[230]

So, according to Popcak, everyone is "sexual" in his own way, including celibate priests and virginal nuns. But Popcak did not stop there. When asked to define what Benkovic called "*Catholic sexuality*," Popcak dared to apply an explicit sexual analogy to nothing less than the Holy Sacrifice of the Mass:

> Sexuality as it is understood by the Church is really a very physical prayer.... *The act of lovemaking is to marriage what the consecration is to the Mass.* It's the incarnation of

---

[229]Gregory K. Popcak, *For Better... Forever!: A Catholic Guide to Lifelong Marriage*, (Our Sunday Visitor Press, 1999), page 202.
[230]"Birds, Bees, Love and Parenting," *The Abundant Life*, broadcast of November 15, 2001.

love in that moment....[231]

The idea that the physical act of "lovemaking" is a form of prayer is grossly offensive to the *sensus Catholicus*, which understands that there will be no "lovemaking" in Heaven precisely because, in comparison with the life of the spirit, it is a lowly thing that is happily foregone by priests and religious in imitation of Christ and His Blessed Mother, even if it is one of the goods of this world. Popcak's idea that "lovemaking" is analogous to the Consecration during Mass, however, is not merely offensive to Catholic ears but downright blasphemous. Here Popcak exhibits the utter confusion of categories that typifies disordered New Church thinking, or what Romano Amerio has called "the loss of essences"[232] since Vatican II— that is, loss of the ability to distinguish one thing from another. Only someone suffering from profound theological confusion could call carnal relations a prayer and liken what happens in the marital chamber to the sacrifice of the Son to the Father on the altar of God through the mystery of transubstantiation.

In the same episode of *The Abundant Life*, Popcak persisted in his revolting theme, making progressively more outrageous statements with the evident approval of his host. Popcak opined that when a husband and wife engage in marital relations

> they're supposed to be incarnating the passion that God has for each of them. So in my marriage book I talk about what I call a Lover's Prayer, which is what I say before my wife and I are together. I'll say something like 'Lord, help me to kiss her with your lips. Help me to touch her with your hands and to love her with your undying passion, so that she might know how precious she is to both of us.' You know, I want to be the incarnation of His love for my wife. And that's what couples really have to practice and develop that mindset...

Host Benkovic greeted this remark with an approving "Mmmmm. And all of this, of course, is foundational to be able *to*

---

[231]Ibid.
[232]Romano Amerio, *Iota Unum: A Study of Changes in the Catholic Church in the XXth Century* (Kansas City, Missouri: Sarto House, 1996).

*pass that on to our children.*" The "marriage book" Popack referred to is his *For Better… Forever!*, part of EWTN's catalog, wherein we find the following version of his "Lover's Prayer," which he (with EWTN's assistance) has published to the whole Catholic world: "Lord, let me kiss her with your lips, love her with your gentle hands, *consume her with your undying passion*, so that I may show her how precious and beautiful she is to you."[233]

Thus, Popcak and EWTN literally encourage Catholic spouses to develop the mental habit of imagining Our Lord Himself engaging in marital relations as the "incarnation" of His divine love, and further to convey this monstrous idea to their innocent children. It is hard to imagine a more obscene and blasphemous suggestion, yet it was presented as sound Catholicism to EWTN's vast TV audience. Only after the break following this segment of the program did host Johnnette Benkovic belatedly warn: "As you know friends, we're talking about some sensitive material that might require a more mature audience, so it might not be appropriate for your children." *Might* not be appropriate? That there is something gravely wrong with a "Catholic" network whose content is unfit for children seems not to have occurred to the directors of EWTN.

Popcak offered more of his lewd blasphemy during an episode of his own EWTN series. On this occasion, Popcak blithely reported to his Catholic audience that in his "counseling practice" he often heard the complaint that wives cannot show their husbands any sign of physical affection, such as a kiss, "without the husband wanting to jump into bed…." From this lewd remark Popcak proceeded to expound the blasphemy that Catholics must learn to "share the same kind of intimacy *that Christ would share if He were married to our mates*… to offer the same kind of passion to our wives, and wives to your husbands, *that Christ would offer* if He were their partner."[234]

Having perpetrated the public outrage of inviting millions of Catholics to commit blasphemy and risk mortal sin by imagining how a married Christ would show "intimacy" and "passion" to *the viewer's own spouse*, Popcak then proceeded to sexualize the beatific vision! If a marriage is "devoid of passionate, romantic love," said Popcak, then the spouses will not be prepared to stand in God's presence when they die. According to Popcak, one who dies after a

---

[233]*For Better… Forever!*, page 212.
[234]The author has personally taken a verbatim transcription from the audio file, which is no longer available on the EWTN website.

marriage without passionate and romantic love will suffer a case of the spiritual "bends," like a deep-sea diver who is suddenly brought to the surface: "suddenly being thrust into the pervasive passionate presence of God would be becoming just like that diver... thrust into this overwhelming incredible passion..." The Catholic whose marriage wasn't passionate and romantic enough, said Popcak, will find himself standing before God exclaiming: "I don't know what to do with that [the beatific vision]. I'm standing there in front of God and all that power and passion and I don't know how to handle it because my husband or my wife didn't get me ready for it... We need to prepare each other to stand in the fearsome passionate presence of our divine lover..."

Leaving no doubt that he really means to say that the carnal relations of spouses are a preparation for eternal beatitude, Popcak declares in *For Better... Forever!*:

> What could sex possibly have to do with the achievement of eternal life?... [W]hen I die, I am going to stand before the Almighty and all his [sic] glory — in all my glory (so to speak). Every blemish, wrinkle, crease and bump of my physical and spiritual being will be — for all eternity — exposed to his [sic] penetrating gaze, completely vulnerable to his [sic] pervasive touch. Under such circumstances, for me to experience anything other than the sheer terror of hell, I must be able to stand confidently in the presence of that gaze, like Adam and Eve while they still enjoyed their original innocence. *What better way to prepare myself for this awesome responsibility than to challenge whatever vulnerability or shame I may feel when my wife gazes upon me in my nakedness and makes love with me?*[235]

It is not only blasphemous, but absurd, to compare the presence of God in the beatific vision with the "passionate, romantic love" of earthly relations between spouses, such that romance and passion are viewed as essential *training* for eternal beatitude. Popcak's poppycock completely ignores the teaching of the Catholic Church that the celibate state of priests and religious, which involves precisely the *renunciation* of the "passionate, romantic love" of an

---

[235]*For Better... Forever!*, page 203.

earthly spouse, makes one *fitter* spiritually for the service of God and thus *more able* to attain sanctity in this life and the beatific vision hereafter. As St. Paul teaches, and as the discipline of the Church has always reflected, the celibate state of the priest or nun is *higher* than the married state, without denying that the married state is good. Speaking of his own priestly celibacy, St. Paul, teaching infallibly under the inspiration of the Holy Ghost, declared:

> For I would that all men were even as myself. But every one
> hath his proper gift from God: one after this manner,
> and another after that. But I say to the unmarried and to
> the widows: *It is good for them if they so continue*, even as
> I. But if they do not contain themselves, let them marry.
> *For it is better to marry than to be burnt.* (1 Cor. 7:7-9)

As St. Paul made clear, marriage is the divinely appointed vocation of those who are not called to the higher celibate state, and who had better marry if they cannot contain their concupiscence. Following St. Paul and the entire tradition of the Church, the Council of Trent declared infallibly that "If anyone should say that the married state should be preferred to the state of virginity or celibacy and that *it is not better and more blessed to remain in virginity or celibate than to be united in matrimony* [cf. Matthew 19:11; 1 Corinthians 7:25, 38-40], let him be anathema."[236]

That only a tiny minority of the Church's host of canonized saints was married should have given Popcak some inkling of this divine and Catholic truth, even if he is theologically ignorant of the matter. Of course marriage is a sacrament, and the married vocation a noble one, without which the number of the elect could not be filled. But it seems to be lost on Popcak and the rest of the New Church sexuality-promoters that the celibate state on earth only anticipates the higher, perpetually celibate state of all who attain eternal beatitude. When one of the Sadducees (who denied that there was any resurrection) tried to trick Our Lord with a question about the survival of marriage after death, He replied: "The children of this world marry and are given in marriage: But they that shall be accounted worthy of that world and of the resurrection from the dead shall neither be married nor take wives. Neither can they die any more: for they are equal to

---

[236]Council of Trent, Session XXIV, *Doctrine Concerning the Sacrament of Matrimony*, Can. 10, Dz. 980.

the Angels, and are the children of God, being the children of resurrection." (Luke 20:34-37) The theological truth could not be clearer: marriage and marital relations are merely goods of this world which will pass away in the life to come; the bodies of the resurrected will not lower themselves to the "romantic, passionate love" that Popcak attempts to portray as a "very physical prayer."

Apparently, it has never occurred to Popcak to contemplate why there are no marriages or marital relations in Heaven, or why the highest of all participants in the beatific vision is the Blessed Virgin Mary, whose perfectly chaste marriage to St. Joseph was anything but a relation of "romantic, passionate love." Mary, perpetually virgin and devoid of any sort of carnal passion, is God's exalted model of preparation for beatitude while on this earth; and that preparation has nothing to do with experiencing romantic passion to "train" one to receive the beatific vision. Popack's notion is a monstrous debasement of Catholic spirituality, yet he tossed it off on national television without any seeming concern about its vile implications.

Popcak's sexual pop-theology is further developed in his books, which (naturally) EWTN either promotes or sells.[237] *For Better... Forever!: A Catholic Guide to Lifelong Marriage*, for example, contains such spiritually elevating chapter headings as "Holy Sex, Batman!" and "Der Intimacy is Good, Jah?," along with "enlightening" quotations from such sources as the Jewish standup comedian Paul Reiser, the pop music celebrity "Sting" (an apostate former altar boy who abandoned his wife and two children to "marry" someone else), and the *Kama Sutra*, an obscene Hindu work on sexual practices.[238] In *Parenting with Grace*, Popcak enthuses that when parents allow children to sleep in their bed "lovemaking is always creative, especially because—how shall we put this?—you begin with all the horizontal surfaces (and perhaps a few vertical ones) in your home in a new, much more interesting light. In a sense, you could say that the sexual creativity that results from co-sleeping empowers a couple to

---

[237]*For Better... Forever!*, which Popcak referred to as "my marriage book" during his appearance on *The Journey Home*, contains the blasphemous "Lover's Prayer" quoted above. As already discussed, host Benkovic avidly promoted Popcak's *Beyond the Birds and Bees* on *The Journey Home*.

[238]The following quotations and page references from this and Popcak's other books are collected in Bridgette O'Donnell, "Perverse Psychology, Profane Theology: The Contemporary Framework of Gregory Popcak", *Catholic Family News*, July 2003.

make their whole house—from the stairways to the kitchen counter and everywhere in between—a sacred space, overflowing with the couple's love for each other."[239] Only a man without shame could write such things and publish them to the entire Church.

As we can see, Popcak is a devotee of the disordered New Church idea that conjugal relations are some kind of sacramental act that can make places holy—another example of the confusion between one thing and another that arises from the ill-defined and self-contradictory notion of a "theology of the body." Popcak advances a gross distortion of the nature of the marital act that ignores the very reason it does not exist in Heaven. While certainly a good thing because God has ordained it, the marital act has no place in Heaven because there is no concupiscence nor any need for reproduction in the state of beatitude, and the perfect love between the members of the society of the beatified requires no carnal expression. In Heaven, man has moved beyond these elements of his life in a fallen state. And even here on earth the celibate clergy and religious show us the way toward this ultimate perfection of human existence.

The idea that the physical relations between husband and wife are a sanctifying action that should be used to make all the "surfaces" in one's home "holy"—including the stairs—evinces a sybaritic preoccupation with sexuality that is just as extreme as the opposite error of Jansenism. The proper Catholic balance respecting the use of marital relations is expressed by Pope Pius XI in the encyclical already mentioned, *Casti Connubii*:

> The *primary* end of marriage is the procreation and the education of children…. [I]n matrimony as well as in the use of the matrimonial rights there are also *secondary* ends, such as mutual aid, the cultivating of mutual love, and *the quieting of concupiscence* which husband and wife are not forbidden to consider so long as they are subordinated to the primary end and so long as the intrinsic nature of the act is preserved.[240]

Only the sober Catholic spouse, following the traditional teaching of the Church, is able to place the goods of marriage in their proper

---

[239]Gregory K. and Lisa Popcak, *Parenting with Grace: Catholic Parent's Guide to Raising (Almost) Perfect Kids*, page 180; cited in O'Donnell, *op. cit.*
[240]*Casti Connubii* (1930), nn. 17, 59-60.

order and treat them with due restraint and circumspection. Popcak's lurid novelties make a public mockery of Holy Matrimony.

In *Beyond the Birds and the Bees*, Popcak extends the New Church cult of NFP to an obscene extremity when he notes with approval that "I am aware of some families where the brother may chart his sister's temperatures for her, or even some cases *where the mother shares her own NFP chart* (minus the coitus record, of course) with the intent of acquainting the young men and women of the house with NFP. I also know some families who object to this idea on privacy or modesty grounds."[241] But while "some families"—i.e. *Catholic* families—object to this patently immoral and scandalous practice, Popcak presents it as a perfectly legitimate "option":

> You will have to decide whether having boys record *their sister's or mother's* temperatures is an option for your family, but as long as the person whose chart it is (the mother or sister) is not terribly opposed to the idea (you really have to respect her opinion on this), *I feel favorably toward the idea* because it decreases the chances that your young teens will eroticize their sexuality. Treated in this manner, you are more likely to present this kind of information as a literal fact of life as opposed to some glamorous, dangerous, erotic mystery.... Whether or not you decide to enlist your pubescent boys in the charting process, they can begin doing the other thing needed for a healthy marital sexuality. They can pray. In fact, your daughters should do this, too.[242]

This is the very essence of the Modernist subversion of morals: advice to "pray" conjoined with the immoral recommendation that *pubescent boys chart the body temperatures of their own mothers and sisters* for NFP training. And this deliberate initiation into the sexual biology of their own mothers and sisters is supposed to *decrease* the chances that young boys will be eroticized? Pure Modernist double-talk.

Popcak goes even further than EWTN's Fr. Torraco in presenting NFP as a veritable duty of married life. Speaking of the young boy

---

[241]Gregory K. Popcak, *Beyond the Birds and the Bees: The Secrets of Raising Sexually Whole (and Holy!) Kids* (Huntington, Indiana: Our Sunday Visitor Press, 2001), pages 142-143; cited in O'Donnell, *op. cit.*
[242]Cited in O'Donnell, *op. cit.*, July 2003.

who will be charting the temperatures of his mother or sister, Popcak opines that NFP is now a basic "responsibility" of married life:

> Part of that means that if he marries, he will be responsible for working with his wife to determine God's will for their lives, including when to have children and how many children to have. *These are decisions that need to be made every month* in collaboration with his wife and with prayer. After he is married, part of his responsibility will be to help his wife do something called charting, which means that he will write down the different signs that tell how healthy his wife is and when they could have a baby.[243]

In an article promoting his EWTN series on marriage,[244] Popcak enunciates the tortured logic by which NFP proponents attempt to reconcile their novelty with the traditional Catholic teaching that every child is a gift from God and that Catholic spouses are called to be fruitful and multiply. The habitual practice of NFP, says Popcak, allows Catholic couples to "practice two sets of virtues..." The first "set of virtues" — otherwise known as traditional Catholic matrimony — is practiced "when a couple is pursuing conception, [and] they are expanding their generosity, their abilities to identify with the Fatherhood of God, their trust in divine providence, and their opportunities to practice sacrificial love..." When the couple decides not to "pursue conception," however, they can switch to the newly discovered NFP "set of virtues." According to these NFP-related virtues, the couple can "practice this openness to life *responsibly* (by using NFP), [and] they grow in self-control, temperance, prudence, chastity..."[245] The astounding implication here is that NFP is a "responsible" alternative to simply "pursuing conception" while trusting in divine providence rather than human planning and "birth regulation." Apparently, the promoters of NFP think that God would imprudently bestow too many children on Catholic couples unless they "responsibly" intervened with their

---

[243]*Beyond the Birds and the Bees*, pages 142-143; cited in O'Donnell, *op cit.*

[244]"Just a note to let you know that our exciting new television series, *For Better...FOREVER!* is now on EWTN...." See, "A Balancing Act: NFP and the Unitive and Procreative Ends of Marriage," at http://www.catholic-homeschool.com/Library/Articles/Balancing/balancing.htm.

[245]Ibid.

charts and thermometers.

Popcak further opines that "When a couple practices NFP *they discern each month* which set of virtues God is calling them to exercise in their marriage. Through prayer and intimate communication, the couple asks each other if *this month* God is calling them to celebrate their life giving love by conceiving, or if God is calling them to work on strengthening their marriage in other ways so that in the future — perhaps next month — the couple will be able to celebrate a love so powerful that, as Scott Hahn says, 'in nine months it has to be given a name.'"[246] By what authority do NFP cultists determine that God has ordained a monthly decision-making cycle for procreation? Where in Sacred Scripture is this notion revealed? Which Pope or council in the entire history of the Church has taught that God calls upon married couples to make monthly determinations of whether they are to have children? This "doctrine" of New Church, like all the rest of its novelties, is a pure invention.

So Popcak (citing Scott Hahn, whose contribution to the "sexualization" of theology is discussed below) posits Catholic marriage as a month-to-month decision on whether God is calling the couple to trust in divine providence, be generous and practice sacrificial love, or rather to exercise "self-control," temperance, prudence and chastity—as if these two "sets of virtues" were mutually exclusive! Popcak and his fellow NFP cultists seriously advocate the idea that a couple can decide that in the month of May, for example, God is calling them to "pursue conception," but that in June He is calling for the avoidance of conception, whereas in July He is calling again for the pursuit of conception, and that in each given month God is calling for the exercise of a different "set of virtues" according to whether conception is to be pursued or avoided. Popcak would have us believe that in any given month God could be asking a couple to trust in divine providence and be open to life, but in the next month *not* to trust in divine providence but rather to avoid conception.

It hardly needs to be demonstrated that this nonsense, which the NFP cult has simply made up as it goes along, is contrary to the entire tradition of the Catholic Church. And yet this is the basic advice EWTN dispenses to its followers—and not only through Popcak. In its "expert" forum, for example, EWTN, working with the

---

[246]Ibid.

New Church group "NFP Outreach," offered the following advice to a woman who wondered if she could deliberately plan on a small family to accommodate her academic career:

### Question from Reena on 9/8/2005:

Hello, I'm a female university student interested in pursuing graduate studies and working in the field after graduation. I also don't believe I have a vocation to be a nun and intend to marry if I find the right man. I was wondering whether it would be morally acceptable to use NFP and have a small family (2 or 3 children) in order to be able to work in my field of study. I don't believe I would be able to handle work and a large number of children at the same time. Thank you for your help, Reena

### Answer by NFP Outreach on 9/15/2005:

Yours is a theoretical question because you are not even married. However, if God is calling you and a future husband to have a small family (*and you discern that almost day to day or month by month*—sometimes what you discern at the beginning of the marriage may change after some years), then what you propose is not wrong or sinful. Thanks for writing.[247]

Thus, EWTN teaches its followers that one's earthly career can be placed ahead of bringing immortal souls into the world for the glory of God, and that marriage involves a month-to-month or even a day-to-day decision on whether to have children. Implicit in this wholly un-Catholic idea is a Protestant notion of illuminist spirituality, according to which one's life is governed not by faith in the divine counsels of the Church, including the counsel to be fruitful and multiply while trusting in divine Providence, but rather by continuous private "discernment" of God's latest instructions, determined according to interior "illuminations" that one is apparently supposed to receive like radio signals. This is not to say that one should not pray to discern God's will in some difficult

---

[247]See, EWTN Q&A Forum, advice of NFP Outreach (to Reena) of September 15, 2005 on "Job and NFP".

matter requiring a decision. But it is patently absurd to reduce procreation, the primary purpose of marriage, to a monthly or daily "consultation" with God for the latest "illumination" on whether to conceive a child, especially when, given our fallen nature, "The heart is perverse above all things, and unsearchable, who can know it?"[248] It is far too easy to deceive ourselves into believing that what we would prefer in our human weakness is "God's will." This is the very error of Protestant illuminist religion, as seen also in such New Church aberrations as "Catholic charismatic" spirituality, which purports to have recourse to the Holy Ghost for direct instructions at any moment, delivered by "speaking in tongues."

This, then, is the New Church vision of Catholic marriage EWTN promotes to the world: The "mysticism of charting" wifely body temperature; pubescent boys "charting" their own mothers and sisters, and then later their own wives in order to compile "coitus records"; monthly and even daily decisions on whether to have a child; "responsible" procreation pitted against trust in divine Providence; the deliberate avoidance of conception for such reasons as the mere furtherance of a career. EWTN preaches the sickness of the NFP cult in full bloom, and thereby undermines the divinely ordained purpose of Holy Matrimony: the procreation and rearing of children for the glory of God and Holy Church.

EWTN's program of "sexualizing" Roman Catholicism does not end with its promotion of a nebulous "theology of the body" and the cult of NFP. The most subtle of EWTN's theological sexualizers is the former Protestant minister, Scott Hahn. Hahn, an engaging writer and compelling speaker, has become a veritable lay "doctor" of New Church theology. His influence has become so great in New Church circles that people actually speak of being "Hahn-verts" as opposed to converts.[249] Hahn is EWTN's theological superstar, co-hosting at least five EWTN series, two of which are named after, and serve as promotional vehicles for, his books of popular theology.[250] One of

---

[248]Jeremias 17:9.

[249]"My husband was an evangelical Christian until he became a 'Hahn-vert' by reading and listening to Hahn's reasons for becoming Catholic." *See,* http://books.philosophyarchive.com/free.php?in=us&asin=0898704782 (review of *Rome Sweet Home*). "I don't consider myself a 'Hahn-vert' but I am a convert."

[250]"First Comes Love," "Our Father's Plan," "Swear to God," "Hail Holy Queen," "The Lamb's Supper." The set of "Swear to God" is dominated by a huge blowup

these series, "First Comes Love," is based entirely on Hahn's book by the same title, and the series is a kind of extended infomercial for the book.[251] In *First Comes Love* Hahn expounds his pet notion that the Holy Trinity is a "covenant family" to which the human family of father, mother and child must correspond. (Hahn never does explain how his analogy applies to a family with multiple unique children, there being only *one* unique divine Son in the Trinity.)

According to Hahn's self-proclaimed "findings," the Holy Spirit should be seen as the "mother" of the Trinitarian "family" — as "maternal," "the uncreated principle of maternity," "bridal" and "feminine" in its operations.[252] He even declares that "by divine actions that are *bridal and maternal*, we may come to discuss *a divine bridal-maternity* in the Holy Spirit."[253] There is, of course, no basis whatever in Church teaching for this kind of talk. Our Lord Himself (whom Hahn does not get around to quoting until the end of the chapter on his theory) declared of the Holy Ghost: "It is expedient for you that I go: for if I go not, the Paraclete will not come to you; but if I go, I will send *Him* to you. And when *He* is come, *He* will convince the world of sin, and of justice and of judgment."[254] What more needs to be said about the temerity of tampering with God's own affirmation of the masculine gender (analogically speaking, of course, as God is neither male nor female) of the Holy Ghost? Our Lord's own words, the foundation of Catholic doctrine on this question, should have been the beginning and the end of Hahn's inquiry. But Hahn and the other "creative" theologians who roam the anomic landscape of the post-conciliar Church are like those characters in science fiction films who awake to find that some great catastrophe has overtaken the world and they are the only survivors. Hahn, like Popcak and the rest of EWTN's gallery of innovators, can just *do* theology and no one will stop him, just as the movie characters can plunder stores and steal cars because the police are gone.

It is hardly surprising that Hahn cites in support of his theory none other than arch-Modernist Yves Congar, whom Hahn describes

---

of Hahn's book by the same title, with Hahn's name as author prominently on display before the camera.

[251]Scott Hahn, *First Comes Love* (New York: Doubleday, 2002). As the series blurb on EWTN's website states: "The series is based on Dr. Hahn's new book, 'First Comes Love.'" - http://www.ewtn.com/vondemand/audio/selectseries.asp.

[252]These terms appear in *First Comes Love*, pages 127-145.

[253]*First Comes Love*, page 138.

[254]John 16:7, 13; cited in *First Comes Love*, page 144.

as "the great theologian."[255] According to Congar, says Hahn, "there must be in God, in transcendent form, something that corresponds to masculinity and something that corresponds to femininity."[256] Congar was stripped of his teaching positions by Pope Pius XII in 1954, before his disastrous resurrection as a *peritus* at Vatican II. Congar's Modernist tome *True and False Reform of the Church* (1950) was suppressed by order of the Vatican. In a fawning tribute to Congar by that notorious ultraliberal dissenter from Catholic doctrine, "Father" Richard P. McBrien,[257] we read of Congar's petulant complaint that "from the beginning of 1947 to the end of 1956 I knew nothing from [Rome] but an uninterrupted series of denunciations, warnings, restrictive or discriminatory measures and mistrustful interventions (*Dialogue Between Christians*, page 34)."[258] The poor thing! McBrien calls Congar "a prophet" and "the most distinguished ecclesiologist in the history of the church [sic]," which is almost as telling as an endorsement by the devil himself. This is Hahn's "great theologian."[259]

Hahn, following Congar, wishes to introduce us to the mysterious feminine aspect of God. But in doing so Hahn issues a disclaimer: "I must raise a caution here. This does not mean that we call God 'Mother': divine revelation does not call God by that name. Nor is it to be found anywhere in the Church's living tradition."[260] (Notice that Hahn does not say we must not call *the Holy Ghost* "mother.") Hahn also states that "we may not speak of God as having

---

[255]*First Comes Love*, page 135.

[256]Ibid., pages 135-136.

[257]Among his other heresies, McBrien has notoriously denied papal infallibility, the Church's teaching against contraception and the ordination of women, has claimed that the authority of the Catholic Church derives from the consensus of the faithful, and has declared that "Not all men are called to the Church, nor is the Church the ordinary means of salvation" and "There is no advantage to being a member of the Church in terms of ultimate salvation." A handy summary of some of McBrien's heresies, along with page citations to the quoted statements, is found in "Father Richard McBrien's Church" by Emanuel Valenza, at http://www.sspx.ca/Angelus/1985_January/Fr_McBriens_Church.htm.

[258]"The 'blessed cross' of Yves Congar", *The Tidings*, March 19, 2004.

[259]In one of his many stupefying acts, John Paul II made Congar a Cardinal at the age of 91, only months before Congar died. John Paul II's equally stupefying decision to make Hans Urs von Balthasar a Cardinal at the end of *his* life did not come to fruition: von Balthasar dropped dead only hours before receiving his red hat.

[260]*First Comes Love*, page 138.

masculine or feminine qualities, even though the first two Persons are properly named Father and Son."[261] (Notice how Hahn avoids the truth that the Holy Ghost is *also* "properly" referred to *only* in the masculine.) Informed Catholics, however, are quite familiar with Hahn's sort of disclaimer. The writings of the Modernists are replete with examples of how they elaborately unveil their outrageous propositions while insisting they do not mean to propose precisely what they are proposing.

Hahn does the same thing in *First Comes Love*. Having issued his disclaimers as fig leaves to cover his novelties, he proceeds to refer to the Holy Ghost repeatedly and exclusively as motherly, feminine and bridal (but never as "He") even if he does not explicitly *call* the Holy Ghost "Mother." Hahn likens the role of the Holy Ghost in the Trinitarian "family" to the role of his wife, Kimberly, whom he describes as "the Holy Spirit of our home."[262] He then explains the theological basis on which he has taught his children why "blaspheming the Holy Spirit is treated differently than [sic] every other sin and blasphemy by their earthly and heavenly fathers. Dad's first law is: You'd better not make *Mom* mad."[263] So, sins against the Holy Ghost are sins against the divine Mom. What can one say?

Hahn goes on to speak of the "Holy Spirit's *motherly* role as comforter and consoler" and claims that "what a *mother* does in the natural order, the Holy Spirit accomplishes in the supernatural order."[264] Hahn asserts that because the Hebrew word for "spirit" in the Old Testament, *ruah*, "is a feminine noun," as is the Hebrew word for "glory cloud," *shekinah*, "For many rabbis, these usages were sufficient evidence for the bridal-maternal character of the Holy Spirit."[265] So what? In the first place, rabbis do not even believe in the Holy Spirit as a distinct divine Person as such, but only as a manifestation or presence of God; hence rabbis do not address the issue of the proper gender reference to the Holy Ghost. At any rate, the New Testament was written in Greek, and as Hahn well knows the Greek word for spirit is *pneuma*, which is neither masculine nor feminine. As Hahn also knows, in the official Latin Vulgate text of the Bible, canonized as normative for the Church by the Council of Trent, the word "spirit" has for 1600 years been translated as *"spiritus,"*

---

[261] *First Comes Love*, page 134.
[262] *First Comes Love*, page 130.
[263] Ibid.
[264] *First Comes Love*, pages 130-131.
[265] *First Comes Love*, page 132.

which is a *masculine* noun. Furthermore, "the Latin text of the Sacred Scriptures had existed *from the earliest times of Christianity...* and had certainly come from the *first days of the Faith...*"[266] — that is, even before St. Jerome's Vulgate. Thus, from the first days of the Faith the Holy Ghost has been referred to solely in the masculine gender. Besides, if the mere usage of a feminine noun for "spirit" by rabbis proved that the Holy Ghost is in some way feminine, then Hahn would have proved too much: by his logic, the Church should have called the Holy Ghost "She" from the beginning, and has erred in failing to do so.

Hahn's novelty is no mere harmless speculation. Its destructive effect on Trinitarian theology can hardly be underestimated. Hahn admits in *First Comes Love* that "some might object that this familial understanding (or 'social analogy') of the relations of the Trinity [i.e., that the Trinity is a "family" with a father, "mother" and child] clashes with the traditional 'psychological' analogy proposed by the two greatest lights of the Western theological tradition, St. Augustine and St. Thomas Aquinas."[267] In other words, "some" — that is, *every* orthodox Catholic who knows Catholic dogma — would object that Hahn is attacking *the infallible de fide teaching of the Catholic Church* on the two "internal" processions of the Trinity: the procession of the Son from the Intellect of the Father by generation, and of the Holy Ghost from Father and Son as an act of will born of the mutual love between Father and Son without the aid of any "maternal" operation of God.[268] Respecting the first procession — the Son from the Father — the Athanasian Creed declares infallibly: "The Son is from the Father alone, not made or created but generated."[269] Respecting the second procession — the Holy Ghost from the Father and the Son — the Council of Lyons declares infallibly: "In faithful and devout profession we declare that the Holy Spirit proceeds eternally from the Father *and* the Son, not as from two beginnings but from one beginning, not from two breathings, but from one breathing. The most Holy Roman Church, the mother and teacher of all the faithful, has up to this time professed, preached and taught this; this she

---

[266]"Revision of Vulgate," *Catholic Encyclopedia* (1907 Ed.).

[267]*First Comes Love*, page 139.

[268]Both teachings are *de fide*. Cf. Ott, *Fundamentals of Catholic Dogma*, (Fourth Edition; Rockford, Illinois: TAN Books and Publishers, reprinted 1974), Book One, Part II, Chapter 3, § 11 and § 12, pages 62-64.

[269]*The Creed "Quicumque" (which is Called "Athanasian")*, Dz. 39.

firmly holds, preaches, declares and teaches; the unchangeable and true opinion of the orthodox Fathers and Doctors, Latin *as well as Greek*, holds this."[270]

Thus, neither of the two processions can involve in any way a "maternal" operation of the Holy Ghost: the Son proceeds from the *Father*, not a "mother," while the Holy Ghost *Him*self, referred to exclusively as *He* in Catholic theology, proceeds *from* the Father and the Son, and thus cannot be "mother" of either the Father or the Son, even analogically speaking. These dogmatic truths negate Hahn's specious analogy between the Trinity and a merely human family, wherein a mother begets children.

In an article in the June 2004 issue of *New Oxford Review*, Edward O'Neill offered an admirably concise explanation of how Hahn's idea makes a shambles of the Church's infallible teaching on the divine processions:

> [I]f the Spirit has bridal and maternal aspects, they must be in reference to the other two Persons. Brides have husbands and mothers have children, so which of the other two Persons is the Husband and which is the Child? There seem to be only two possible combinations. One is that the Father is the Husband of the Spirit and the Son is the Child. Yet this would contradict what we already know about the processions within the Godhead, since the Son proceeds from the Father alone (without the aid of a maternal principle), and the Spirit proceeds from the Father and the Son. The second combination would be that the Son is the Husband of the Spirit and the Father is the Child. This also contradicts what we know about the processions in the Godhead, since the Father proceeds from no one.[271]

Hahn himself acknowledges that "the traditional model," as he calls it[272] (otherwise known as Catholic dogma on the subject) involves the two processions just discussed, but then proceeds to

---

270Dz. 460.

271"Scott Hahn's Novelties," *New Oxford Review*, June 2004.

272*First Comes Love*, page 140, "The traditional model understands the first procession to be a matter of the mind of God… and the second procession to be a matter of the will of God…"

ignore "the traditional model" in favor of his own novelty.[273] Objectively speaking, then, Hahn is teaching heresy, or is at least suspect of heresy, whether or not he subjectively intends to depart from Catholic dogma. It is thus morally incumbent on Hahn (and EWTN, which promotes his views) to affirm the Catholic Faith unambiguously and unequivocally on this point.

Aside from contradicting defined Church teaching (i.e., teaching heresy) on the very nature of God, Hahn's idea produces further theological absurdities, as O'Neill observed in his *NOR* piece:

> Honoring the known processions of the Trinity while viewing the Holy Spirit as "bridal-maternal" results in further absurdities. In Hahn's paradigm, the Trinity must certainly represent the only Family in existence in which a Father and a Son cooperate to have a Mother! Hahn sketches a parallel between the procession of the Spirit from the Son and the Father and the creation of Eve from the side of Adam, who was created by God. This preserves the genders he wants and the sequence of Persons, but it still poses problems for the alleged "bridal-maternal character" of the Spirit. Eve was Adam's wife. *Is the Spirit the wife of the Son?...*

Hahn's own admirer and fellow theologian, Monica Miller, Ph.D., voiced similar objections to Hahn's theological tinkering. In an earlier piece for *NOR*,[274] Dr. Miller, while professing her profound love and respect for Hahn, does not hesitate to lay it on the line:  In *First Comes Love* Hahn is proposing "that the Trinity is a family and thus the human family of father, mother, child is based on this supernatural truth. Within the human family [says Hahn], *maternal activity is the historical expression of the Third Person* of the Trinity..." Dr. Miller offered a critique of what she (rightly) sees as "Hahn's theology on the *feminine nature* of the Holy Spirit." Hahn is on the wrong track, wrote Dr. Miller, because "The Holy Trinity is not a Father, Mother and Child that has a strict biological correlation here on earth." But, she concluded, "*Scott is seeking that strict parallel*" when he declares in *First Comes Love* that "In the family we become three-in-one, imaging the Triune God." The obvious problem with Hahn's novelty of the

---

[273]*First Comes Love*, page 140.
[274]"The Gender of the Holy Trinity," *New Oxford Review*, May 2003, pages 27-35.

Trinity as "family" is

> ... *who's who?* Do the Son and the Father beget the Holy
> Spirit? So the Holy Spirit is their child? But Jesus is not a
> Mother; He is the Son. Or is the Holy Spirit the mother?
> But we know the Holy Spirit proceeds from the Father
> and the Son, so He can't be the mother. If there is a
> "child" in the Trinity we know it is the Son, eternally
> begotten of the Father but *without* the aid of a divine
> mother. We see that trying to create literal parallels
> within the human family to image the persons of the
> Trinity *doesn't work.*

Dr. Miller concluded "There is certainly not a shred of evidence
in the biblical account of the Incarnation that the Holy Spirit has a
maternal role." In rejecting Hahn's suggestion that Mary is the
"created replication" of the Holy Spirit, Miller asks: "Is Mary's
maternity her own, or is it the Holy Spirit's as well? And if it is the
Holy Spirit's as well, *then Christ has two mothers* — and that will never
work." But such problems do not deter Hahn or EWTN in their
promotion of Hahn's departure from the "traditional model" of
Trinitarian theology.

Hahn argues further that the two different processions suggest
a "wifely/motherly" work of the Holy Ghost—that of loving—
versus the "husbandly/fatherly" work rooted in the divine
intellect and knowledge. For Hahn, this "motherly" difference in
the procession of the Holy Ghost means something for the mode of
our salvation: "We can look at our salvation in legal terms, as
justice... We can see our justification, then, as a work of the Son,
the Logos." But, on the other hand, "We can describe our
sanctification, then, as a work of the Holy Spirit, the Sanctifier—
and a work that is *bridal-maternal* in nature."[275] To demonstrate his
justification/sanctification disjunction in the order of grace (so
that he can assign the latter aspect of grace to his "bridal-
maternal" Holy Ghost), Hahn lays out a chart to illustrate what he
imagines to be the feminine attributes of the Holy Ghost's
procession as compared with the Son's procession:

---

[275]*First Comes Love*, pages 140-141.

| Procession of the Son | Procession of the Spirit |
| --- | --- |
| Knowing | Loving |
| Intellect | Will |
| *Justification* | *Sanctification* |
| *Husband/Father* | *Wife/Mother* |
| Legal | Liturgical |
| Justice | Mercy |

This idea, which Hahn invented solely to lend support to his faulty analogy, undermines Catholic dogma on the nature and effect of sanctifying grace. Justification cannot be distinguished from sanctification in the manner Hahn proposes—i.e. that the former is a work of the Son, while the latter is a work of the "maternal" Holy Ghost—for as the Council of Trent teaches, justification and sanctification are *both* simultaneously effected by sanctifying grace in one's soul: "sanctifying grace is the sole formal cause of justification... This means that the infusion of sanctifying grace effects the eradication of sin [justification] *as well as* inner sanctification."[276] As the Council of Trent further declared: "Justification... is not merely the remission of sins, but *also* the sanctification and renewal of the interior man... whereby an unjust man becomes a just man, and from being an enemy becomes a friend [of God]...."[277]

Now, sanctifying grace, which simultaneously effects *both* justification and sanctification, is a created supernatural gift of God given to man as a work by *all three* Persons of the Trinity in common, for "the operations of God *ad extra* [e.g. from God to man] are common to the three Persons."[278] This dogmatic truth follows of necessity from the dogma of the absolute simplicity of God as defined infallibly by the Fourth Lateran Council and the First Vatican

---

[276]Ott, *Fundamentals of Catholic Dogma*, Book Four, Section II, Chapter 1, § 17, pages 251-252.
[277]Council of Trent, *Decree on Justification*, Chapter 7; Dz. 799.
[278]Ott, Book Four, Section II, Chapter 1, § 20, page 259.

Council—i.e., that God is a pure spirit Who is not composed of elements, either metaphysical or physical, which could be said to act separately from each other.[279]

St. Peter, the first Pope, taught infallibly: "He has given us most great and precious promises, that by these you may be made partakers of the divine nature." (2 Peter 1:4) The Council of Trent taught that this participation in the divine nature is called sanctifying grace. The Council further taught that sanctifying grace is a *created* participation in the divine nature. It is not God Himself but this created quality given to the soul that makes the soul godlike. Sanctifying grace is thus distinct from the *uncreated* grace of the divine indwelling of the three Persons of the Most Holy Trinity in the soul.

The presence of sanctifying grace in a soul is what makes it a worthy dwelling place for the Most Holy Trinity. As the *Catholic Encyclopedia* notes, in this life "[t]he crowning point of justification is found in the personal indwelling of the Holy Spirit.[280] Because a soul is in the state of sanctifying grace, the Holy Ghost, together with the Father and the Son, takes up His abode in that sanctified soul. As Our Lord Himself declares: "If anyone loves Me, he will keep My word. And My Father will love him, and *We* will come to him and make Our abode in him."[281] St. Paul likewise teaches infallibly: "Know you not that you are the temple of God and that the Spirit of God dwells within you?"[282]

Therefore, it is false, confusing and misleading to speak as Hahn does of justification "as a work of the Son," while sanctification is "a work of the Holy Spirit... that is bridal-maternal in nature." The action of God in a soul cannot be neatly divided between "husband/father" and "wife/mother" to accommodate Hahn's novel and objectively heretical scheme.

Rightly outraged by Hahn's novelties, *New Oxford Review* editor Dale Vree has even called for the burning of *First Comes Love*. After

---

[279]Lateran Council IV: "Firmly, we believe and we confess simply that the true God is one alone... indeed, three Persons, but one essence, substance or nature entirely simple." Dz. 429. Vatican Council I: "The Holy, Catholic, Apostolic, Roman Church believes and confesses that there is one, true, living God... He is one, singular, altogether simple and unchangeable spiritual substance." Dz. 1782.

[280] "Sanctifying Grace," *Catholic Encyclopedia*.

[281] John 14:23.

[282]1 Corinthians 3:16. As Ott observes: "[T]he indwelling of the Holy Ghost inevitably implies the indwelling of the Three Divine Persons." *Ott*, loc. cit.

citing various magisterial texts commanding that the Holy Ghost be referred to (and thus worshipped) exclusively in the masculine gender, Vree took Hahn up on his offer[283] to consign the pertinent pages of *First Comes Love* to the flames: "Now that Dr. Hahn knows what the Magisterium teaches, we trust he'll order Doubleday to recall all the copies of his book from Barnes & Noble and all the other stores and, along with the copies in the warehouse, pile them up in the parking lot and burn them. What a bonfire that'll be!"[284]

In the same article Vree pointed out (as Dr. Miller did) that as Mary is female, it follows that "if the Holy Spirit is female or feminine, then Jesus had two mommies, and presto 'gay' is good and so is 'gay' marriage. Dr. Hahn goes so far as to say the Holy Spirit is 'bridal' and that 'Mary's maternity is mystically one with that of… the Spirit.' The imagery is blatantly and scandalously lesbian." Vree is not exaggerating this concern. Mary *conceived* by the Holy Ghost and for this reason She is traditionally known as "the spouse of the Holy Ghost." As St. Louis Marie Grignion de Montfort explained in *The Secret of Mary*: "The Holy Spirit espoused Mary and produced *His* greatest work, the incarnate Word, in Her, by Her and through Her. *He* has never disowned Her and so *He* continues to produce every day, in a mysterious but very real manner, the souls of the elect in Her and through Her."[285] Thus, if words are understood according to their objective signification, Hahn's positing of a "maternal" or "bridal" operation of the Holy Ghost necessarily implies (even if Hahn does not explicitly say so or even subjectively intend it) nothing short of a homosexual abomination — two mothers cooperating in the Incarnation — just as Vree suggests, as well as two mothers cooperating in the creation of all the members of the elect. This is so only analogically, of course, since (to anticipate the banal objection) the Godhead has no gender in the literal, physical sense, as even Hahn readily acknowledges. It is just that what one says *analogically* of God has profound implications for what theologians call "the opposition of relations" between the Persons of the Trinity and the two processions of the Trinity — the basis for all Catholic theology on the pure distinction between the three Persons of the Triune God. And this is why the Church has never permitted the

---

[283]See *First Comes Love*, page 129.
[284]Dale Vree, "Burn, Baby Burn," *New Oxford Review* (September 2002).
[285]*The Secret of Mary*, 13 °7. See http://www.ewtn.com/library/Montfort/ SECRET.HTM.

feminization of the Holy Ghost.

Hahn's novelties, so avidly promoted by EWTN, add nothing to Catholic theology but further confusion at a time when the Church is already afflicted by diabolical disorientation. But, worse than this, Hahn's thinking serves quite well the aims of feminist theology. As Vree rightly observed in his *NOR* piece: "Feminist theologians and their queer cheerleaders have been campaigning for a feminine Holy Spirit for decades. How odd — how depressing, actually — to see Dr. Hahn jump on the bandwagon." Hahn would of course protest that he hasn't jumped on the feminist bandwagon, just as he would protest that he hasn't actually *called* the Holy Ghost "Mother" or "She." But if Hahn's words are taken according to their objective meaning (as opposed to *post hoc* interpretations of what he "really means") he has done precisely that, whether he admits it or not.

When all is said and done, *what is the point* of Hahn's attempt to "sexualize" the Holy Ghost (even as he denies that he is doing so)? What need does the Church have for the theological inventions of this layman and former Protestant minister? No need at all. Hahn's speculations are as gratuitous as they are dangerous. Yet to watch Hahn and his fellow EWTN innovators at work is to conclude that they seem intoxicated by their own capacity for invention, unrestrained by any authority willing to enforce a sober adherence to the dogmas of the Faith.

Greg Popcak, intoxicated by his own "sexualized" idea of God (which is clearly influenced by Hahn's thinking), has even gone so far as to take up the obscene question posed by the New Age guru and "healer" Deepak Chopra: "Does God have orgasms?" Popcak writes: "I, like Chopra believe the answer is 'Absolutely yes.' My own faith tradition teaches that God is a lover and that the cosmological orgasm physicists refer to as the Big Bang... is the model for human sexuality. Who wouldn't give their eyeteeth for a night like that with their beloved?"[286] Popcak repeats his obscenity with even more explicitness in the EWTN-promoted *For Better... Forever!* in a chapter entitled "Holy Sex, Batman (or Why Catholics Do It... Infallibly)":

> To experience sacred sex is to experience the cataclysmic
> eruption of love that was the cosmological orgasm we

---

[286]Gregory K. Popcak, *The Exceptional Seven Percent – The Nine Secrets of the World's Happiest Couples* (New York: Birch Lane Press, 2002), cited in O'Donnell, *op. cit.*

call the "Big Bang" through which the entire universe was created and from which the entire universe continues to reel even today. Who wouldn't give his eyeteeth for a night like *that* with his beloved?[287]

Showing us just where Scott Hahn's sexualization of the Trinity leads the minds of New Church spokesmen, Popcak continued: "When Christian married couples celebrate holy sex, it is just one more way they celebrate the 'trinity' that the human being images…"[288]

That EWTN would showcase a man capable of such insane and blasphemous filth is almost impossible to believe, but such is the state of New Church theology. Popcak defended his blasphemy with these remarks:

> God enjoys his [sic] own 'sexuality' and because he [sic] is generous, he shares that sexuality with us…. Some of you are probably appalled by what must seem to be a hopeless anthropomorphism on my part. But when I refer to God's 'sexuality' or even God's 'orgasm,' I don't mean it in the physical way we humans understand it. Rather, God's 'sexuality' is expressed in his joy in loving all things, uniting all things, creating all things. What we mortals refer to as our sexuality is the power God lends us to join him in loving, uniting and creating both on a physical level (through lovemaking which leads to children) and on a spiritual level (through lovemaking) which strengthens the unity of the couple and actualizes their values, ideals and goals.[289]

So, even as he attributes "sexuality" to God, Popcak (like Hahn) denies that he is doing the very thing he is doing. It is just a manner of speaking, he protests. But why choose *that* manner of speaking if Popcak does not mean to sexualize God? In just this way does the Modernist inject his poisonous doctrine into what St. Pius X called "the very veins and heart of the Church": advancing an error while insisting that the error is not being advanced. So it goes at EWTN and throughout the New Church establishment, and always under the

---

[287]*For Better… Forever!*, page 203.
[288]Ibid., page 28.
[289]*The Exceptional Seven Percent*, cited in O'Donnell, *op. cit.*

pretense that corruptions of the Faith are consistent with orthodox Catholicism.[290]

---

[290]Popcak defends his revolting opinions on the grounds that his books carry a "Nihil Obstat" and "Imprimatur" or have been submitted for review to "theologians." Given the current state of the Church, however, such "local" credentials are hardly a guarantee of sound theology or morals. The Church today is awash with "approved" books, including filthy sex-education curricula and heretical catechisms, which are positively inimical to the Faith. This is one of the symptoms of the very crisis Cardinal Ratzinger described as "a process of decay" following Vatican II. As Catholic apologist Robert Sungenis put it: 'The words "Nihil Obstat" and "Imprimatur" are only as good as the censor librorum who has read and examined the material at issue, and only as good as the caliber of the bishop who approves it.... Furthermore, there is a great difference between dogmatic error and one's scandalous and profane personal opinion.... [T]here may be no [explicitly defined doctrine] against Popcak saying that God had a spiritual orgasm in the Big Bang [and that is simply because up until now no Catholic has ever dared to think—much less say in public, especially on television—such a blasphemy], but anyone with common sense and an eighth grade education in theology knows that such concepts are hurtful to pious ears and degrade the Trinity...."

# Chapter 15

# "Cool" Catholicism

EWTN's liturgical and theological novelties aside, any traditional Catholic who has watched the network's current range of programming for any length of time will have been disgusted by its attempt at a fusion of Catholicism with the American rock-and-roll culture. Michael J. Matt, editor of *The Remnant*, has coined the term "cool Catholicism" to describe this grotesquerie.

The best example of this is EWTN's most popular show: *Life on the Rock*, a play on the Rock of Peter, but also a reference to rock music. The show takes place on a set called "the Rock House," and viewers are urged to contact the show at rock@EWTN.com. As the show's title suggests, *Life on the Rock*, which is supposedly designed to confirm teenagers in the Faith, is filled with rock music from beginning to end. Apparently EWTN thinks that teenagers best respond to the Gospel when it is accompanied by pounding drums, wailing electric guitars, and whining vocals. The running theme of *Life on the Rock* is that Catholicism *is* "cool"—cool, cool, cool. Cool may be the single most used word on the show. On one recent episode the host, Fr. Francis, declared that "about the coolest thing you can do is to become a Catholic priest." The priesthood, he added, is "an awesome vocation of life." We know the priesthood is "cool" because during the opening sequence of the show (while the rock band pounds away) we see Fr. Francis sinking a 20-foot jump shot as he prances backward on a basketball court in his Franciscan robe. Very cool. Also very "cool" is Fr. Francis's refusal to speak like an educated adult possessed of the dignity of a priest. His speech is littered with common slang, and he habitually drops the endings of words—talkin', goin', showin'—in apparent effort to "relate" to young people by speaking just like them, thereby contributing to the general deterioration of language and manners among the young.

During a recent "cool" episode—typical of the consistently lame and embarrassing content of the show—a young man sang a rock ditty he had composed entitled "These Beads." The lyrics (if one can call them that) were set to the tune of "These Dreams," a Top 40 hit by Heart, a "glam rock" band from the 1980s. As the youngster, who could barely carry a tune, crooned "These beeeeeads, etc., etc." to a pre-recorded rock soundtrack—the New Church version of karaoke—he held up Rosary beads in one hand and a copy of *The Complete Idiot's Guide to Understanding Catholicism* in the other. He sang about how *The Complete Idiot's Guide* had recently converted him to the Catholic Faith—or what he thinks is the Catholic Faith.[291]

Father Francis pronounced this ludicrous performance "awesome"—a word he employs almost as much as "cool." Neither he, nor his guest, nor the live audience seemed to appreciate the irony that nothing could be more suitable for a complete idiot than the image of Catholicism presented by *Life on the Rock*. What intelligent person would consider abandoning a comfortable life of vice in order to join *that* silly religion? The singing guest's website asks: "What do you get when you cross authentic Catholic teaching with 'Weird Al' Yankovic?" Oddly enough, the website never answers the question, but the answer is clear enough: What you get is a blasphemous joke that makes the Faith look ridiculous. The same is true for the rest of EWTN's attempt to combine Roman Catholicism with rock culture.

Even when *Life on the Rock* attempts to address a serious moral issue, its insistence upon presenting the matter in a "cool" way with "cool" people only succeeds in vulgarizing the truth and sending mixed messages. Another recent episode featured a lay crusader against "pornography addiction" who described his struggle to become "free of the stuff." If one read a transcript of the show, one would see that on paper the man has many good things to say. But if one *watched* the show, one would see that this crusader against pornography was sporting a ponytail and a *crucifix earring.* The sight of the very symbol of our Faith dangling as a vanity item from the ear of a pony-tailed man undid the whole message of purity and spiritual progress the show was trying to convey.[292] Then there was the "commercial" break, during which the supremely ridiculous Stan

---

[291]*Life on the Rock*, February 3, 2005. The online audio file of this program (#397: Fr. Francis Mary with Nick Alexander) was available in EWTN's archives as of November 13, 2005.
[292]*Life on the Rock*, February 24, 2005 (online audio program #400).

Fortuna, the so-called "rapping priest," gave a sidewalk talk on "discipline" riddled with crass and undisciplined language—including plenty of "yos" and double negatives—while he strutted, rapper style, down a New York City street. In manner and appearance, Fortuna was indistinguishable from one of the homeless men who roam Manhattan. A worse looking spokesman for "discipline" could hardly be imagined. And this was a *priest*.

Still worse is EWTN's treatment of "teen issues" during its call-in segments. For example, during one episode of *Life on the Rock* teenagers were allowed to call in their explicit questions about sexual temptations and sins of impurity which were then discussed on the air, when such matters belong strictly in the privacy of the confessional or the home. The impact of such scandalous talk on the souls of innocent children who might have been watching cannot even be calculated. EWTN wantonly disregards the teaching of Pope Pius XI that *even in the privacy of the home* a parent should never descend to such details, because in the very attempt to address such matters a parent might actually destroy the child's innocence:

> Hence it is of the highest importance that a good father, while discussing with his son a matter so delicate, should be well on his guard and not descend to details, nor refer to the various ways in which this infernal hydra destroys with its poison so large a portion of the world; otherwise it may happen that instead of extinguishing the fire, he unwittingly stirs or kindles it in the simple and tender heart of the child.[293]

Even more dangerous than the indiscrete parent in this delicate area is EWTN's attempt to take the place of parents with nationally broadcast public discussions of such intimate matters.

Still more offensive to good morals is EWTN's repeated public airing of "testimonies" by men who were once involved in what the show persistently calls "the lifestyle" of sodomy. On another episode of *Life on the Rock* (typical of this content)[294] a man openly discussed his formerly sodomite "lifestyle," including how he "came out in New York" and "had a lover." Now, however, with prayer and therapy, he had left "the lifestyle" and his attitude toward women

---

[293]Pius XI, *Divini Illius Magistri* [On the Christian Education of Youth] (1929).
[294]*Life on the Rock*, broadcast of February 20, 2003 (online audio program #297).

had changed: "Could I ever have s-- with a woman?" he asked himself on camera. "Of course I could," he answered. Speaking of so-called "monogamous relationships" between sodomite "couples," the guest referred to his own ten-year relationship with a man and said: "It can be very nice. I'm not saying it's not..." But, the guest had concluded, "we're not made that way." Yet, he said, "other couples" who remain in "the lifestyle" are "still searching" and in this "search" they engage in "night prowling" to "fill that need—it's a legitimate need... everybody wants somebody [but] we're not made that way."

Not once did the guest or the host, Fr. Francis, even suggest that sodomy is wrong not simply because "we're not made that way" or because it is a bad "lifestyle," but because sodomy is abomination and one of the four sins (sodomy, murder, oppression of the poor, defrauding a day laborer of his wages) that cry out to Heaven for vengeance.[295] To those who might object that such a condemnatory approach would be "counterproductive," I would reply that the topic should not be addressed at all if the full measure of God's reprobation of this vice must be covered over with euphemism and ambiguity. The very discussion of this abomination on the air as if it were a badly chosen "lifestyle" instead of a sin especially worthy of divine retribution, can only tend to undermine the sense of horror and abhorrence that any Catholic—indeed any man—should have for it.

In any event, it is absolutely inadmissible that such a topic should be discussed on a supposedly Catholic show seen by potentially millions of children. Well into the show (and with the usual pounding rock music soundtrack in the background) a slick announcer's voice intoned: "Due to the sensitive nature of this program, parental discretion is suggested." Something is gravely wrong with a "Catholic" television network whose content carries a parental warning. *Nothing* broadcast in the name of the Faith should be unfit for children; but on EWTN much of the content is.

EWTN's "original programming" is shot through with profane, indecent and scandalous attempts to purvey a "cool" Catholicism that only impugns the dignity of the Faith and the priesthood, while

---

[295]From the Catechism of St. Pius X (The Vices and Other Very Grievous Sins):

Q: Which are the sins that are said to cry to God for vengeance?

A: The sins that are said to cry to God for vengeance are these four: (1) Willful murder; (2) The sin of sodomy; (3) Oppression of the poor; (4) Defrauding day laborers of their wages.

threatening the innocence of children. It would require a book in itself to document all of the examples, but one additional example should suffice to make the point: a performance in a Las Vegas lounge, hosted by EWTN news commentator Raymond Arroyo... on *Christmas Eve*. The Christmas Eve lounge act included a comic's impressions of that famous "Rat Pack" of drunken, womanizing entertainers from the 1960s (Frank Sinatra, Sammy Davis, Jr. and Dean Martin). One elderly Catholic viewer contemptuously described this spectacle as "the Three Wise Men meet the Beatles." It was actually much worse than that.

Need one say more? This sort of programming is the dismal result of EWTN's misguided attempt to combine Catholicism with pop culture in order to make it appealing to a mass audience. But who would be attracted to the Catholic Church by such trash? And what does it say about the direction EWTN has taken in Mother Angelica's absence that this kind of thing would be presented on the very eve of the celebration of Our Lord's birth? At EWTN religion has been fused with show business, and the Faith is cheapened and disfigured in the vain pursuit of popular appeal.

In sum, what EWTN presents as traditional Catholicism is nothing but a destructive New Church substitute for the real thing. If this is considered rock solid orthodoxy today, it is no wonder the Church is in crisis.

# Chapter 16

# The Assault on Fatima

As I noted in the Overview, by Tradition is meant the totality of the perennial doctrine, dogma, liturgy and practice of the Faith, just as it existed with unbroken continuity at the start of the Second Vatican Council — the way Catholics always believed and the way they always worshipped. As our experience since the Council has shown us, the so-called post-conciliar revolution is nothing but an attack on Tradition.

Cardinal Suenens observed that Vatican II was "the French Revolution in the Church," while the equally liberal Cardinal Congar likened it to the Russian Revolution of 1917. When an organization like EWTN partakes of the post-conciliar revolution and its revolutionary spirit, and not only refuses to condemn its evils but actively promotes many of them, it will tend inevitably to regard as "enemies of the People" faithful Catholics, commonly known today as "traditionalists", who have refused to embrace the revolution. And, indeed, the faithful Roman Catholic *is* a natural adversary of the post-conciliar revolutionaries in the Church. For the Catholic, animated by love of the Faith, charity and a zeal for souls, instinctively opposes unheard-of novelties that undermine Tradition and thus the integrity and mission of the Church, which is the salvation of souls. He does so because, as St. Pius X taught in *Pascendi*, he *must* do so if he is to be worthy of the name Catholic.

In an almost incredible reversal of the proper order of things, however, Catholics who adhere to this perennial Catholic attitude — who conserve with devotion the heritage, doctrine, and practices of the Church, as they are enjoined to do by all Popes, Councils, Fathers and Doctors of the Church — are now painted as ecclesiastical outlaws and even "schismatics," while the revolutionaries and those who defend them hold themselves out as the guardians of sound orthodoxy. As in the world, now in the New Church of EWTN, evil is called good, and good evil.

Nowhere is this intolerable reversal more evident than in EWTN's treatment of "the Fatima priest," Father Nicholas Gruner—the favorite whipping boy of major New Church apostolates. Father Gruner has been singled out for denunciation because no Catholic has been more effective than this Canadian priest in exposing and opposing the disastrous trends in the Church since Vatican II. Accordingly, no one has come under more sustained attack by EWTN than Father Gruner.

There are no fewer than 66 entries in EWTN's database impugning Father Gruner as "schismatic," "suspended,"[296] "disloyal" to the Pope and unfaithful to the "Magisterium," and urging everyone to "shun" his apostolate. These attacks are *not supported by a single quotation* from Father Gruner's writings or speeches or from the publication (*The Fatima Crusader* magazine) with which he is associated. No quotations are provided because what Father Gruner preaches and teaches is nothing but traditional Roman Catholicism, combined with right reason and common sense. Merely to quote the man is to make his case for him. EWTN knows this.

Many of the attacks EWTN has published on its website refer to a supposedly definitive piece on Father Gruner by Mr. Donovan, acting as "Vice President for Theology." The details of Donovan's piece, which I have refuted elsewhere,[297] will not be recapitulated again here. Suffice it to say that Donovan hurled the usual accusations of "schism," "suspension," "disobedience" to the "Magisterium" and "disloyalty" to the Pope without providing the least proof that Father Gruner is guilty of any of these charges. Donovan cited no evidence for the simple reason that he has none.

This tactic of the unsubstantiated smear, so typical of revolutionary movements in political society, has now found its way into the Catholic Church. As Professor Philip Davidson observed in

---

[296]For a complete refutation of the claim that Fr. Gruner is suspended, see "Actually, Virginia, Father Gruner is *Not* Suspended," http://www.fatima.org/apostolate/defense/notsusvir.asp. A printed copy is also available from The Fatima Center, 17000 State Route 30, Constable, New York 12926.

[297]See, "The Ignorant Advice of Colin Donovan," - http://www.fatimaperspectives.com/fg/perspective33.asp; see also, "The Art of Pious Calumny," *The Fatima Crusader*, Issue #68, Autumn 2001, pages 29-36 (http://www.fatimacrusader.com/cr68/cr68pg29.asp). A printed copy is also available from The Fatima Center.

his monumental study of the use of propaganda in the American Revolution, the most effective way to attack the established order and justify rebellion is not "reason, or justice or even self-interest, but hate. An unreasoning hatred, a blind disgust, is aroused not against policies but against *people*."[298] That is precisely what EWTN has done in the case of Father Gruner and other prominent defenders of the Church's doctrine, dogma, liturgy and traditional practice.

EWTN's campaign of calumniation against Father Gruner only intensified after the recent scandal at the Fatima Shrine. As readers of *The Fatima Crusader* are well aware, Fr. Gruner took the lead in opposing the plans of the Shrine's rector, Fr. Luciano Guerra, to convert that hallowed ground into a center for interreligious activity. As Guerra declared in connection with the interreligious congress of Buddhists, Hindus, Muslims and assorted Protestants and schismatics which he hosted at the Shrine in October 2003: "The future of Fatima, or the adoration of God and His Mother at this holy Shrine, *must pass through the creation of a shrine where different religions can mingle*."[299]

Only a few months later Guerra made good on his plans by inviting a Hindu "priest" and his followers to use the Fatima Shrine for their rituals.[300] As coverage by Portugal's SIC television network showed on the videotapes obtained by Father Gruner's apostolate, the Hindu "priest", wearing the vestments of a Hindu "priest", went up to the altar in the Capelinha (little Chapel) in the Shrine—an altar consecrated for the Holy Sacrifice of the Mass on the very spot where

---

[298]Davidson, Philip, *Propaganda and the American Revolution*, (Chapel Hill, North Carolina: University of North Carolina Press, 1941), page 139.

[299]See John Vennari, "Fatima to Become Interfaith Shrine? An Account From One Who Was There", *The Fatima Crusader*, Issue #75, Winter 2004, pages 16ff (http://www.fatimacrusader.com/cr75/cr75pg16.asp) and at http://www.fatima.org/news/newsviews/sprep111303.asp; see also "Fatima to Become Interfaith Shrine", printed and on-line editions of *The Portugal News*, November 1, page 4; and "Sanctuary of Various Creeds", the Fatima weekly newspaper, *Notícias de Fátima*, October 24, 2003 edition, page 1.

[300]The entire event is meticulously documented in *The Fatima Crusader*, Issue #77 (http://www.fatimacrusader.com/cr77/toc77.asp), including numerous still photographs taken from the videotape by SIC television in Portugal, and direct quotations from the participants in the sacrilege. See also "Pictures of a Desecration: Photo Report of Hindu Ritual at Fatima" (http://www.fatima.org/news/newsviews/0704desec.asp) with the accompanying photo report (http://www.fatima.org/news/newsviews/0704desecrep.asp). Printed copies of Crusader #77 and the Photo Report are also available from The Fatima Center.

Our Lady of Fatima appeared. The Hindu "priest" then stood at the altar and proceeded for several minutes to intone the *Shanti Pa*, the Hindu "Prayer for Peace," which is addressed to the Hindu god Vishnu. As he did so, the Hindu "pilgrims" in the "congregation" actively participated in the ritual by their presence, posture and gestures, which included a procession by three Hindu women into the sanctuary to make an offering of flowers to the statue of Our Lady, whom the Hindus described as "the Holy Mother" — the Hindu term of endearment for the goddess Devi, as SIC, the National Portuguese TV station, reported.[301]

Only days before this sacrilege took place, EWTN, conducting the usual cover-up, invited leading Father Gruner-basher Fr. Robert J. Fox to attack Father Gruner on a live interview show. Fox ridiculed as "fabrications" Father Gruner's well-documented concerns, soon to become a reality, that the Shrine would be opened to the worship of pagan gods.

Donovan and his theological committee refused to admit that anything improper would happen at the Shrine. "I guess you heard then there was a rumor that Fatima was going to become some sort of ecumenical place of worship. I guess you probably heard that," Peterson told Donovan. Donovan replied "Oh no, that will never happen, that will never happen." As Peterson told me, "I got to where I couldn't believe anything they said, because everything they said [would not happen] always came true."

Even after the Hindu sacrilege had occurred and was captured on videotape, EWTN remained determined to cover it up and to denounce Father Gruner for having revealed the truth. In private form letters sent to concerned EWTN supporters (some of which were forwarded to Father Gruner's apostolate), EWTN's Manager of Viewer Services, Gordon Sibley, and others attempted to obfuscate the issue. Sibley's letters gratuitously asserted that Father Gruner "is misrepresenting the facts," even though the facts were plainly evident on the videotape. The letters also contain the usual *ad hominem* attacks: Father Gruner is "suspended," Father Gruner is disloyal to the Pope, etc. Fr. Fox, on the other hand, is "in good standing" and "a personal friend of the bishop of Fatima..." — as if this had anything to do with the scandal at the Fatima Shrine. Finally, descending to the crudest of calumnies, Sibley condemned Father

---

[301]Ibid.

THE ASSAULT ON FATIMA

Gruner and "Grunerites" as rebellious souls who will be forced to confess to Christ on Judgment Day that they "shook their fist" in the Pope's face and "followed a renegade priest rather than give obedience to your Church!" Unable to address the plain fact that the rector of the Fatima Shrine had allowed an unprecedented sacrilege to take place at a Catholic altar on the very ground where Our Lady appeared to the Fatima seers, Sibley resorted to the favorite tactic of New Church demagogues: the mindless, hysterical denunciation.

In the same vein was a letter from one Mark Jefferson in EWTN's Viewer Services department, dated September 7, 2004. Jefferson was responding to a concerned EWTN supporter who had written to EWTN concerning a story by John Vennari in *Catholic Family News* (CFN) on the Fatima Shrine scandal. Ignoring all evidence of what had actually happened at the Shrine, Jefferson insisted that "Contrary to what *Catholic Family News* and certain other publications are reporting [*The Fatima Crusader* carried photos of the event as well], no pagan ritual took place at the Shrine. The Hindu pilgrims shown in the news article [in *Catholic Family News* and *The Fatima Crusader*] were simply offering a prayer for peace." In other words, Jefferson and EWTN want Catholics to believe there was no Hindu ritual involved in a Hindu "priest" intoning the *Shanti Pa* at a Catholic altar to petition the god Vishnu for peace, followed by an offering of flowers to the goddess Devi, whom the Hindu pilgrims were worshipping via the statue of the Blessed Virgin! What was Jefferson's "explanation" if not an out-and-out deception designed to conceal the evidence of sacrilege?

Jefferson huffed that "EWTN does not take seriously the scandal mongering of *Catholic Family News* or their print and web partners." So, first Fr. Fox denied on EWTN's interview show that Hindu ceremonies or other pagan rituals would ever occur at the Fatima Shrine, pronouncing Father Gruner's concerns in this regard as "fabrications." But once the scandal actually occurred, EWTN denounced *CFN*'s and Father Gruner's accurate reports as "scandal mongering." By "scandal mongering" EWTN means nothing other than *telling the truth* about a public outrage in the Church that needs to be denounced and for which public reparation to God must be made, along with measures to ensure that it never happens again. By "scandal mongering" EWTN means the righteous protest of a faithful Catholic priest against a public insult to God and His Blessed Mother, on the very ground where She appeared at Fatima.

To deride speaking this truth as "scandal mongering" is to indulge in the hypocritical "scandal" of the Pharisees and the Sadducees, who made a great show of being gravely offended by Our Lord when He was doing a positive good, such as working cures on the Sabbath. The scandal of the Pharisees means the ruse of crying "scandal" against someone who is doing good, in order that the good deed might be prevented. EWTN follows the example of the Pharisees when it sounds the alarm, not against the perpetrators of the Hindu sacrilege at the Fatima Shrine, but against those who *oppose* the sacrilege. This is not just hypocritical; it is perverse. The Pharisees of New Church, like the Pharisees of old, profess to deplore "scandal mongering," when what they really deplore is the proclamation of Catholic truth, by which they are convicted of error and complicity in offenses against the Faith.

In an effort further to confuse the issue and intimidate the recipient of his letter, Jefferson played the "obedience" card, a staple of New Church arguments in defense of the indefensible: "[W]hat they [Father Gruner and *CFN*] call 'healthy criticism' is actually rejection of the governance of an ecumenical council and the recent popes, dressed up as fidelity to Tradition." Come again? What does Father Gruner's just criticism of Msgr. Guerra's scandalous doings at the Fatima Shrine have to do with the teaching of Vatican II and the recent Popes? Where did the Council or the recent Popes authorize the use of Marian shrines for Hindu ceremonies? Nowhere, of course. In typical New Church fashion, Jefferson tried to quell legitimate opposition to outrages against the Faith by suggesting that "obedience" requires one to accept the outrages.

Jefferson, following Donovan's lead, went on to denounce *CFN* as "a frankly schismatic publication that dissents from the Holy Father and the Magisterium." Like Donovan, however, Jefferson made no effort to prove the charge, relying entirely on the ecclesial politics of hate instead of evidence and reasoned argument. Jefferson then repeated the accusation that Father Gruner is "suspended" — yet another repetition of a false charge which, in any event, has nothing to do with what happened at the Fatima Shrine.

It tells us a great deal about the depths to which the New Church establishment will sink in its defense of the indefensible that even the Vatican apparently reacted with alarm over the events at the Fatima Shrine. As John Vennari reported in the November 2004 edition of *CFN*, *Correio da Manhã*, the second largest newspaper in Portugal, ran a front page story under the headline: "Vatican is shocked with Fatima."[302] According to the newspaper, said Vennari, the Vatican "censured the prayer of the Dalai Lama [an earlier sacrilege little known in the Catholic world] and that of the Hindu priest in the Shrine," and instructed the Portuguese Episcopal Conference (PEC) to replace the Bishop and Shrine Rector. If not, the Vatican would assume direct control of the Fatima Shrine." After Guerra denied the report, *Correio da Manhã* responded by publishing the following on its website:

> Rome has already made known to the Portuguese Episcopal Conference (PEC) that it must change the Bishop of Leiria-Fatima, D. Serafim Ferreira e Silva (with the excuse that he is at the end of his career), and replace the Rector of the Sanctuary, Monsignor Luciano Guerra. Otherwise, the Vatican will take over direct management of Fatima.[303]

Rome has never denied this report. And, as a matter of fact, Guerra himself has since attempted to repudiate his own actions and to suggest that others were responsible. On November 4, 2004, *The Universe,* the United Kingdom's largest Catholic newspaper, reported that at a press conference concerning the reports of imminent Vatican action against him, "Guerra admitted that the Hindu ceremony 'was a little beyond his control', and promised that *he would never again permit a visit of the Hindu group* 'in the same manner'." Guerra's belated attempt at contrition was in stark contrast to his earlier defiant statements defending the Hindu event he had personally authorized.

EWTN, however, continues to deny that anything objectionable took place at the Fatima Shrine. EWTN's function here—and this is typical of the New Church establishment as a whole—is to provide cover for neo-Modernist Churchmen in order to preserve EWTN's vital, and apparently quite lucrative, attachment to the New Church

---

[302]"Vatican Calls for Resignation of Bishop of Fatima and Shrine Rector Guerra: But Controversy Remains," http://www.fatima.org/news/newsviews/120804 vatican.asp. See also *The Fatima Crusader*, Issue #78, Autumn 2004, pages 92-94 (http://www.fatimacrusader.com/cr78/cr78pg92.asp). A printed copy is also available from The Fatima Center.

[303]See "ROMA QUER GERIR FÁTIMA", published September 29, 2004 on *Correio da Manhã* web site: www.correiomanha.pt/noticia.asp?id=132667&idCanal=10.

bureaucracy. There is big money in post-conciliar correctness, as EWTN's approximately $30 million annual operating budget and its staff of 250-300 would suggest. It takes real money to provide live coverage of Las Vegas lounge acts on Christmas Eve.

It is hardly surprising that the same people who are willing to cover up sacrilege at Fatima, which is just one sign of the foretold crisis in the Catholic Church, are just as willing to cover up the Fatima Message and what Pius XII called its "divine warning against the suicide of altering the Faith, in her liturgy, her theology and her soul." In fact, they are desperate to do so. For nothing excites the loathing of New Church more than the traditional Catholic understanding of the Message of Fatima as a call for the conversion of Russia and the Triumph of the Immaculate Heart of Mary, failing which the world will be chastised, various nations will be annihilated and apostasy will grip the Church. Such notions are profoundly disturbing to the New Church status quo, which looks upon the growing apostasy and labors to make us think that it is good. Hence the Fatima Message must be subjected to the historical revisionism that characterizes all revolutionary movements, and those who promote the authentic Message must be declared non-persons.

Accordingly, Jefferson's letter also presents EWTN's New Church version of the Message of Fatima, whose chief exponent is EWTN's fellow New Church propagandist, Fr. Robert Fox. Instead of listening to Father Gruner, Jefferson declared, one should listen to Fr. Fox, who "truly is a child of Fatima" and who "has spoken the truth about Our Lady and Fatima, Portugal and would be appalled at any sacrilege that would occur there."

But a sacrilege *did* occur there, and Fr. Fox is manifestly *not* appalled. Quite the contrary, Fr. Fox defends the sacrilege as an entirely legitimate use of the Shrine. As for this "child of Fatima" telling the truth about the Fatima Message, here is Fr. Fox's version of the "truth" about Fatima:

- Russia was consecrated to the Immaculate Heart of Mary in 1984, even though today Russia is an abortion-ridden, alcohol-sodden, militaristic neo-Stalinist dictatorship under Vladimir Putin, wherein the Catholic Church is barely allowed to function and almost no one practices either the Catholic or the Orthodox religion.

- The conversion of Russia promised by Our Lady of Fatima

does not mean "a Russia suddenly turning itself into a people of converted holiness and even as Roman Catholics...." In other words, according to the "true child of Fatima," Our Lady of Fatima never promised us a miracle following Russia's consecration—in which case, what was the point of the Fatima apparitions and the Miracle of the Sun?

- The conversion of Russia actually means the "rebirth" of Russian Orthodoxy, which virtually no one in Russia is practicing today. Thus, according to the "true child of Fatima," Our Lady of Fatima prophesied that Russia would become what it already was in 1917—a Russian Orthodox nation. According to the "true child of Fatima," Our Lady of Fatima is really Our Lady of the Orthodox.

All of this is detailed in my article "Father Fox's Modernist Assault on Fatima" and need not be repeated here.[304] Suffice it to say that by the time this "true child of Fatima" is done with the Fatima Message, we have a consecration that is not a consecration, a conversion that is not a conversion, and world peace that is a continual state of war. In splendid New Church fashion, Fr. Fox "interprets" the Message of Fatima to mean exactly the opposite of what it actually says.

In the New Church assault on Fatima, EWTN "expert" Father Fox has a major ally in Karl Keating of San Diego. Keating, who heads the aforementioned Catholic Answers, is another self-appointed New Church inquisitor of Father Gruner and others he deems "extreme traditionalists"—i.e., faithful Roman Catholics who have conscientiously declined to join Mr. Keating and the New Church establishment in embracing the ruinous novelties of the past forty years.

Keating is on EWTN's roster of "experts" together with Catholic Answers staffers Fr. Vincent Serpa and Rosalind Moss. As already discussed, Serpa and Moss are helping EWTN promote the Judaizing agenda of the Association of "Hebrew Catholics," headed by Moss's brother, David.

---

[304]http://www.fatima.org/news/newsviews/062504frfox1.asp. A print version is available from the Fatima Center, 17000 State Route 30, Constable, New York 12926.

In the January 2003 issue of *This Rock*, the Catholic Answers magazine of which Keating is editor, there is a "Feature Article" entitled "Are There Cults in the Catholic Church?" According to the author, Jay Dunlap, contrary to what many Catholics believe, and what even many ex-members insist, groups such as the crazed, pan-denominational "Charismatic Renewal,"[305] the semi-secret, cult-like Opus Dei,[306] the pan-religious Focolare[307] and the openly heretical

---

[305]In "'Catholic' Charismatic Extravaganza," (*Catholic Family News*, August 1997), Catholic journalist John Vennari provides a definitive exposé, supported by audio and videotapes, of the history and current activity of the "Charismatic Renewal." This "renewal," which began in 1967 with some Catholics receiving "a Protestant mock-sacrament of 'baptism of the spirit'" at the hands of a Protestant minister, leads Catholics into a world of frenzied, pan-denominational gatherings, "speaking in tongues," bizarre dancing, gyrating and other manifestations of spiritual disturbance that are both horrifying and embarrassing to behold. This movement destroys the sound piety and inward composure exemplified by the saints of the Church, and obliterates the boundaries between the Catholic Church and the Protestant sects. As Vennari reports, "anointed" Protestant ministers commonly preach to Catholics at these pan-denominational gatherings.

[306]Abundant documentation and testimony against Opus Dei's secretive, cult-like methods and operation have been provided by former members, and can be found at the Opus Dei Awareness Network's website: http://www.odan.org/tw_how_opus_dei_is_cult_like.htm. A review of the material on the website will reveal that, like EWTN, Opus Dei combines good and bad elements into a novel substitute for authentic Roman Catholicism. Like all other New Church organizations, Opus Dei is opposed to any restoration of the traditional Latin Mass and the other recently obscured or suppressed elements of traditional Roman Catholicism.

[307]Focolare was founded by a woman named Chiara Lubich in 1943. Today, according to its website, "The Movement is made up of persons of all ages, races and walks of life. It is ecumenical. *Members of the world's religions as well as persons of no religious affiliation also participate in the life of the Movement in varying degrees.*" The movement's website reveals that Chiara and company are engaged in promoting a pan-religious utopia: a "New Humanity," "New Families" and, of course "world peace." In February 2001, Lubich was in India to "open channels of dialogue with Hinduism," according to the Zenit news organization. (See "Chiara Lubich: On What Christians and Hindus Can Agree On," Zenit News interview, February 9, 2001.) Here is what Lubich said about this "dialogue": "Dialogue means... *putting aside our thoughts, our affections of heart, and our attachments; putting everything aside and 'entering' the other...* This dialogue makes universal fraternity a reality, in whose name we wish to act. Thus, it is possible to be united even with the most distant and different people." Lubich, in other words, is promoting the Masonic ideal of the "brotherhood" of all religions, rather than the Catholic Church's divine commission of making disciples of all nations.

Neo-Catechumenal Way (discussed further below) are not cults at all, but perfectly Catholic, officially approved "new ecclesial movements." In short, Dunlap sees no problem with any of the novel "ecclesial movements" that have sprung up over the past forty years, even though all of these "movements" avidly promote, more or less, the rotten fruits of the conciliar "renewal" while opposing any restoration of integral Tradition—most especially the traditional Latin Mass, which they all reject. Like the Protestant sects, these "movements" all agree on one thing: the Church must move beyond "pre-Vatican II" Roman Catholicism and embrace the new "ecumenical orientation" of the Church. The very existence of such movements in the Church has no precedent in her history.

While endorsing all these "ecclesial movements" away from Tradition, however, Dunlap warns that Catholics must be on their guard against one movement: Father Gruner and his International Fatima Rosary Crusade! What exactly is wrong with Father Gruner and his organization? Dunlap offers no evidence—again, because there isn't any—but contents himself with observing that Father Gruner "has been in conflict with the Church for two decades." By "the Church" Dunlap means several members of the Vatican apparatus, led by Cardinal Sodano, who have sought to impede Father Gruner's incardination and concoct a bogus "suspension" (for "failing" to be incardinated!) because his work incenses them. By "the Church" Dunlap means the same Vatican bureaucrats who preside over the worst collapse of faith and discipline in Church history, while they hound Father Gruner, a wholly orthodox Marian priest. As the Indian archbishop who incardinated Father Gruner, despite the interference of these bureaucrats, declared: "Evil forces have conspired to destroy your [Father Gruner's] work of love... Bureaucratic forces cannot stifle God's work."[308]

Compare *This Rock*'s call to shun Father Gruner with, for example, its endorsement of the Neocatechumenal Way in the same article. "The Way," as its followers call it, is a Judaized, semi-gnostic, intra-ecclesial sect that conducts private, closed-door Saturday night "liturgies" which have been dispensed from all compliance with even the radically liberalized liturgical laws of the Novus Ordo. The Judaized liturgy of this sect has no Offertory, and the congregation dances the *horah* around the altar-table. The congregants consume a

---

[308]Decree of the Archbishop of Hyderabad, November 4, 1995.

Host the size and consistency of a personal pan pizza, which tends to crumble and leave fragments all over the floor. The sect claims, however, that by a special prayer of its "ostiari" (those who handle the sacred vessels at these liturgies), the fragments on the floor are *deconsecrated*.[309] The sect's lay founders, an "existentialist" painter, Kiko Arguello, and a chain-smoking ex-nun, Carmen Hernandez,[310] exhibited a shocking familiarity with John Paul II (Carmen called him "Father" instead of "Holy Father"). These two characters have invented a "catechism" by which the movement's adherents are brought into varying levels of gnostic initiation into "the Way". The "catechism" of Kiko and Carmen is rife with heresy, including the proposition that the Church went astray after the eighth century and became obscured by an accretion of unnecessary customs and structures — precisely what the Protestants say — until Vatican II freed the Church's essence again.

An Italian priest, the late Father Enrico Zoffoli, wrote an extensive exposé of "the Way"[311] in which he compiled testimony and documentation of the movement's heresies and gross liturgical abuses in Italy, where (as in the United States) it is systematically undermining the parish structure and the integrity of the family by dividing spouses from each other. The movement's heretical catechism and gnostic characteristics have also been exposed by former "neocatechumenate" Mark Alessio in a series of articles in *Catholic Family News*.[312] Despite the demonstrable heresy of its

---

[309]Father Enrico Zoffoli, *Verita Sul Cammino Neocatecumenale*: *Testimonianze e Documenti* (The Truth About the Neo-Catechumenal Way: Testimonies and Documents), (Edizioni Segni: Udine, Italy, 1985), page 142.

[310]The English newspaper *The Tablet* reports that on the day Cardinal Stafford of the Pontifical Council for the Laity issued a document approving the statutes of "the Way," the mood was "relaxed and celebratory and was punctuated throughout with outbursts of laughter at quips and side-of-the-mouth remarks by Miss [Carmen] Hernandez, the group's feisty female co-founder. Wearing a black cotton T-shirt marked in gold with Chinese characters, she repeatedly ignored a laity council official's attempts to cut short her 20-minute improvised speech, complaining jokingly: 'They never let women talk.' In the council's corridors afterward, chain-smoking slim cigarettes, she broke into an Italian television interview with Mr. Arguello to teasingly heckle the TV reporter for asking questions about the group's controversial reputation." Cited in "To Deceive the Elect," *Christian Order*, October 2002 (see http://www.christian order.com/editorials/editorials_2002/editorials_oct02.html).

[311]*Verita Sul Cammino Neocatecumenale*, cited above.

[312] See *Catholic Family News*: "The Neo-Catechumenal Way: What do the Founders

doctrine, "the Way" recently received approval of its statutes by Rome, apparently without any doctrinal examination of its teaching. The English journal *Christian Order* notes that "Father Gino Conti, an expert on the Way, had warned that 'If the approval of the statutes does not also include the total revision of the catechesis, there is the danger that very many will abandon the Church altogether.'"[313]

So, here again, the New Church establishment condemns a defender of Tradition, Father Gruner, while endorsing yet another avenue to apostasy. And, here again, New Church encourages the Judaizing tendency.

Keating has used his position as EWTN's apologetics "expert" to launch further attacks on Father Gruner. On EWTN's Q&A forum, Keating fielded a purported complaint from one "Rose," concerning "a lady" who was allegedly rude to her while proffering a petition for the Consecration of Russia to the Immaculate Heart of Mary. What "Rose's" purported complaint had to do with apologetics was far from apparent. At any rate, instead of discussing the alleged rudeness of the anonymous Fatima petitioner, Keating launched into a mini-diatribe against Father Gruner, asserting that the petitioner "seems to be pushing his party line." Keating claimed that Fr. Gruner has "built his reputation on... supposedly having an inside track on the Third Secret [and] claiming that the consecration of Russia wasn't done right."

First of all, Father Gruner has never claimed to have an "inside track" on the Third Secret. Having read the same sources available to anyone who cares about the subject, and exercising his own common sense and powers of deduction, Father Gruner reached the same conclusion as Mother Angelica, noted at the beginning of this book: that the Third Secret has not been fully revealed. (EWTN has observed a studious silence concerning Mother Angelica's opinion.)

As for the Consecration of Russia not having been "done right," 22 years after the Vatican ceremony in which Russia was never mentioned, any fool can see that Russia shows no signs of the religious conversion promised by Our Lady of Fatima. Confronted with this undeniable fact, Keating and Catholic Answers have devised a New Church dodge around it. In reply to a letter from a

---

Really Believe?", March 1996; "An Update on the Neo-Catechumenal Way", July 1997; "The Catechist in the Neo-Catechumenal Way", July 1997; "Neo-Catechumenal Way Gathers No Moss", Parts I and II, October and November, 2002.
[313]"To Deceive the Elect," *Christian Order*, October 2002.

nun defending Father Gruner, Catholic Answers Apologist James Akin argued that "[T]he Portuguese word converterá [will convert] does not require conversion to the Catholic Faith. It can indicate simply turning from a course of destructive behavior." So, according to New Church, the entire Catholic world misread Our Lady of Fatima from the beginning—along with Sister Lucy herself! All Our Lady had in mind was a political change of course in Russia, leading to a neo-Stalinist dictatorship under Vladimir Putin, the persecution of the Catholic Church, and an average of five abortions for each Russian woman. That is what EWTN and the New Church establishment would have us believe.

But not only does this Big Lie concerning Fatima contradict the plain meaning of the word "convert," especially when spoken by the Mother of God, it also contradicts the unvarying testimony of Sister Lucy herself. In 1976 Father Joaquin Alonso, probably the top Fatima expert of the twentieth century, summarized his many interviews with Sister Lucy on this point as follows:

> ... we should affirm that Lucia always thought that the "conversion" of Russia is not to be limited to the return of the Russian People to the Orthodox Christian religions, rejecting the Marxist atheism of the Soviets, but rather, it refers purely, plainly and simply to *the total, integral conversion of Russia to the one true Church of Christ, the Roman Catholic Church*.[314]

For those who are not content with such fantasies but prefer to deal with facts, the dismal results of the 1984 ceremony are easily explained: a consecration of Russia really needs to *mention* Russia, but John Paul II's advisors told him not to do it for fear of offending the Russian Orthodox and harming "ecumenical dialogue." As we learned in the November 2000 issue of *Inside the Vatican*, a leading Cardinal, identified only as "one of the Pope's closest advisors" (in fact, it was Cardinal Tomko) admitted that "Rome fears the Russian

---

[314]*La Verdad Sobre el Secreto de Fatima, Fatima sin mitos*, Father Joaquin Alonso, (2nd edition, Ejercito Azul, Madrid, 1988) p. 78. English translation by Joseph Cain. Original Spanish reads: "... *podríamos decir que Lucía ha pensado siempre que la 'conversión' de Rusia no se entiende solo de un retorno de los pueblos de Rusia a la religión cristiano-ortodoxa, rechazando el ateismo marxista y ateo de los soviets, sino que se refiere pura y llanamente a la conversión total e integral de un retorno a la única y verdadera Iglesia, la católica-romana.*"

Orthodox might regard it as an 'offense' if Rome were to make specific mention of Russia in such a prayer, as if Russia especially is in need of help when the whole world, including the post-Christian West, faces profound problems..." Yes, it was most impolitic for Our Lady of Fatima—that is to say, God, for Our Lady is only His messenger—to single out Russia for special attention! The ecumenical diplomats of New Church have overruled God, and Mr. Keating, it seems, quite agrees. To recall the phrase employed by EWTN's Fr. Levis, this is just another case of enlightened "modern shepherds" bringing God up to date on the latest post-Vatican II thinking.

The whole story of New Church's impudent evasion of the Consecration of Russia has been detailed copiously in *The Fatima Crusader*, and I can only refer the reader to its many articles on the subject,[315] all of which exhibit something utterly lacking in the polemics of New Church spokesmen: common sense and the marshalling of *facts*, against which there is no argument. Keating, however, is not interested in discussing such common sense factual matters as the necessity of *mentioning* the thing to be consecrated. Instead, he tells "Rose" that she was "right not to sign the petition" for Russia's consecration. After all, says Keating, "who is likely to have a better understanding of what Our Lady asked for—this woman or the Pope?"

What exactly is there to "understand"? To consecrate a thing, one must identify what one is consecrating in order to set it apart from what is *not* being consecrated. A bishop who insisted that he could consecrate a new church for sacred worship by consecrating his whole diocese, and who refused to consecrate the new church specifically, would be regarded as a lunatic. Yet New Church "Fatima revisionists" insist one can consecrate Russia by consecrating the world. This is nonsense, and the Pope must have known it. That is why the Pope stated during and after the 1984 ceremony, in words addressed to the Blessed Virgin Herself, that Russia is *still awaiting* consecration to the Immaculate Heart.[316] That is why Sister Lucy told

---

[315]See http://www.fatima.org/consecrussia/relateddocs.asp

[316]As reported in the March 26-27, 1984 Italian edition (and the April 10, 1984 English edition) of *L'Osservatore Romano*, at a certain point Pope John Paul II departed from his pre-published prepared text during the ceremony, spontaneously adding these words addressed to the Virgin: "Enlighten especially the people whose consecration and entrusting *you are awaiting* from us." Several

the press afterwards that the 1984 ceremony had not fulfilled Our Lady's request.[317] And the Pope's advisors understood this as well, which is why they told the Pope in the first place not to mention Russia, so that *the Russians would not be offended by seeing their nation singled out for consecration.* But a singling out of Russia is precisely what Our Lady asked for. As Sister Lucy's letter of May 18, 1936 to her confessor records, Our Lord Himself told her that the specific Consecration of Russia was required for Russia's conversion "Because I want My whole Church to recognize that consecration as a triumph of the Immaculate Heart of Mary, so that it may extend its devotion later on, and put the devotion to this Immaculate Heart beside the devotion to My Sacred Heart."

Rather than addressing these facts, Keating, like his fellow New Church spokesmen, tries to reduce the matter to a mindless invocation of papal authority: only the Pope can "understand" what "consecration of Russia" means, and never-you-mind that Russia does not appear to have been consecrated. New Church wants us to blind ourselves to reality while Russia, the world and the Catholic Church continue to suffer the consequences of the failure to honor Heaven's most simple request.

Keating concludes his attack on Father Gruner by advising "Rose" to "stay away from Father Gruner's group and from people— such as that woman—who push his party line…. [Y]ou want to make sure you don't fall in with people who use the Tridentine Mass as a cloak to hide their fringey ideas." What does Keating mean by

---

hours *after* the Act of Consecration, as reported in *Avvenire* (March 27, 1984), the Pope again publicly addressed the Virgin, this time inside St. Peter's Basilica before 10,000 people, where he declared: "We wished to choose this Sunday, the Third Sunday of Lent, 1984—still within the Holy Year of Redemption—for the act of entrusting and consecration of the world, of the great human family, of all peoples, especially those who have a very great need of this consecration and entrustment, of those peoples for whom You Yourself *are awaiting* our act of consecration and entrusting." Respecting the 1982 consecration ceremony, which also failed to mention Russia, *L'Osservatore Romano* reported that the Pope explained his failure to mention Russia by saying that he had "tried to do everything possible in the concrete circumstances." (May 19, 1982) The same rationale is used to explain the failure to mention Russia in 1984.

[317]In a 1985 interview in *Sol de Fatima*, Sister Lucy was asked if the Pope fulfilled the request of Our Lady when he consecrated the world in 1984. Sister Lucy replied: *"There was no participation of all the bishops, and there was no mention of Russia."* She was then asked, *"So the consecration was not done as requested by Our Lady?"* to which she replied: *"No. Many bishops attached no importance to this act."*

"fringey ideas"? He means, apparently, these ideas:

- the consecration of Russia needs to mention Russia;

- Vladimir's Putin's neo-Stalinist dictatorship could not possibly represent the promised conversion of Russia;

- the Third Secret, as Mother Angelica herself believes, has not been fully disclosed;

- the Church is in the midst of what John Paul II himself called a "silent apostasy";

- this apostasy is predicted in the Third Secret, as John Paul II's own personal theologian has revealed and the future Pius XII foresaw;

- the crisis in the Catholic Church has resulted from an attack on the Church's doctrine, dogma, liturgy and very identity as the ark of salvation;

- the abandonment of the traditional Latin Mass, as the former Cardinal Ratzinger and Monsignor Gamber have both admitted, was a disastrous break with Tradition;

- Tradition—doctrine, dogma, morals, liturgy—must be restored;

- Tradition cannot be restored until the chastisement of the Church is ended by the honoring of Our Lady of Fatima's requests.

In short, the "fringey" Father Gruner is a Roman Catholic priest who takes Our Lady of Fatima at Her word, and who wishes to see the Roman Catholic Church restored for the good of souls and the peace and safety of the world.

Now, the New Church establishment, of which Keating is such a prominent member, certainly does not view itself as "fringey." Anything but that! No, it views itself as the standard of responsible, "mainstream" orthodox Catholicism in the Church today. Here is what New Church considers "orthodox" Catholicism, according to the evidence I have presented here:

- the destruction of the Roman Rite, as Msgr. Gamber called it, by replacing the traditional Latin Mass of 1500 years' standing with a new Mass that, as even Mother Angelica observed, accomplishes the same goals accomplished by the Protestant rebels of the sixteenth century: elimination of the Latin language, the Roman Canon, the Offertory, the eastward-facing priest and altar, and Communion on the tongue;

- changing the words of Our Lord from "for many" to "for all," when not even the Protestant rebels dared to do this—an act Msgr. Gamber (in a book endorsed by Cardinal Ratzinger) rightly calls scandalous and truly problematical;

- the sacrilegious abuse of Communion in the hand, distributed even by lay people, which allows Hosts to be stolen and marketed to Satanists;

- a "new interpretation" of the infallible dogma that outside the Church there is no salvation, which, according to EWTN, "modern shepherds" interpret "more generously" than "previous documents"—i.e. more generously than the infallible pronouncements of Popes and Councils;

- the refusal to state that Protestants, schismatics, Jews and infidels are bound for eternal damnation by not joining the Catholic Church;

- the advice that it is "very possible" that schismatics will attain eternal life, when the Church has taught infallibly that schismatics cannot be saved as such;

- the abandonment of the return of the dissidents to Rome in favor of an ecumenical "convergence";

- the consequent loss of conversions and vocations, threatening the very existence of the Church in many countries and endangering countless souls;

- outdoor "Pontifical" rock Masses attended by vast crowds of gyrating, immodestly clad teenagers;

- the introduction of pagan rituals into Catholic worship, even at Pontifical Masses;

- the desecration of the Fatima Shrine by Hindu worship;

- the Catholic celebration of Seder suppers, "Hebrew Masses," Jewish holidays and the wearing of rabbinical prayer shawls and yarmulkes;

- the creation of a "Hebrew Catholic" branch of Catholicism with its own calendar and liturgy in order to correct the "failure" of the Catholic Church for 1800 years to allow "Israelites" their just vocation in the Church;

- the Judaization of Catholic dioceses through the neo-Catechumenal Way and the episcopal celebration of Seder suppers with rabbis;

- the destruction of the traditional three-part, fifteen-mystery Rosary, which even Paul VI refused to change;

- the "sexualization" of Roman Catholicism, including, the practice of young boys "charting" the reproductive cycles of their own mothers and sisters;

- the combination of Catholicism with rock music and popular culture, including a Las Vegas lounge act broadcast by EWTN on Christmas Eve.

In sum, the New Church version of "orthodox" Catholicism is actually the *disintegration* of orthodox Catholicism. The New Church version of the Faith is precisely what Pius XII foresaw in his prophecy of the "suicide" of unprecedented innovations in the

Church. Yet the promoters of this counterfeit religion have the supreme audacity to proclaim in their neo-Pharisaical pride that the defenders of Roman Catholic Tradition are "fringey." What could be more diabolical than this inversion of the truth?

It seems that in EWTN's view Mother Angelica herself is guilty of harboring "fringey ideas," otherwise known as the faith of a traditional Roman Catholic. As if to confirm its total attachment to New Church, and its clean break with the militantly traditional direction in which Mother had been taking the network, EWTN is now *censoring the tapes of Mother Angelica's old broadcasts*. Dr. Peterson recounts how in the Fall of 2003 he received an email from Donovan advising that "before any of Mother's tapes would be heard they would be edited for theological content by Colin Donovan."

Thereafter, when Peterson had to "look up things for people" from Mother Angelica's past broadcasts, he would notice "red or yellow" markings to indicate on the transcript of the broadcast what had been edited out of the tape. "And I thought, well, this is amazing. This is a lady who, a nun who has built up an enormous organization based on truth and Catholicism, and here we have a Modernist who is going to edit what she said. It was just stupendous to me."

If Mother Angelica herself is now being required to hew to the New Church party line, it follows that every other employee at EWTN must do so. The fate of Dr. Peterson is a case in point. Having been assigned the task of answering letters and phone calls from EWTN's viewers, many of whom were expressing grave concern about the direction the Church was taking, Peterson found himself increasingly compelled to provide frank answers that were not in accord with "official EWTN dogma." These responses included "articles that were favorable to the traditional Latin Mass, why it should be continued."

As he listened to other employees in the Viewer Services Department advising callers to shun Father Gruner and his apostolate, Peterson would quietly (and out of earshot of the others) advise callers to "listen to every side and evaluate the situation as to whether they felt Russia had been converted or not." He began sending written replies, perhaps 50 in all, containing the other side of the story on such issues as Fatima, including "some of Father Gruner's periodicals..."

"Quite frankly," said Peterson, "I had gotten to the point where I almost couldn't take it any more... I'm very loyal towards a job, but it was—I could take it no more." Peterson was finally terminated from his employment by Gordon Sibley in February 2004, after it was discovered that he had bucked the EWTN "dogma" by sending one viewer a copy of an article on why the Consecration of Russia had not been accomplished in 1984, along with another article supporting a return to the traditional Latin Mass. The New Church party line required that Peterson be purged as surely as Mother Angelica was censored.

We have seen, then, how EWTN and its fellow partisans of New Church combine in an effort to bury the truth, defend sacrilege in the holiest of places and, as New Church opinion-makers always do, lend support to the ongoing post-conciliar revolution. Trading on their "prestige" and "good standing" in the Church, and relying entirely on mindless epithets and irrelevant arguments from authority, the partisans of New Church labor to make outcasts of faithful Catholics, while giving aid and comfort to enemies of the Church and the Fatima Message. The Pharisees themselves were no more skillful in using positions of influence to oppose the Truth and advance error.

It is worthwhile to conclude this chapter by noting that EWTN's ceaseless attacks on traditional Catholics, including Father Gruner, and its deafening silence on the crisis in the Church, were finally too much to bear for EWTN supporter Dr. John Turner. In a scathing, publicly posted email to another of EWTN's theological "experts," Dr. William Carroll (whose field of expertise is history, not theology), Turner provided an able summary of the grounds for the justified anger many Catholics feel about EWTN's self-righteous posturing and selective indignation:

> I have peripherally followed Fr Gruner (not an adherent) and watched in amazement at the strength and focus of attacks on this priest. It is remarkable given the range of heresy and disobedience that unfortunately marks our clergy and religious in this age—and goes unpunished. Given recent Vatican focus, it appears that Rome considers the Priestly Fraternity of St Peter, The Remnant, Catholic Family News, those who prefer the Tridentine Mass, those who quote scripture ("we resist you to the face" - people really need to READ the article) and Fr Gruner are the most significant challenge facing the Church today. It seems clear to me that our troubles

are far more serious and really lay elsewhere.[318]

Turner then zeroed in on the heart of the matter with deadly accuracy, exposing EWTN's culpable silence in the face of the auto-demolition of the Church. The following passages — again, from one of EWTN's own supporters — say it all:

> Why is Cardinal Hoyos making a point of Fr Gruner? Is "showing contempt" (whatever that means) for other Fatima apostles the problem? Many don't even believe in Fatima. How is that for contempt? Is thinking that the Church is in need of a return to historic teachings, liturgy, and practice the problem? If so, then Mother Angelica is in trouble.... *What is Fr Gruner actually doing that is worthy of such high level attention and censure? Mr Donovan slanders without evidence. This is treacherous and uncharitable behavior.*

> To any objective observer, there is a decided shift in Rome to stamp out Traditionalist movements at all levels. Cardinal Hoyos [head of the Congregation for the Clergy] seems to be leading the charge. Where is the action on gay masses, liturgical abuses, heretical retreat centers, heretical teachers in Catholic institutions, — or dare I mention pedophilia in the clergy, etc....? Is Fr Gruner really the leading candidate for excommunication in this troubled time? *Where is your outrage at this ludicrous proposition?*[319]

Dr. Turner went on to examine Donovan's baseless charges that Father Gruner is not only "suspended" but "schismatic." Where, Turner demanded to know, is the evidence?

> I really suspect that EWTN "experts" have overstated, in fact, what has happened to Fr Gruner [concerning his alleged "suspension"] — as well the status of other "branded" groups of Catholics. It is too bad that you have not provided the factual data necessary to begin to

---

[318]See, EWTN Q&A Forum, question from John Turner, Ph.D. of October 25, 2001 on "Intellectual Integrity".
[319]Ibid.

sort this out for ourselves. If you and Mr Donovan are going to call Fr Gruner "schismatic", you had better say specifically why he meets the complex definitions and conditions presented by Mr Donovan. It is not at all clear to me that he does.[320]

Turner next considered the curious post-conciliar solicitude toward the schismatic Orthodox, while traditional Catholic priests are cast into outer darkness:

Further, you better have some solid arguments explaining why communists installed as priests in Russia (who do not recognize the authority of the Pope, who do not share even our theology of the Trinity, and who deny Catholics access to the sacraments out of territorial rivalry) are worthy of kisses and ecumenism while Fr Gruner (and for that matter, the Pius X Society) are objects of schism and worthy of excommunication....[321]

Turner also asked EWTN to explain its silence on the moral and doctrinal pollution in the Catholic seminaries at the same time it was denouncing Father Gruner, a wholly orthodox priest, for unproven offenses:

When will someone get around to clearing the heretics out of our seminaries and Catholic Universities? Isn't that important? *Why doesn't EWTN call for action there?* Which Vatican congregation is focusing on that problem?[322]

Dr. Turner concluded by expressing his shame over EWTN's resort to demagoguery against a Catholic priest who simply exercises his priesthood as priests have done for 2,000 years, while it turns a blind eye to the crisis in the Church:

Your (and Mr Donovan's) replies on this subject are an outrage to any thinking Catholic and should be swept aside.

---

[320]Ibid.
[321]Ibid.
[322]Ibid.

You should be ashamed of yourselves. I am ashamed that I have supported EWTN over the years with my prayers, my funds, and our visits. I am ashamed of what our Church is doing to people who believe in the historical continuity of our Faith and the importance of liturgy in passing on that Faith. I am ashamed at the way that Rome is turning its back on the blood of the martyrs. I am ashamed by my own participation in nutty liturgies and heretical CCD.

The Church is in crisis. It totters on the edge of disintegration. The people are confused at the bizarre actions of our hierarchy. You have turned this vital discussion into posturing, name calling, and theological parsing. May God have mercy on us.[323]

Unable to mount a serious reply to this unanswerable rebuke, Carroll could only refer vaguely to "the judgment of the Church on him [Father Gruner]"—a "judgment" neither Carroll nor Donovan had substantiated in the first place. Ignoring the thrust of Dr. Turner's objection—that EWTN ignores the enemies of the Church while condemning defenders of tradition—Carroll pleaded lamely: "How can you be ashamed of your support for EWTN when you consider how much good it has done?" But how much good *has* EWTN done by not only refusing to oppose, but also actively covering up and even promoting the post-conciliar revolution?

Although Mr. Donovan later modified one of his pieces on Father Gruner to remove the explicit accusation of schism (following an email exchange with me), EWTN retains on its website another piece by Mr. Donovan in which he repeats virtually the same calumnies.[324] Thus, in fulfilling its ongoing role as a facilitator of the post-conciliar revolution, EWTN continues to engage in precisely what one of its own exasperated supporters was compelled to condemn: posturing and name-calling rather than rational argument—the politics of hate in the Catholic Church.

---

[323]Ibid.

[324]See, EWTN Q&A Forum, Donovan's reply of January 12, 2001 to question from Maria Gualberti on "Father Nicholas Gruner".

# Part III

# Summing Up

# Chapter 17

# Did They Love You,
# John Paul II?

When Pope John Paul II passed from this earth on April 2, 2005 at 9:37 p.m. Rome time, it was a new beginning for him and for the Church of which he was head. Seventeen days after John Paul's death, Pope Benedict XVI, formerly Joseph Cardinal Ratzinger, ascended to the throne of Peter. Only God knows where this papacy will take the Church, and prognostications in this regard are worthless. We can only hope that we will witness the triumph of the Immaculate Heart which Our Lady of Fatima promised, and not the annihilation of nations of which She warned.

As the pontificate of Benedict XVI takes shape, however, we can profit from an examination of how **EWTN** and New Church, in cooperation with the mass media, assessed the pontificate of John Paul II. Instead of mourning the Pope in prayer and circumspection and beseeching Heaven for a new Pope who would restore the Church, EWTN joined the media in "spinning" the death of John Paul II the way the world spins its coverage of everything Catholic: in favor of revolution and against Roman Catholic Tradition.

In the days immediately following the death of Pope John Paul II, Catholics with any sense of dignity and tradition were horrified to see the organs of world opinion, as if by some prearranged signal, conducting a campaign to make of our late Pope a veritable icon of the New World Order—literally the first Pope in Church history deserving of the world's unanimous praise. An endless parade of dignitaries without the least respect for the teaching authority of the Catholic Church was instantly produced to hail John Paul II, not as the Roman Pontiff that he was, but as an esteemed leader of "the global community"—a community that will never, of course, submit to any Pope.

How is it that a world in the grip of apostasy, as John Paul II himself observed, had nothing but praise for the Pope whose moral teaching the world simply ignored? On every major television network politicians of the Left and the Right, conservative and liberal journalists and political commentators, Protestant ministers, rabbis, Imams, Hindus and Buddhists, rock stars and even MTV video jockeys—spokesmen of every conceivable persuasion and political orientation—unanimously offered unstinting tribute to the Pope. How does one explain this seeming paradox? Part of the explanation is that even in its apostasy, the world implicitly recognizes that the Catholic Church is the one true Church and that the papal office is a divinely instituted monarchy. The religion the world most detests is also the only religion it takes seriously, for "the devils also believe and tremble". (James 2:19) Thus the world's attention is naturally riveted on the death of any Roman Pontiff.

But there has to be more to the explanation than this, for the Church has never seen anything like the unceasing hosannas offered to John Paul II by virtually every organ of world opinion. Far more is involved here than the usual expressions of worldly respect for a deceased Pope. What we saw in the incredible non-stop, 24-hour-a-day coverage of the death of John Paul II is the world's attempt to install in our minds, as the model for the future of the Church, a Pope who would be a kind of spiritual politician, leading only by moral example and with the consent of whoever cares to be his subject. We were reminded of Pius XI's condemnation of similar efforts to reduce the papal office by the fledgling "ecumenical" movement of the 1920s: "Among them there indeed are some, though few, who grant to the Roman Pontiff a primacy of honor or even a certain jurisdiction or power, but this, however, they consider not to arise from the divine law but from the consent of the faithful."

This is the figurehead Pope of Masonic dreams: loved and admired, but never feared; respected, but not obeyed, unless it pleases one to obey him; an eminent leader among the leaders of the world's religions, but no more than this. This is the kind of Pope the "modern world" wants to see emerge from the next conclave—the kind it has *always* wanted to see emerge from the next conclave. And that is why the world tried to appropriate to itself the memory of John Paul II.

Consider *what* the leaders of the world were praising in the pontificate of John Paul II. Mikhail Gorbachev lauded the late Pope as "the number one humanist on this planet." Kofi Annan eulogized him as "a tireless advocate of peace, a true pioneer in interfaith dialogue and a strong force for critical self-evaluation by the church itself." Fox News called him "a tireless and outspoken campaigner for world peace and humanitarian causes." European Commission President Jose Manuel Barroso said that the Pope had played "an essential role in the reunification of Europe and in the advance of ideas of freedom and democracy in our continent." George Bush (who at least referred to the Pope as a "fearless priest" and "the Bishop of Rome") hailed him as "a champion of human freedom," who "spoke of our providential Constitution, the self-evident truths about human dignity in our Declaration, and the blessings of liberty that follow from them." Israeli Foreign Minister Silvan Shalom said that "Israel, the Jewish people and the entire world lost today a great champion of reconciliation and brotherhood between the faiths." The Dalai Lama expressed "deep appreciation for the pope's mission to bring peace to the world." CNN summed up the tributes of the world this way: "Pope John Paul II was remembered Saturday as a 'champion of human freedom,' a 'tireless advocate of peace' and a man with a 'wonderful sense of humor'.... The pope was known for his energy, intellectualism and activism on the global stage."

Even more telling than all this worldly praise of the late Pope was the eulogy by none other than Abe Foxman, head of the B'Nai B'rith Anti-Defamation League. This is the same Christophobic bigot who led the effort to destroy Mel Gibson and scuttle *The Passion of the Christ*. It is hard to think of a more vicious enemy of the Catholic Church today, yet here is what Foxman said of John Paul II:

> Pope John Paul II's moral inspiration and leadership was a shining light to the world. Throughout his lifetime the Pontiff defended the Jewish people... John Paul II worked tirelessly to repair the Church's painful 2,000-year history with the Jewish people.
>
> Pope John Paul II revolutionized Catholic-Jewish relations. He denounced anti-Semitism as a "sin against God and humanity." He was the first Pope in history to visit the central synagogue in Rome, where he recognized Jews as elder brothers, announcing to the Chief Rabbi of Rome and Jews around the world: "I am Joseph, your brother." He normalized relations with the

Jewish people and the Jewish State of Israel, and then made his historic pilgrimage to the Holy Land, where he visited Yad Vashem and prayed at the Western Wall.

In his exceptional teachings, writings and pronouncements, John Paul II has denounced the evils that led to the Holocaust and questioned whether the Church's attitudes provided an environment for the deadly anti-Semitism in Europe in the 1930s and 1940s.

Most importantly, the Pope rejected the destructive concept of supersessionism and has recognized the special relationship between Christianity and the Jewish people, while sharing his understanding of Judaism as a living heritage, of the permanent validity of God's covenant with the Jewish people...[325]

The world, then, praises the late Pope entirely for reasons unrelated to his office as the Vicar of Christ. He is praised for his effect on social and political relations in the world. And, as Foxman's eulogy shows us, the world viewed John Paul II as more worthy of admiration than any Pope before him because he, unlike any of his predecessors, was willing to lend credence to many of the world's accusations against the Catholic Church, especially the accusations of the Jews. To appreciate this, one need only compare the world's opinion of Pius XII with its opinion of John Paul II.

But wherever the papal office *as such* was actually exercised authoritatively during John Paul's reign, the world is now silent or even critical. Hence there was no praise from the world, but only criticism, for the Pope's definitive ending of the debate on women's ordination and his "inflexible" stand on such moral questions as contraception, abortion, euthanasia, and homosexual "marriage" and adoption. Then again, the world is at this very moment praising the Pope's personal opposition to the death penalty, a view he never imposed upon the Catholic faithful and which represented a departure from the constant teaching of the Church.

The conclusion is inescapable: Whatever the Pope's subjective intentions might have been (and these are known only to God), the

---

[325] "ADL Mourns the Loss of Pope John Paul II", April 2, 2005, http://www.adl.org/PresRele/VaticanJewish_96/4679_96.htm

world's unprecedented praise for John Paul II clearly arises from the perception that his pontificate, unlike any other, *served the world's interests* as opposed to the "narrow" sectarian interests of the Roman Catholic Church. As Colin Powell put it in his own tribute to the Pope: "His *faith for the world* transcended his Catholic background." Whether or not one wishes to argue that the perception is unjustified, the world thinks of John Paul II as a Pope whose Catholicity was merely part of his "background"; it hails him as a "moral and spiritual leader" for the members of all religions or none, whose leadership did not involve any idea of submission to the Roman Pontiff. How did this perception arise? Is the world not responding to the Church's own "opening" to it at the Council? Is the world not rejoicing in the legacy of a Pope it sees as having, at long last, brought the Church down to earth, dispelling once and for all its aura of divine majesty as the one and only City of God, ruled by a king who is Christ's Vicar?

Here too the words of our departed Pope confirm the reality as opposed to the myth EWTN and the other New Church hagiographers are already beginning to construct. As I noted earlier, in his 1986 encyclical *Dominum et Vivificantem* the Pope wrote that in assessing the Second Vatican Council's supposed fruits "one must learn how to 'discern' them carefully from everything that may instead come originally from the 'prince of this world.' This discernment in implementing the Council's work is especially necessary in view of the fact *that the Council opened itself widely to the contemporary world*, as is clearly seen from the important Conciliar Constitutions *Gaudium et Spes* and *Lumen Gentium*." Thus the Pope himself depicted Vatican II, precisely *because* of its unprecedented "opening to the world," as a council whose fruits must be carefully distinguished from what comes from the devil! No other ecumenical council in the history of the Church has carried such a papal caveat. And now, with the Pope gone, we reap the whirlwind. A state of silent apostasy is what the new Pope now confronts in the Church's ceaseless war against the world, the flesh, and the devil. This is the reality John Paul II left behind, as his own words confirm. What sort of love for the Pope would make EWTN pretend that this silent apostasy does not exist?

The Catholic instinct is to be suspicious of the world's praise, for we are always mindful of our Lord's admonition to His disciples: "If the world hates you, know that it has hated Me before you. If you were of the world, the world would love its own: but because you are not of the world, but I have chosen you out of the world, therefore the world hates you." (John 15:18-19) But EWTN was only too happy to join the world in elevating one Pope above all others. EWTN's anchorman, Raymond Arroyo, summoned by the powers of the world to provide commentary on Fox News, declared: "This was not a man who went around with the tiara on his head or in the *sedia* being carried about. He was the people's Pope. He used to pull his hand back whenever someone went to kiss it. He didn't like all the trappings. There were no red tassels on this guy's shoes."

Arroyo thus blithely undermined respect for John Paul II's predecessors, many of them great saints, by suggesting that, unlike "the people's Pope," they were vainglorious royalists and popinjays partial to red tassels. This is New Church hubris at its height: the Church of today is so much more enlightened than the medieval kingdom of forty years ago. New Church luminary George Weigel spoke in the same vein: "He was not interested at all, and in fact was embarrassed by, some of the rituals that traditionally were extended to the pope; for instance, the kissing of his ring." But even Pope John Paul I reportedly consented to be carried in the *sedia* as a gesture of *humility*, once it was pointed out to him that his own embarrassment over the tradition was no reason to deny the dignity of his supreme office, which was no merit of his. And even a child understands that to kiss the papal ring is not to honor the man who wears it, but rather the office conferred by Christ Himself, who allowed His own feet to be kissed and anointed by a weeping sinner.

EWTN's implicit denigration of the pre-conciliar Popes (a basic element of New Church thinking) continued on Marcus Grodi's show *The Journey Home*, where Grodi opined that John Paul II had made Protestants "feel welcome" in the Church, whereas before his reign "there was not that welcome." One wonders why Grodi failed to mention something of which he is surely aware: the millions of defections from the Church into Protestant sects *since* 1978. A few moments of statistical research would reveal that in 2002, 24 years into the pontificate of John Paul II, there were only 80,000 adult baptisms in the United States as compared with 126,000 in 1965, when Protestants supposedly felt less welcome in the Catholic Church. Is Grodi really unaware of these irrefutable and widely published statistics of drastic Church decline since Vatican II?

A Catholic does not love the Pope by attempting an immediate revision of the history of the past 26 years. Wild declarations that the Pope transformed the whole world, restored the faith of the multitudes and gave hope to all of humanity are not expressions of love for the Pope, but only flattery. That John Paul II took strong stands on moral issues, resisting all pressure to change the Church's teaching, cannot be doubted. This is admirable, but it is also what the faithful have the right to expect from every Vicar of Christ. That the Pope was a giant on the world scene is also beyond question, although one may be permitted to debate what lasting effect his presence had on world events. But the love we owe the Pope — the love of Christian charity, as opposed to pleasing sentiments — requires us also to acknowledge the state of the Church the Pope left behind, as *he himself* described it: a "silent apostasy." This is not to blame the Pope for everything that has happened in the Church since 1978. It is, rather, to admit the reality we must face in the coming years, the reality the Pope himself acknowledged not long before his death, rather than deluding ourselves that the end of this pontificate finds us in the Promised Land.

Arroyo at least made some effort to reconcile his eulogizing with reality when he asserted that while the Church had declined "numerically" during John Paul II's reign, what was left was "a fervent small body of believers" from which the "renewal of the Church will take place." Does it really help the Church, do we really show love for the Pope, by presenting mass defections from the Faith as a great pontifical *success*, as if John Paul II had deliberately put into play a kind of survival-of-the-fittest plan of spiritual privation? Arroyo here echoed Cardinal Ratzinger's claim that the Church has undergone a "qualitative renewal" since Vatican II. But how does one determine the "quality" of the remaining faithful, and how could this "quality" counterbalance a loss of "quantity," when that "quantity" represents immortal souls in need of salvation? As Peter's net is drawn up with increasingly meager catches, is it not ridiculous to marvel at the imagined plumpness of each fish — as if human souls were fungible goods whose total combined "weight" is all that matters? The Pope himself, however, did not marvel at the quality of the diminishing catch when he spoke of Europe's "silent apostasy" near the end of his reign, as we saw in the Overview. Why do those who say they love the Pope not admit with him that he reigned during a silent apostasy? Why, instead, do they build up one Pope by tarnishing the memory of sainted predecessors who presided over a robust and expanding Church?

This ready denigration of the pre-conciliar Church by EWTN celebrities demonstrates that the world's praise of the last pontificate has only come at the expense of what Saint Pius X called "the Catholic name." Indeed, as Kofi Annan's eulogy suggests, the world very much appreciates that during John Paul II's pontificate the Church was, for the first time in her history, subjected to public "critical self-evaluation" by a Pope. Annan was referring to the nearly 100 apologies the Pope had issued for the alleged offenses of deceased Catholics, handily collected and published to the world in *When a Pope Asks Forgiveness* by Luigi Accattoli. In his own retrospective in *The New York Times* the day after the Pope's death, Robert D. McFadden described this feature of John Paul II's papacy in just the way the world perceives it: "a daring, unprecedented apology for the errors of his church and individual Catholics over the past 2,000 years, a catalog of sins that included episodes of religious and cultural intolerance and of historic injustices against Jews, women, indigenous peoples, immigrants and the poor." As the Chief Rabbi of Wales, Dr. Jonathan Sacks, put it: "Pope John Paul II was a global leader for a global age. Few Jews will forget his visit to the synagogue in Rome or his deeply moving pilgrimage to the Western Wall in Jerusalem. That one act of *atonement for the suffering caused to Jews by the Church* was one of the great healing moments of our time."

Quite simply, the world lauds one Pope alone because it perceives that during his reign alone, the Catholic Church finally agreed with the world's condemnations of her. This should give any Catholic pause. But EWTN is undeterred, as it joins the world in clamoring for the elevation of one Pope above all others, and thus the novelties of New Church, of which the world heartily approves, above the constant traditions of authentic Roman Catholicism. EWTN is leading the charge to dispense with all formalities and simply declare John Paul II a saint immediately. On *Life on the Rock* the show's host Father Francis openly declared that people must "whip everyone into a frenzy" to declare the late Pope to be John Paul the Great—a *frenzy*, which is to say, the abandonment of reason. And the abandonment of reason is, in the end, what Modernism means, as the religion revealed by God and safeguarded by an unchanging Magisterium is replaced by mere sentiment and opinion surrounded by a few Catholic trappings, including even a few pieces of sound doctrine mixed in with the latest novelties. Behind a façade of

Catholicity, EWTN is promoting the reduction of the Faith to an ever-evolving cult centered about the person of the currently reigning Pope, as opposed to the Petrine office itself and the infallible, unalterable dogmas of the Faith that office was divinely commissioned to protect. And there is no reason to doubt that EWTN will labor mightily to create a cult of Benedict XVI, just as it did with the cult of John Paul II.

Catholics can only object to this whole eerie spectacle, the likes of which the Catholic Church has never seen before. Whoever wishes to love our late Pope as he ought to be loved must be willing to say now, in charity and in truth, that John Paul II was a ruler whose words often said one thing while his actions said another, and that the contradictions which marked his reign have produced enormous confusion in the Church that must be undone by his successor. Even the liberals can see this. Giovanni Ferro, editor of *Jesus* magazine, told CNN that John Paul II "was what you might call a revolutionary conservative. In some areas, such as the preparedness to enter into dialogue with other religions, he was very forward-minded. In other areas, however, he was an extremely reactionary, traditionalist pope. *He maintained all sorts of opposing currents in the church*, with the result that his successor will probably be faced with a great crisis of direction."

A great crisis of direction caused by opposing currents is precisely what Benedict XVI will have to resolve. We saw the opposing currents at work even in the funeral liturgies for Pope John Paul II, where the Vatican appears suddenly to have rediscovered the ecclesiastical necessity of Latin and chant, while the rest of the Church suffers the degradation of funerals and other vernacular liturgies whose utter lack of dignity offends even Protestants. Every word of the liturgical text for the ceremonies surrounding the procession of the Pope's body into St. Peter's (before the day of the funeral Mass) was intoned in Latin, every vestment was of the most dignified traditional design, and there was not a woman, lay reader or guitar in sight. Even the choir was composed entirely of men. It was as if the "liturgical renewal" of the past 35 years had never happened, as if the Vatican were finally admitting that the new liturgy is simply not suitable for serious worship. All of this magnificent solemnity in prayers for the deceased Pope, and rightly so, but no such solemnity on the very altars where the divine sacrifice of Our Lord Himself is presented anew amidst the banalities and even the profanations of the Novus Ordo. How can those who say they love John Paul II not insist *in his name* that the dignity rightly accorded to the body of a Pope also be accorded to the Body of Christ—on every altar in the world?

For 26 years the New Church establishment, led by EWTN, chanted "John Paul II, we love you!" But did they love the Pope as a Pope should be loved, in charity and in truth, being willing, as St. Thomas Aquinas teaches, to admonish even the Pope should the danger of scandal to the Faith arise? Or did they love instead the cult they themselves had built up around the man in sports stadiums and at the World Youth Days which were among EWTN's most popular broadcasts? As he viewed the Pope lying in state in St. Peter's Basilica during EWTN's coverage, Marcus Grodi said that people must develop an appreciation not only for the Catholic Faith, "but for the meaning of John Paul II." When the person of a Pope is raised to the level of a "meaning" that is held to be something over and above the Faith itself, we are witnessing a process of papal deification that is foreign to our religion and must arouse in us no little fear of what is to come in the days ahead.

As we pray that Benedict XVI will restore the Catholic Church, we must pray as well for our departed Pope. But we should also watch and learn from EWTN's startling elevation of John Paul II above all his predecessors. The rock star Bono said this in tribute to the Pope: "he was the best front man the Roman Catholic Church has ever had... I was so taken by this showman, even if I didn't agree with everything he said..." The world, like EWTN, says it loves John Paul II. But what, really, do they love, and does it come from God? Or, as the Pope himself warned us concerning the implementation of the Second Vatican Council, does it come from "the prince of this world"? We need to be most wary of what EWTN and the voices of the world are now praising, and what they might well be praising during the new pontificate.

# Chapter 18

# What the Evidence Shows

At the outset of this discussion I said that I would prove that since the departure of Mother Angelica, **EWTN** has taken a sharp turn toward Modernism and is now promoting a Modernist counterfeit of Roman Catholicism. I said that the evidence would show that

1) EWTN has endorsed and advanced the liturgical destruction of the past forty years;

2) EWTN has helped undermine Catholic adherence to the infallibly defined dogma that outside the Roman Catholic Church no one can be saved, and the constant teaching of the Roman Pontiffs that the only means of achieving Christian unity for those who are not Catholics but claim to be followers of Jesus Christ is the return of the Protestant and schismatic dissidents to the one, Holy, Catholic and Apostolic Church;

3) EWTN has promoted and encouraged a Judaizing tendency in the Church not unlike that which confronted the original Jewish Apostles, while undermining the Church's infallible teaching on the abrogation of the Old Covenant with the coming of the New Covenant;

4) EWTN has publicized, excused, defended and outright promoted sacrilege in Catholic holy places;

5) EWTN has contributed to the tendency to substitute a common-denominator natural religion for adherence to the truths of revelation expounded by the Catholic Church as necessary for salvation;

**6)** EWTN has advocated a senseless and un-Catholic idolatry of the Pope's person that does a grave disservice to the Pope, the Church and the Faith;

**7)** EWTN is leading the way toward destruction of the traditional Rosary, whose traditional form was defended against innovation even by that unprecedented liturgical innovator, Pope Paul VI;

**8)** EWTN has promoted an obscure sexual gnosticism that scandalously attempts to "sacramentalize" marital relations and make NFP into a mystical cult;

**9)** EWTN has generally corrupted and cheapened the Faith and image of the Church by trying to combine Roman Catholicism with rock music and show business in a vain effort to make Catholicism "cool" and appealing to the base instincts of a mass audience;

**10)** EWTN has attacked and attempted to ostracize from the Church defenders of Roman Catholic tradition and the authentic Message of Fatima, with its warning of a crisis in the Church.

The evidence has clearly proven these claims. Simple honesty compels the conclusion that Pius XII and every one of his predecessors would view with horror, and absolutely condemn, the collection of destructive doctrinal and liturgical novelties EWTN broadcasts to the entire world as "traditional" Catholicism. Our eyes do not deceive us: despite the good elements that remain in its programming, EWTN is powerfully assisting the Modernist program of the very "innovators" of whom Pius XII spoke in the prophecy he uttered in light of the Message of Fatima. Let us recall that prophecy once again:

> I am worried by the Blessed Virgin's messages to little Lucy of Fatima. This persistence of Mary about the dangers which menace the Church is a divine warning against *the suicide of altering the Faith, in her liturgy, her theology and her soul*.... I hear all around me innovators who wish to dismantle the Sacred Chapel, destroy the

universal flame of the Church, reject her ornaments and
make her feel remorse for her historical past.... A day
will come when the civilized world will deny its God,
*when the Church will doubt as Peter doubted.* She will be
tempted to believe that man has become God. In our
churches, Christians *will search in vain for the red lamp*
where God awaits them. Like Mary Magdalene, weeping
before the empty tomb, they will ask, "Where have they
taken Him?"

The evidence presented here shows beyond question that EWTN
has endorsed and promoted the alteration of the Faith in the
Church's liturgy, theology and soul—even to the point of
commending the creation of a "Hebrew Catholic" branch of the
Church (as if such a thing could exist).

Let us also recall once again what Pope John Paul II's theologian,
Cardinal Ciappi, revealed: "In the Third Secret it is foretold, among
other things, that the great apostasy in the Church will begin at the
top." Our Lady clearly indicates this in the opening words of the
Third Secret: "In Portugal, the dogma of the Faith will always be
preserved..." The Third Secret, then, prophesies an apostasy that will
begin at the top and will involve an undermining of the infallible
*dogma* of the Church. The Church's liturgy, theology and soul will
come under attack by the "innovators" Pius XII knew were preparing
a major assault on the Church. Through the medium of television, a
medium that exerts a most powerful influence on countless millions
of souls, EWTN has contributed substantially to this Modernist
assault on the Church by legitimating throughout the world a
"conservative" compromise with the innovators—a compromise that
is constantly moving in an ever more Modernist direction; a
compromise that has the appearance of being "the most Catholic
thing out there," but which in truth is a horror by any objective
standard of Roman Catholicism. And the same is true of the rest of
the New Church establishment.

Moreover, as the evidence has shown, EWTN compounded its
role in this apostasy by denouncing, calumniating and trying to
ostracize from the Church faithful Catholics who defend the Church's
liturgy, theology and soul against the innovators. Transgressing the
very injunction of Holy Scripture, EWTN portrays the defenders of
the good as evil, and the promoters of evil as good.

The modern mass media have immense power. Television, radio, film and the major print outlets are capable of forming the attitudes of a nation and changing its entire culture. As we Catholics know only too well, the tyranny of public opinion wielded by the mass media can be more oppressive than any government agency.

But in the right hands the mass media can be a force for good. Mel Gibson, for example, was able to make a profoundly favorable impact on our society with a single film: *The Passion of the Christ.* In defending his traditional Catholic beliefs in televised interviews concerning the film, Gibson did not hesitate to point out that the reforms engendered by Vatican II have been disastrous. Gibson, who built his own independent Latin Mass chapel in Malibu, California in order to escape Cardinal Mahony and his hellish Archdiocese of Los Angeles, openly called for a restoration of Tradition. Through his use of television and film, Gibson single-handedly put the word "traditionalist" into the working vocabulary of the average American, and America will never be quite the same again.

It is interesting to note that despite Gibson's notorious abandonment of the increasingly decrepit New Church, the leaders of New Church opinion did not even hint at an accusation of schism or heresy in their adulatory coverage of *The Passion.* Gibson is a celebrity, and the one thing New Church respects is the prestige of celebrity. Hence, during his "exclusive" interview of Gibson on EWTN's show *The World Over*, host Raymond Arroyo astonishingly referred to his guest as simply "Mel Gibson, who is a traditional Catholic." Later in the interview Arroyo, visibly brimming with delight at being in the presence of a world-class celebrity, practically burbled to Gibson: "We share a love of the Latin Mass." (When Gibson replied, "I don't go to any other service," Arroyo quickly moved on to other matters.)

When the Gibson interview was over and *The Passion* was no longer major news, however, EWTN retuned to business as usual: worldwide promotion of the same catastrophic innovations of New Church from which Gibson himself has fled, and which have emptied the pews and seminaries and provoked worldwide defection from the Faith. Having taken advantage of Gibson's celebrity, EWTN resumed its basic function as an enforcer of post-conciliar correctness in the Catholic world. Instead of using the powerful means at its disposal for restoration of the Church, as Gibson has tried to do, EWTN goes on supporting the manifestly ruinous status quo: a debauched liturgy, a destructive ecumenism, a deadly religious indifferentism, a degraded "pop" Catholicism, and a revisionist "interpretation" of the Message of Fatima that would place Our Lady's prescriptions for a Church in crisis forever beyond our reach, if that were possible.

Here it is important to consider a few interesting questions: At a time when the political regimes of individual States and the United Nations are all arrayed against the Catholic Church, and her teachings are hated and opposed more widely than ever before, how is it that EWTN has such vast access to television and radio outlets throughout America and the world? Why is it that EWTN is almost everywhere on television screens? Where does the money for this immense enterprise come from, as it is obviously not being raised entirely by small donations from individual members of the faithful? Where does EWTN obtain $2.3 million a month for its operations, month after month, year after year, with no sign of any major financial distress despite the prevailing economic insecurity? Would EWTN survive for even a month if it truly opposed the spirit of the world by abandoning the rock music and pop culture, and returning to the Church's traditional militancy, liturgy, doctrine and dogma, without compromise or ambiguity? Could it be, then, that the powers of the world are only too happy to let flourish a "conservative" Modernist substitute for authentic Roman Catholicism—a substitute that poses no real threat to the world and whose very ubiquity on TV screens obscures the object of true reform and restoration in the Church? These are questions every Catholic should ponder, as EWTN enjoys ever-greater success in the world while the crisis in the Church continues to worsen.

As this discussion draws to a close, I ask the reader to consider another quotation from the "moderate" Monsignor Klaus Gamber concerning the state of the Church in our time, for Gamber can hardly be accused of being a partisan of Father Gruner and the so-called "extreme traditionalist" view of our situation. As Gamber wrote 12 years ago, even before the homosexual priest scandal had rocked the entire Church:

> Great is the confusion! Who can still see clearly in this darkness? Where in our Church are the leaders who can show us the right path? Where are the bishops courageous enough to cut out the cancerous growth of Modernist theology that has implanted itself and is festering within the celebration of even the most sacred

> mysteries, before the cancer spreads and causes even greater damage?
>
> What we need today is a new Athanasius, a new Basil, bishops like those who in the fourth century fought against Arianism when almost the whole of Christendom had succumbed to the heresy. We need saints today who can unite those whose faith has remained firm so that we might fight error and rouse the weak and vacillating from their apathy.[326]

Who indeed can still see clearly? Who indeed will unite the remaining faithful and rouse the weak and vacillating? Certainly not EWTN and the New Church establishment. By their fruits we have known them. As Msgr. Gamber suggested, today almost the whole of Christendom has succumbed to a heresy even greater than that of Arius in the fourth century. Yes, the Church today needs another St. Athanasius or St. Basil. But she also needs lay faithful like those in the time of the Arian heresy, who are willing to stand in opposition to the spirit of the age when the whole world is against them. For today we face the same situation remarked by St. Basil the Great at the height of Arianism:

> Only one offense is now vigorously punished, an accurate observance of our fathers' traditions. For this cause the pious are driven from their countries and transported into deserts.[327]

Like the Pharisees of old, the Pharisees of New Church strain at gnats while they swallow camels. (Matt. 23:23-24) They use false obedience to destroy obedience, and mindless appeals to authority to destroy respect for authority. They find "schism" where there is really unity with eternal Rome, and "unity" where there is really schism. They assist in the work of devastating the vineyard and then pronounce the devastation a work of Catholic piety.

Why must it be this way? Can those responsible for EWTN not admit the damage caused by the Modernist uprising in the Church — the greatest crisis in Church history? Can they not, with Gamber,

---

[326]Gamber, *Reform of the Roman Liturgy*, page 113.
[327]*Epistles of St. Basil*, n. 243.

recognize "the cancerous growth of Modernist theology that has implanted itself and is festering within the celebration of even the most sacred mysteries"—a cancerous growth EWTN itself promotes? Can they not perceive that the very novelties they themselves incessantly extol and advance have brought on the present darkness and confusion? Can they not recognize apostasy when they see it? Or have they placed themselves in the category of those described in the prophecy of St. Paul in his Second Epistle to Timothy: "For there shall be a time when they will not endure sound doctrine but, according to their own desires, they will heap to themselves teachers having itching ears: And will indeed turn away their hearing from the truth, but will be turned unto fables." (2 Tim. 4:3-4)

The hard truth is that for all its good elements, EWTN is a Trojan horse in the City of God. Like the Greeks' ostensible gift to the city of Troy, EWTN's seemingly impressive façade of Catholicity conceals grave danger to our City. Anyone who cares about true restoration and reform in the Church should recognize this Trojan horse for what it is, and have nothing further to do with it.

It might be said that the format of its content may be a major part of the problem with EWTN. The Catholic Faith cannot but suffer compromise when it is presented as a continuous television show that strives to keep the audience entertained. This is not to say that television cannot convey authentic Catholicism. In the right hands, it can, provided that prudence, sobriety and dignity are strictly observed. But, EWTN's televised "pop" Catholicism is, in some ways, even more insidious than commercial television for the very reason that its Catholic packaging makes it easier for people to swallow the bad with the good. One must therefore be especially careful to avoid exposing impressionable children to EWTN's mutilated and corrupt version of the Faith. When a child encounters on this "Catholic" network such things as pounding rock music, "rapping" priests, immodestly dressed teens, open discussions of sexual matter that belong in the confessional, men wearing ponytails and Crucifix earrings, the constant use of street slang by priests and others, a Las Vegas lounge act on Christmas Eve, and even the image of a Host in a monstrance juxtaposed with a rock soundtrack, that child will be all the more easily habituated to the myriad evils in the rest of "TV land" and contemporary popular culture as a whole. After all, if a "Catholic" television network is presenting such things, what could possibly be wrong with them? This is one of the most disturbing facts about EWTN: that a Catholic parent *would be negligent in allowing little children or even adolescents to watch it unattended*. EWTN is, in fact, a gateway to the loss of innocence, as its own parental warnings implicitly concede.

In sum, like the rest of New Church, EWTN does not preach the pure and unadulterated Gospel of Jesus Christ that was handed down to us. Quite the contrary, EWTN has become a vehicle of the Modernist apostasy in the Church. Further, given the power of television to mold public opinion, EWTN may be the *premiere* vehicle of Modernist apostasy; for contemporary Catholics, like men everywhere today, have been habituated to accept as true whatever appears on their TV screens. Therefore, EWTN ought to be considered anathema — that is, something Catholics should avoid like the plague.

To those who might view this advice as shocking and intolerable, I would pose this question: If, as St. Paul taught, we must view as anathema even an Apostle or angel from Heaven when he departs from the Gospel, how can we not do the same with a mere lay-operated *television network* which, as I have shown here, promotes manifest errors against the Faith, scandal and even sacrilege? Moreover, if EWTN can effectively anathematize Father Gruner and other people they term "extreme traditionalists" by urging people to shun them and their organizations, by what standard of justice are Catholics who defend the dogma, doctrine and traditional practice of the Church required to remain silent while EWTN blatantly undermines the Faith on the Internet and in televised broadcasts seen by millions? Indeed, is any truly faithful Catholic free *not* to oppose what EWTN is doing?

# Chapter 19

# What Should We Do?

What can the lay faithful do in this age of apostasy, when even "the most Catholic thing out there" is contributing to the confusion and darkness remarked by Gamber? The first thing they can do is to recognize that *it is EWTN and the whole New Church establishment that must be shunned*, not Catholics and Catholic organizations standing fast in Tradition. There was a time, before the removal of Mother Angelica from her position of control, when EWTN seemed poised to become an ally in the movement for a return to Tradition. But that time was brief, and is now over. As we have seen in abundance, today EWTN is in the hands of lay directors, many of them ex-Protestants, who have no intention of using the network to restore authentic Roman Catholicism in all its integrity — the perennial doctrine, dogma, liturgy and spirituality of the Church, all of which have been thrown into confusion by the post-Vatican II revolution.

If this book has shown anything, it has shown what a tragic mistake of judgment it was for Mother Angelica to end her direct resistance to Modernist prelates and yield to their pressure by resigning from EWTN's board and subjecting her apostolate to lay control. No doubt her intentions were good, even noble. But the evidence is overwhelming that Mother ought to have continued to follow the example of those sainted prelates of the Arian crisis — St. Athansius, St. Eusebius of Vercelli — by continuing her resistance to the widespread attack on the Faith in our time, which exceeds even the Arian crisis in its scope. Just as those great prelates of the fourth century refused to allow demands for a false "obedience" or the prestige and power of their Arian persecutors to cow them into abandoning their resistance, even though the whole Church, including Pope Liberius, seemed to be siding with Arius, so should Mother have continued her resistance to New Church by using the powerful means at EWTN's disposal. Better to be declared an outcast or even "excommunicated" in defense of the Faith, as St. Athanasius was, than to give ground to error and subversion of the Church.

Sad to say, Mother abandoned the path of a forthright and conscientious resistance in the hope that an expedient corporate maneuver would save her apostolate by somehow allowing it to co-exist with the very prelates who wanted to destroy it. As we have seen in the preceding pages, her plan failed. In consequence, EWTN has become what all the lavishly funded New Church apostolates have become: a servitor of revolution in the Church; an organization whose "prestige" and financial resources allow it to compound the damage caused by Modernist innovation, while posing a major obstacle to the Church's restoration. The Church can never be restored by a compromise with Modernism, but compromise with the Modernist heresy is precisely what EWTN now presents as Catholic orthodoxy: an abhorrent marriage of the sacred and the profane in place of the timeless and unchanging faith of our fathers which built Christendom and Western civilization on the bedrock of unbroken apostolic and ecclesiastical tradition. The evidence compels the conclusion that Catholics ought to have no part of EWTN and its compromise with the Modernists. Catholics ought to abandon all support for this network gone wrong.

Once we have abandoned EWTN and the rest of the New Church establishment, we must seek out the still-existing sources of Tradition in the Church and cling to those, for Our Lord has not deserted us and we can still find the authentic goods of the Church if we look for them. We must find priests who offer the traditional Mass and traditional catechesis. We must find traditional Catholic schools for our children or else school them at home. We must study and impart to our children the unchanging doctrine and dogmas of the Faith, just as the laity did during the Arian crisis when, as Cardinal Newman observed, it was the "Church taught" more than "the Church teaching" that kept the Faith alive. We must pray the Rosary every day, frequent the traditional Mass and sacraments, and strive to advance in a traditional Catholic spiritual life.

As we do these things, we need to keep in mind constantly the gravity of this crisis: authority in the Church has broken down and simply cannot be trusted without the greatest of discernment by each of us, and always with Tradition as our infallible reference. Let us recall the advice of St. Vincent of Lerins that if:

some new contagion should seek to poison, not only a little part of the Church, but the whole Church at once then his [the Catholic's] greatest care should once again be to adhere to antiquity, which obviously cannot be seduced by any deceitful novelty.

If this assessment seems presumptuous or excessive, consider Cardinal Newman's description of the Arian crisis and recognize that what has happened in the Church before is happening again before our very eyes—only this time our situation is even worse:

> The body of bishops failed in their confession of the Faith.... They spoke variously, one against another; there was nothing, after [the Council of] Nicea [325 A.D.] of firm, unvarying, consistent testimony, for nearly sixty years. There were untrustworthy Councils, unfaithful bishops; there was weakness, fear of consequences, misguidance, delusion, hallucination, *endless, hopeless, extending into nearly every corner of the Catholic Church.* The comparatively few who remained faithful were discredited and driven into exile; the rest were either *deceivers or deceived.*[328]

No matter how long this crisis lasts we must not relax our grip on Tradition. We must not allow any part of Tradition to be diminished in our eyes, be it doctrine, dogma, morals, liturgy, spirituality or other observance handed down to us. We must hold fast to Tradition even though, as during the Arian crisis, the comparatively few members of the hierarchy who have remained faithful to Tradition are (like Father Gruner) being "discredited and driven into exile" by the holders of high offices and positions of influence in the Church, who are "either deceivers or deceived." St. Athanasius, hammer of the Arians, was "excommunicated," only to be canonized as one of the Church's greatest saints. His "excommunication" did not change the truth of the infallible dogma he defended: that Christ is true God as well as true man. Indeed, his unjust sentence was a badge of his fidelity. So it is today.

With good reason did Pius XII link his prophecy of the ecclesial

---

[328]John Henry Newman, *On Consulting the Faithful in Matters of Doctrine* (Kansas City: Sheed and Ward, 1961), page 77.

crisis we now endure to the "persistence of Mary" regarding a "divine warning" at Fatima about "the dangers which menace the Church." With good reason did Pius XII describe those dangers as a suicidal attempt to change the Church in her liturgy, theology and very soul—precisely what we have seen since Vatican II.

Exactly how is this crisis linked to the Message of Fatima? At Fatima God laid a divine precept upon His Church, conveyed to us by His own Blessed Mother: "In the end My Immaculate Heart will Triumph. The Holy Father will consecrate Russia to Me, which will be converted and a period of peace will be given to mankind." By divine precept, the Triumph of the Immaculate Heart of Mary, the conversion of Russia and peace in the world will come *only* when the Virgin's request for the Consecration of Russia is honored. Only then will the Fatima blessings be conferred upon the Church and the world.

Now, what happens when God lays down a divine precept to which a blessing is attached and His subjects evade obedience to that precept? As Holy Scripture teaches us time and again, the blessing becomes a curse, even a deadly curse, for God will not be mocked.

In the Book of Leviticus, for example, God enumerates the many blessings that will accrue to the Jews if they obey all of His specific precepts: "If you walk in My precepts," says God to the Jews, they will receive abundant harvests, a land "without fear" and "peace in your coasts... You shall pursue your enemies, and they will fall before you... I will look on you, and make you increase; you shall be multiplied..." (Lev. 26:3-9) But, God warns them, "if you will not hear Me, nor do *all* of My commandments," they will be visited with drought, famine, disease, and defeat in war. (Lev. 26:15-23) That is, the Jews will be cursed for their disobedience: "I will chastise you seven times more for your sins... I will bring seven times more plagues upon you for your sins..." (Lev. 26:18, 21) God then enumerates with even more specificity the elements of the divine curse that will result from disobedience: pestilence, starvation, deliverance into the hands of enemies, the destruction of cities, reducing them to wilderness, *sanctuaries reduced to desolation*, and the destruction of the whole land. (Lev. 26:24-38) Only when the Jews "confess their iniquities and the iniquities of their ancestors... " will the curse be lifted. (Lev. 26:39)

In the New Testament we find a particularly apt example: the stunning account of the fate of Ananias and Sapphira, who, as they each appeared before Saint Peter, were struck dead on the spot for trying to evade their duty to give alms to the Church by holding back a portion of the proceeds from land they had sold. (Acts 5:2-10) If they had given alms honestly in true obedience to God, they would have received His blessing. Instead, they were cursed. God's curse was not imposed because Ananias and Sapphira wished to retain part of their property for themselves (which they could have done in justice had they been honest about it), but rather because *they pretended to give God all that they had* when in truth they did not.

Today, likewise, certain members of the Vatican apparatus wish to pretend that they have given God all that He has asked respecting the Consecration of Russia, when in fact they have held back what is due to Him. Thus the Fatima blessings have been withheld and a Fatima curse imposed instead: the Church is being swept by apostasy, Russia has failed to convert, the world is racked by war against the born and the unborn.

This, then, is why Pius XII specifically tied his prevision of the crisis in the Church to the Message of Fatima. He could see that the crisis would result from a failure to heed "the divine warning" of the Message: "If My requests are not granted, Russia will spread her errors throughout the world raising up wars and persecutions against the Church, the good will be martyred, the Holy Father will have much to suffer, various nations will be annihilated." The Third Secret is obviously a continuation of this warning, with specific reference to the consequences for the Church outside of Portugal. "In Portugal the dogma of the Faith will always be preserved" the Secret begins, and it is now manifest that Pius XII knew what follows these words: a prophecy of apostasy beginning, as Cardinal Ciappi has revealed, "at the top"—an apostasy caused by suicidal changes in the Church.

The Fatima curse will not be lifted until the divine command of Fatima is obeyed. But obedience, when it comes, will have to be exact, for God does not accept human substitutes for His precepts. What is "close enough for government work" is not nearly close enough for God. Just as the Old Testament figure of Naaman, the leader of the Syrian army, could not be cured of leprosy unless he did *exactly* as God's prophet had instructed him—bathe seven times in the River Jordan, not six times or in some other river—so also the Church will not be cured unless the Pope and the bishops do exactly as God commanded through His Mother in the Message of Fatima:

consecrate Russia, not the world, to the Immaculate Heart of Mary.[329] By such tests of obedience does God measure the faith of His subjects.

Sooner or later, God will obtain the obedience of His subjects. The Pope and the bishops will consecrate Russia, the Immaculate Heart will triumph, and the ecclesial crisis predicted in the Third Secret will be ended. Our heavenly Mother has promised us that "in the end" all these things will come to pass. No one can thwart God's will, even if He tolerates disobedience for a time.

Meanwhile, however, it falls to us to weather the consequences of the Fatima curse and to labor as best we can to secure the obedience that will lift the curse from us before we incur the ultimate sanctions, including the annihilation of nations. At the moment, humanly speaking, we are on our own. And yet we are hardly without resources. Although so much of the human leadership of the Church is failing at present, we have the Faith to guide us. And, above all, we have recourse to Jesus and Mary. Here we ought to remember the simple advice of Sister Lucy:

> We should not wait for an appeal to the world to come from Rome on the part of the Holy Father to do penance. Nor should we wait for the call to penance to come from our bishops in our dioceses, nor from the religious congregations. No! Our Lord has already very often used these means and the world has not paid attention. That is why now, it is necessary for *each one of us to begin to reform himself spiritually. Each person must not only save his own soul but also help all the souls that God has placed on our path.*

Sister Lucy also said that there can be no neutrality in this crisis: "From now on we must choose sides. Either we are for God or we are for the devil. There is no other possibility." Our choice, then, is clear: the Church of all time, as seen at Fatima and in 2,000 years of Tradition, or New Church, as seen on EWTN. If we wish to remain in the Church of all time and save our souls, we must flee the pied pipers of New Church and reform ourselves by practicing the perennial Faith without alteration or compromise: liturgical, doctrinal, dogmatic, moral and spiritual Tradition, including the

---

[329] 4 Kings 5:1-15, referred to in some Bibles as 2 Kings 5:1-15.

offering of penance to stay the hand of God. And, as Sister Lucy said, we must help others to do the same, while we work and pray for the day when the Fatima curse is lifted through obedience and the Fatima blessings are bestowed upon the Church and the world.

At the beginning of this discussion I said that the defenders of Tradition should no longer allow themselves to be framed by their Modernist accusers, and that it is the accusers, not the accused, who ought to stand trial for their views. That has been the burden of the arguments presented here. I believe I have met that burden.

But the aim of this exercise has not been to win an argument for the sake of winning an argument. My aim has been to serve the truth—the truth that more and more Catholics of good will are coming to see because it is simply undeniable, because it is completely and unavoidably obvious: that the Church is undergoing an apostasy, and that EWTN is part of it. It is fitting to conclude, however, not with a declaration that an indictment has been sustained, but with a plea to our brothers at EWTN to reconsider their course of conduct—for their own good, the good of the Church and the good of countless souls they could help bring back to the whole and entire Catholic Faith, if only they provided an uncompromising defense of authentic Roman Catholicism against those who have come so close to destroying it these past forty years. But this they have thus far refused to do, preferring instead to ally themselves with the destroyers while claiming to represent the standard of Catholic orthodoxy.

As our time grows short and apostasy spreads throughout former Christendom, more and more Catholics are coming to realize that nothing less than a total restoration of Roman Catholic Tradition is necessary to end the crisis in the Church and the world. While we look to our new Pope, Benedict XVI, to lead this restoration as only the Roman Pontiff can, each of us must assist in the work according to his station in the Church and his own opportunities and abilities. The directors and celebrities of EWTN have willingly taken upon themselves a high station indeed, and with that station comes a grave duty to the entire Church. This they must ponder in their hearts as the evidence of catastrophe mounts against their vain effort to make compromises with Modernism and the spirit of the world. So must we all ponder our respective duties, as we too are inclined in our weakness to compromise and thus betray our mission as confirmed soldiers of Christ.

I began this book with the observation that the men and women responsible for what EWTN has become since Mother Angelica's departure might believe they are doing a service to the Church and that they have the right to engage in their public mission, but if they consider attentively the evidence of what they are promoting they will no longer have the refuge of good faith. For the evidence shows beyond any doubt that what EWTN is broadcasting to the world is nothing other than a form of the Modernist heresy.

To recall what St. Pius X said of the Modernists in *Pascendi*: "There is no part of Catholic truth from which they hold their hand, none that they do not strive to corrupt." And so it is with EWTN. As we have seen, from liturgy, to theology, to traditional devotions such as the Rosary, to Catholic decency, modesty and sobriety, there is nothing EWTN has not in some way corrupted in its collaboration with the New Church establishment. I have shown that this corruption has extended even to the outright contradiction of infallibly defined dogmas of the Faith—first and foremost the dogma that there is no salvation outside of the Roman Catholic Church, a dogma on which the eternal welfare of every soul in the world depends. And surely *even EWTN's own directors* would have to admit that no one would be quicker to pronounce EWTN's "updated" version of Catholicism a Modernist corruption than St. Pius X himself, the very hammer of Modernism. Indeed, could anyone at EWTN seriously argue that that sainted Pope would be anything but horrified and outraged by the evidence I have presented here?

Those who have made EWTN what it is today, therefore, are confronted with two choices: abandon the network entirely for the Modernist corruption it now is, or else restore it immediately to sound orthodoxy in every department. The choice is theirs, and they cannot evade it, for the peril to countless souls who imbibe the corrupted Catholicism EWTN presents to the masses is beyond human calculation, and God will demand an accounting for every soul who is harmed by it. But if they will neither abandon nor correct their wayward enterprise, then faithful Catholics can only regard them, whatever their subjective intentions might be, as enemies of the Faith. Never again should they dare to hold themselves out as the standard of orthodoxy, when in truth they owe a great debt of reparation to the Church they have helped to damage and the good Catholics they have calumniated for nothing more than holding fast to Tradition.

Meanwhile, the continuing chastisement of the Church, the growing apostasy we see all around us, the looming annihilation of nations — these are Heaven's warnings that God will never accept any substitute for that which He entrusted to His Church to be handed down, completely intact, until "the consummation of the world". (Matt. 24:14) Nor will He accept anything less than what He commanded through the Virgin of Fatima for the salvation of souls, the welfare of the Church and peace among men in this epoch of human history. It is not possible for any informed Catholic to deny in good faith these unmistakable signs of the times. As the Third Secret of Fatima unfolds throughout the Church and the world, let those responsible for EWTN, let every Catholic in every nation, heed those signs and work for the salvation of souls and true reform in the Church, before an even greater chastisement is visited upon us all.

# INDEX

Accattoli, Luigi
  on apologies of John Paul II, 242
Act of Consecration of Pius XI, 117, 127, 224
  on status of Jews as former chosen
    people, 117
Akin, James
  claims conversion of Russia does not
    mean to Catholicism, 222
Albigensian heresy
  ended by Rosary, 166
Alessio, Mark, 220
Alonso, Father Joaquin, 222
Amerio, Romano, 32, 180
  on loss of essences in post-conciliar
    thought, 180
**apostasy**, i, ii, 3, 9, 19, 21, 25, 27, 41, 150,
    178, 216, 225, 236, 239, 241, 247, 251,
    252, 253, 257, 259, 261
  and contents of Third Secret, 27
  and Great Apostasy at end of time, 20
  and loss of consecrated souls, 20
  as induced by changes in Church since
    Vatican II, 41
  as promoted by EWTN, 49
  as rebellion against Church, 19
  as rebellion against Divine
    commandments, 20
  as resurgence of Modernist heresy, 13
  as revolt against Divine
    commandments, 23
  as turning away from Catholic Faith,
    25
  Book of Apocalypse on, 20-21
  broader sense of, 19-23
  caused by altering liturgy and theology
    of Church, 56-59, 69
  definition of, 19-21
  ignored by EWTN, 157
  Judaization of Church as avenue to,
    150, 221
  Latin Mass as bulwark against, 57-59
  Modernism as, ii
  not seen in Church before Vatican II, 23
  of Emperor Julian (331-363), 19
  of entire West, 22
  of Europe, 21, 22
  Pope John Paul II at Fatima, 20
  sense used in this book, 20
  silent apostasy, noted by John Paul II,
    21, 23, 24, 40, 241
  since Vatican II, 9
  St. Thomas Aquinas on, 20
  Third Secret's warning of, 5, 25, 26
Aquinas, St. Thomas, 19, 21, 23, 48, 118,
    129, 160, 163, 165, 194, 244
  on apostasy, 19
  on right to rebuke Pope causing
    scandal, 163
*Arcanum Divinae Sapientiae*, 175
Arguello, Kiko, 220
Arroyo, Raymond, 1, 2, 3, 4, 5, 6, 54, 153,
    154, 155, 208, 240, 241, 248
  defends pagan rituals at papal
    liturgies, 151
  disparages John Paul II's pre-Vatican II
    predecessors, 240
**Association of Hebrew Catholics
  (AHC)**, 122, 123, 124, 125, 130, 131,
    137, 140, 142, 143, 146, 147, 148, 149
  advocates separate Catholic
    community for baptism of Jews,
    123
  claims Catholic Church has become
    Gentile community, 123
  EWTN's aggressive promotion of, 122-
    123
  Original Manifesto of, 123
  planning Hebrew para-liturgy in
    Church, 148
  promotes celebration of Jewish
    holidays and Sabbath by Catholics,
    147
  promotes creation of Hebrew Catholic
    canonical community, 122-124
  promotes Hebrew calendar for
    Catholics, 147
  rejects assimilation of Jewish people
    into Gentile Church, 123-124, 134-
    138
  revises Sign of the Cross formula, 147
Athanasian Creed, 42, 194
Augustine, St., 72, 106, 122, 128, 129, 160,
    194
*Avvenire*
  reports Pope's acknowledgment he did
    not consecrate Russia in 1984, 224
Bacci, Antonio Cardinal, 56
Bandas, Msgr. Rudolph
  on Vatican II causing blight of Church,

24

baptism
    drastic decline of after Vatican II, 109
    necessity of for salvation, 74
Barrack, Marty, 149
Basil, St., the Great, 250
    on persecution of traditional Catholics
        by Church authorities, 250
Benedict XVI, Pope, i, 15, 26, 32, 35, 101,
    113, 159, 235, 243, 244, 259
    election of, 235
Benedicta, St. Teresa, 145
Benkovic, Johnnette, 179, 180
Bernard, St., of Clairvaux
    on pope in danger of hell for allowing
        bad bishops, 161
Billington, Professor James, 37
Bonacci, Mary Beth, 174
Boniface VIII, Pope, 71
Bono, rock star
    lauds John Paul II as showman, 244
Bruskewitz, Bishop Fabian, 122
    on right to rebuke Pope for
        malfeasance, 161
Bugnini, Annibale, 171, 172
    role in changing Mass, 172
    sacked and sent to Iran, 172
    tries to change Rosary, 171
Buonaiuto, Father Aldo, 68
Calvin, John, 59
Campaigning for Christ, 139
Cano, Bishop Melchior, 163
    on folly of defending every papal
        decision, 160
Cantate Domino, 72, n. 134
Capelinha (Little Chapel) at Fatima, 211
Carroll, Dr. Willliam, 229
Casti Connubii, 175, 185
Castrillon Hoyos, Dario Cardinal, 230
    admits right to criticize post-Vatican II
        changes in Church, 113
    admits Society of Saint Pius X not in
        schism, 113
    persecution of Father Nicholas Gruner
        by, 230
Catholic Encyclopedia, 44, 89, 194, 199
Catholic Family News, 213-214, 220, 229
Chopra, Deepak, 201
Ciappi, Luigi Cardinal, 9
    on contents of Third Secret, 25, 36
    on Third Secret as warning of apostasy,
        26, 27, 247
    on Third Secret's prediction of

apostasy at top of Church, 41, 257
Communion in the hand, 58, 62, 63, 64,
    65, 66, 67, 68, 226
    as exception to Church law, 58, n. 71
    defended by EWTN, 62-66
    introduction of through disobedience
        to Church law, 58, n. 71
    leads to theft of consecrated Hosts by
        Satanists, 68-69
Communion on the tongue, 58, 59, 62,
    65, 226
    still the law of the Church, 63, 66
Congar, Yves, 192
    book suppressed by Vatican, 192
    on God's alleged feminine aspect, 191
    on Russian Revolution in Church at
        Vatican II, 209
    relied upon by Scott Hahn, 192
Consecration of Russia, 221, 223, 224,
    229, 256, 257
    not done for fear of offending Russian
        Orthodox, 223
    not yet done, 221, 222
Consueverunt Romani Pontifices, 167
Correio da Manhã, 214
Council of Florence, 70, 90, 108, 109,
    120, 121, 130, 134, 148, 149
    condemns adherence to Mosaic rituals,
        118, 120
    condemns refusal to embrace received
        and approved rites of Church, 43
    on conversion of Jews for salvation, 134
    on dogma nulla salus (no salvation
        outside Catholic Church), 108
    on dogma of hell, 70
    on fires of hell, 70
    on no salvation for schismatics, 108
    on supersession of Old Covenant by
        New, 118
    temporary resolution of Greek schism
        at, 108
Council of Lyons, 129, 194
    on torments of hell, 70
Council of Nicea (787 A.D.), 43, 255
    on duty to abhor novelty, 43
Council of Trent, 11, 42, 43, 61, 70, 72,
    88, 91, 96, 98, 152, 160, 183, 193, 198
    on exclusion of unbaptized infants
        from Heaven, 75
    on nature of sanctifying grace, 199
    on necessity of Sacraments for
        salvation, 88
    on pro multis (for many) in

Consecration formula of Mass, 60
on received and approved rites of
Church, 42
on Sacraments as more than spiritual
nourishment alone, 96
on simultaneity of justification and
sanctification, 198
on the necessity of the Sacrament of
Confession for forgiveness, 98
Cranmer, Thomas, 59
*Crossing the Threshold of Hope*, 71, 156
on eternal punishment, 71
Cyril, St., 127
Dalai Lama, 237
Damian, St. Peter
on conversion of the Jews, 129
Davidson, Professor Philip
on politics of hate, 210
Davies, Michael, 32, 35, 162
dialogue, 10, 14, 30, 47, 102, 111, 125,
139, 140, 175, 218, 222, 237, 243
Diego, Blessed Juan, 152, 153, 155
pagan rituals during beatification of,
151
*Divini Illius Magistri*, 206
**dogma**, 9, 11, 13, 14, 33, 34, 46, 49, 70, 74,
75, 76, 77, 78, 79, 81, 82, 83, 84, 85, 86,
92, 96, 99, 100, 105, 109, 111, 112, 113,
116, 120, 124, 132, 139, 140, 142, 151,
161, 162, 194, 195, 198, 209, 211, 225,
226, 228, 229, 245, 247, 249, 252, 253,
255, 257, 260
attack on predicted in Third Secret, 25
of absolute simplicity of God, 198
of indwelling of Trinity in soul, 199
of necessity of Sacraments for
salvation, 88
of no salvation outside Catholic
Church (*extra ecclesiam nulla salus
est*), 71, 109
of Original Sin, 107
of processions of Trinity, 194
of supersession of Old Covenant by
New Covenant, 118
of the *filioque*, 107
Dominic, St., 166
*Dominum et Vivificantem*, 239
**Donovan, Colin B.**, 61, 101, 109, 110,
112, 123, 156, 178, 210, 212, 214, 228,
230, 231, 232
continues to calumniate Fr. Gruner, 232
defends elimination of kneeling at
Communion, 61

defends Pope kissing Koran, 157
EWTN's Vice President for Theology,
123
falsely accuses Father Nicholas Gruner
of schism, 210
heads EWTN's theological committee,
54
questions permanency of Pope Leo
XIII's teaching on invalidity of
Anglican orders, 100
refuses to admit sacrilege occurred at
Fatima Shrine, 212
refuses to recognize failure of
ecumenism, 110
Dreher, Rod, 161, n. 200
*Ecclesia in Europa*, 21
ecumenism, 10, 30, 47, 55, 101, 109, 110,
111, 112, 175, 231, 248
can be criticized according to John Paul
II, 111
not a doctrine, 30
Eucharistic Prayer II, 60
resembles Protestant Communion
Service, 59
Eugene IV, Pope, 72
**EWTN**
abandons necessity of return of
dissidents, 116
abandons *nulla salus* dogma, 115
advises that conception of children a
daily decision, 188
as Trojan horse in Church, 251
attacks Father Nicholas Gruner sixty-
six times, 210
broadcasts Las Vegas lounge act on
Christmas Eve, 208
calls attachment to Tradition
schismatic, 113
censors Mother Angelica's shows, 228
claims reversal of Church teaching, 84,
140
covers up sacrilege at Fatima Shrine,
212-216
defends Communion in the hand, 62-
67
defends Hindu scandal at Fatima
shrine, 157
defends interreligious Assisi events,
including witch doctors, 156
defends Pope kissing Koran, 157
demotes traditional form of Rosary,
165
denounced by former supporter, 229-

232
denounces Catholics who reject
  innovation of Church, 247
double standard concerning schism,
  112, 113
endorses Association of Hebrew
  Catholics, 123-124
exempts Mel Gibson from its
  condemnation of Catholics
  opposed to changes in Church, 248
falsely accuses Father Gruner of
  schism, 112
falsely accuses loyal Catholics of
  schism, 112
good elements of, 8
ignores "silent apostasy" admitted by
  John Paul II, 239
inconsistent view of schism, 112
joins New World Order in elevating
  John Paul II above predecessors,
  235-242
liberalization after Mother Angelica's
  departure, 5, 10
loses militancy after Mother's
  departure, 4
"moderate" Modernism of, 53
Modernism of, 12, 15, 49
more insidious than overt liberalism, 7
opposes restoration of traditional Latin
  Mass, 40, 67
papal idolatry of, 158
parental warnings concerning content
  of, 181, 207, 252
practices politics of hate in Church, 211
preaches "fullness" rather than
  salvation, 99-100
promotes Association of Hebrew
  Catholics, 122-125, 134-139
promotes blasphemous interpretation
  of marital relations, 181
promotes Catholic karaoke, 205
promotes changing of Rosary, 165
promotes error that all religions are
  more or less good and
  praiseworthy, 79, 115
promotes Hahn's undermining of
  Trinitarian theology, 190-196
promotes Judaizing movement in
  Church, 122-150
promotes mistranslation of *pro multis*
  in Mass, 59
promotes New Mass, 40, 59-69
promotes NFP as mystical experience,

177
promotes NFP cult, 176-178
promotes novelty in Church, ii
promotes pagan rituals during Mass,
  151
promotes rock music, 204
promotes same Modernist innovations
  condemned by Pope Pius XII, 246
promotes theology of the body, 174
promotes Zionism, 142-145
pronounces New Mass superior to
  traditional Mass, 67
revises Message of Fatima, 216-224
seeming orthodoxy of, ii
turn toward Modernism of, i
undermines Catholic doctrine on
  return of the dissidents, 85-116
undermines dogma on no salvation
  outside Church, 76-84
undermines dogma on supersession of
  Old Covenant, 120-142
undermines necessity of Sacraments
  for the salvation of all men, 91-100
Ex Quo
  on necessity of reunion of Orthodox
  with Rome for salvation, 107
Fahey, Father Denis, 129, 136
  on Talmud, 136
*Fatima Crusader, The*, 110, 159, 210, 211,
  213, 215, 223
Fatima Shrine, 211, 227
  sacrilegious scandal at, 157, 211, 212,
  213, 214, 215
Ferro, Giovanni
  on opposing currents let loose by John
  Paul II, 243
Flummerfelt, Robert, J.C.L., 64
  defends Communion in the hand for
  EWTN, 64
Foley, Bishop David
  conflict with Mother Angelica, 3
  decree banning Mass facing altar, 3
  decree banning televised Masses facing
  east, 3
  instigates Vatican investigation of
  Mother Angelica, 3
Fortuna, Fr. Stan, 206
  EWTN's rapping priest, 206
Fourth Lateran Council, 71
  on absolute simplicity of God, 198
Fox News, 237
Fox, Fr. Robert J., 212, 213, 216, 217, 240
  attacks Father Gruner on EWTN, 212

covers up Fatima Shrine sacrilege on
EWTN, 212
revises Message of Fatima, 216
Foxman, Abraham, 237-238
French Revolution, 36, 209
Cardinal Ratzinger on, 37
Cardinal Ratzinger on Church's
attempted reconciliation with, 38
**Gamber, Msgr. Klaus**, 10, 32, 38, 39, 55,
57, 59, 60, 225, 226, 249, 250, 253
criticizes mistranslation of *pro multis* in
Mass, 60
on destruction of Roman Rite, 39
on dire state of Church today, 249
on failure of Vatican II, 38
on need for new St. Athanasius in
Church, 249
on New Mass as break with Church
Tradition, 39
on Protestantization of Catholic
worship, 9
on spread of Modernism in Church
after Vatican II, 250
Gantley, Mark J., J.C.L., 63, 64
defends Communion in the hand for
EWTN, 63
Geraghty, Richard, 66, 103, 104, 105
defends Communion in the hand for
EWTN, 65
Gibson, Mel, 29, 132, 237, 248
criticizes Vatican II reforms on
television, 248
director of *The Passion of the Christ*, 248
example of what mass media could do
for Faith, 248
refuses to attend New Mass, 248
uses television to promote Catholic
Tradition, 248
gnostic, 174, 219, 220
gnosticism, 14, 174, 176, 246
Goldstein, David
preached Jewish conversion, 139
Good Friday liturgy
prayer for conversion of Jews in, 131
Gorbachev, Mikhail
lauds late John Paul II, 236
Great Western Schism, 161
Gregory the Great, Pope St., 72
Gregory XVI, Pope, 73, 104, 115
condemns mixed marriages with
schismatics, 105
condemns religious indifferentism, 83,
104

Grodi, Marcus, 94, 95, 96, 97, 98, 99, 102,
123, 134, 135, 240
extols the "meaning" of John Paul II,
244
suggests Protestants not welcome in
Church before Vatican II, 240
**Groeschel, Fr. Benedict**, 78, 79, 80, 81,
82, 83, 86, 87, 88, 89, 90, 91, 92, 93, 102
afraid of stealing souls from Protestant
clergy, 93
denies necessity of Holy Communion
for salvation, 89
denies necessity of Sacraments for
salvation, 87
denies *nulla salus* dogma, 78
disparages teaching of Pius XI, 87
suggests Orthodox Masses fulfill
Sunday obligation for Catholics,
102
Gruner, Father Nicholas, 15, 28, 112,
210-214, 216-217, 219, 221, 224-225,
228-232, 249, 252, 255
EWTN's false accusations of
denounced by EWTN supporter,
231
Guerra, Father Luciano
allows Hindu "priest" and followers to
use altar at Fatima Shrine, 211
attempts to distance himself from
Fatima Shrine scandal, 215
hosts congress of Buddhists, Hindus,
etc. at Fatima Shrine, 211
invites heretics and schismatics to use
Fatima Shrine, 211
says all religions must mingle at
Fatima Shrine, 211
Haas, John, 174
**Hahn, Scott**, 188, 190, 191, 192, 193, 194,
195, 196, 197, 198, 199, 200, 201, 202
admits novelty of view on Trinity, 194
claims Holy Ghost is bridal and
feminine, 191
claims Trinity a family, 191
confusion caused by, 201
departs from Catholic Trinitarian
dogma, 195-201
dubious theology criticized by Dale
Vree, 200
dubious theology criticized by Dr.
Monica Miller, 197
dubious theology criticized by Edward
O'Neill, 195
dubious theology criticized by *New*

*Oxford Review*, 195, 196
EWTN celebrity, 190
false disjunction between justification
and sanctification of, 197-199
likens Holy Ghost's role to that of his
wife, 193
novelties of criticized by *New Oxford
Review*, 195
service of feminist theology by, 201
undermines Catholic dogma of Trinity,
194
**Hebrew Catholics**, 5, 122, 124, 125, 130,
131, 134, 135, 137, 138, 139, 140, 141,
142, 145, 146, 147, 148, 149, 150, 217,
227
Association of, 122
distinguish themselves from other
Catholics, 124
promoted by EWTN, 122, 124-125, 134-
139, 247
seek Hebrew para-liturgy in Church,
148
seek separate community and baptism
in Catholic Church, 123
*see also* Association of Hebrew
Catholics
hell, 21, 33, 82, 96, 161, 182
dogma of, 70
John Paul II on eternal punishment in,
71
not empty, 70
Our Lady of Fatima on, 176
torments of, 70
Heras, Msgr. Michael, 154, 155
defends pagan rituals during papal
liturgies for EWTN, 153
Hernandez, Carmen, 220
Holy Office, 48, 56
affirms teaching of popes on return of
dissidents to Church, 85
Hoyos, see Castrillon Hoyos, Dario
Cardinal
*Humani Generis*, 76
*Humanum Genus*, 37
ICEL
mistranslation of *pro multis* by, 60
Ignatius, St. (Church Father), 128
Immaculate Heart, 34, 216, 221, 256, 258
Consecration of Russia to, 223
triumph of, 235
Innocent III, Pope, 71
*Inside the Vatican*, 29
on Pope John Paul II being advised not

to consecrate Russia, 222
interreligious dialogue, 10, 30
Irenaeus, St., 128
Israeli Foreign Minister
lauds late John Paul II, 237
**Jews**, 14, 80, 81, 99, 102, 108, 117, 121,
123, 124, 125, 126, 127, 128, 129, 130,
131, 132, 133, 134, 135, 136, 137, 138,
139, 140, 141, 142, 143, 144, 145, 146,
148, 150, 160, 226, 238, 242, 256
benefit of Mass to remainder of the
elect, 60
called elder brothers by John Paul II,
237
calling of (to convert to Christ), 129
cut off from olive tree (Christ), 127
must be grafted into Christ, 128
no salvation for outside Church, 71, 73
opinion on conversion of at end of
history, 129
prayers for conversion of on Good
Friday, 130
**John Paul II, Pope**, i, 1, 6, 9, 13, 15, 20,
21, 24, 25, 28, 40, 71, 87, 100, 101, 111,
112, 139, 151, 154, 156, 157, 159, 161,
163, 165, 175, 177, 178, 192, 220, 222,
223, 225, 235, 236, 237, 238, 239, 240,
241, 242, 243, 244, 247
changes Rosary, 164
death of, 235
decline in conversions during reign of,
240
in Mexico City 2002, 151
kissing of Koran by, 163
lauded by head of UN as pioneer of
interfaith dialogue, 237
lauded as number one humanist by
Mikhail Gorbachev, 236
lauded as showman by rock star Bono,
244
lauded post-mortem by Colin Powell
for his faith for the world, 239
lauded post-mortem by Fox News for
humanitarianism, 237
lauded post-mortem by head of B'Nai
B'rith Anti-Defamation League, 237
lauded post-mortem by Israeli Prime
Minister, 237
lauded post-mortem by MTV, 236
lauded post-mortem by press and
world leaders after death, 236
listing of scandalous actions of, 158
on decline of vocations and births

during reign of, 176
on hell, 71
on opening to the world at Vatican II, 24
on "silent apostasy" in the Church, 20, 27
on Vatican II fruits being confused with devil's designs, 24
one hundred apologies of, 242
praised for criticizing Church's attitude toward Jews, 238
theology of the body of, 174
John XXII, Pope, 163
denounced for heresy, 162
erroneous theology of, 162
retracts error on deathbed, 162
John XXIII, Pope, 23, 24, 32, 35, 151
defends Latin Mass against innovators, 39
on "opening to the world" at Vatican II, 23
Johnston, George Sim, 174
*Journey Home*, 94, 95, 123, 124, 134, 137, 139, 142, 146, 148, 184, 240
Julian the Apostate, 19
Kasper, Walter Cardinal, 101, 102, 120, 121
claims Old Covenant never revoked, 120
claims Old Covenant still saves Jews, 120
denies supersession of Old Covenant by New Covenant, 120
questions Pope Leo XIII's teaching on Anglican orders, 101
rejects Church teaching on return of dissidents, 101
**Keating, Karl**, 217, 221, 223, 224
attacks Father Gruner for EWTN, 221
calls for shunning Fr. Gruner, 217, 224
claims Consecration of Russia done, 223
EWTN expert, 217
Modernist views of, 225
on alleged "fringey" ideas of traditional Catholics, 224
promotes Association of Hebrew Catholics, 218
Keck, Doug
transforms content of EWTN, 5
urges Mother Angelica to resign, 5
**Latin Mass**, 7, 26, 29, 35, 44, 56, 66, 69, 103, 152, 172, 218, 219, 225, 226, 228,
229, 248
attended exclusively by Mel Gibson, 248
bulwark against heresy, 57
defended by Pope John XXIII, 39
defended by Pope Pius XII, 39
EWTN opposes restoration of, 40
five basic elements of, 57
Msgr. Gamber on destruction of, 39
never legally forbidden, 28
Lémann, Fathers
on conversion of Jews, 129
Leo XII, Pope
on no salvation outside Catholic Church, 72
**Leo XIII, Pope**, 37, 101, 166
encyclical, *Humanum Genus*, 37
on absolute inerrancy of the Bible, 89
on invalidity of Anglican priestly orders, 58, 100
on marriage, 175
on Masonic assault against religion, 37
on necessity of Orthodox assenting to all Catholic doctrine and dogma, 108
on necessity of reunion of Orthodox with Rome, 106
on Protestant change of worship to change belief, 59
on the Rosary, 166, 169
Levis, Father Robert, 76, 77, 78, 83, 109, 120, 121, 223
claims Vatican II loosened requirements for salvation, 76
Leviticus, Book of, 256
Liberius, Pope
sides with Arian heretics, 253
*Life on the Rock* (EWTN series), 175, 204, 205, 206, 242
cool Catholicism of, 204
discussion of homosexual lifestyle on air, 206
filled with rock music, 204
on-air discussion of sexual matters, 206
Luther, Martin, 152
attacks traditional Latin Mass, 59
Mahony, Roger Cardinal, 2, 3, 5, 7, 113, 248
agitates Vatican against Mother Angelica, 2
canonical complaint against Mother Angelica, 2
conflict with Mother Angelica, 2

*Marriage… for Better, Forever!* (EWTN series), 178-202
Mary, Father Francis, 204, 242
Matatics, Gerry
on sacrilege at WYD '93, 67
Matt, Michael
on sacrileges at papal Mass, 1980, 68
McBrien, Richard P., 192
*Memoriale Domini*, 58, 63
maintains Communion on tongue as law of Church, 58
**Message of Fatima**, 246, 249, 256, 257
and post-conciliar crisis in Church, 26
as call to conversion, 20
as warning of crisis in Church, 246
attempted debunkation of by Cardinal Ratzinger, 34
defenders of attacked by EWTN, 15
guide to ending Church crisis, 15
Modernist revision of, 35
revised by New Church, 10, 216
stripped of prophetic content by Cardinal Ratzinger's interpretation, 34
traditional Catholic understanding of, 216
undermining of by Fr. Robert J. Fox, 216, 217
Messianic Judaism, 123
defended on EWTN by David Moss, 137
Miller, Dr. Monica, 196, 197, 200
*Mirari Vos*, 83, 85, 104
on cutting off of schismatics from Church, 105
**Modernism**, 2, 13, 45, 46, 48, 53, 84, 242, 245, 254, 259, 260
definition of, 45
essence of, iii
Oath Against, 46
Pope St. Pius X condemns as heresy, i
*See also, Pascendi Dominici Gregis*
**Modernist**, i, ii, 2, 5, 7, 8, 12, 13, 15, 17, 34, 45, 48, 49, 53, 60, 64, 69, 71, 78, 82, 83, 86, 88, 89, 91, 94, 109, 112, 113, 120, 124, 125, 128, 134, 137, 146, 147, 149, 172, 178, 186, 191, 202, 215, 217, 228, 245, 246, 247, 249, 250, 252, 253, 254, 259, 260
as reformer, described, 47
Cardinal Mahony's pastoral letter as, 2
denial of supersession of Old Covenant by New, 120

description of, 45
errors of, 6
uprising of, after Vatican II, 48
writings of, iii
Mondin, Father Giovanbattista
on demissionization of Catholic Church after Vatican II, 110
Morris, Bishop Thomas, 34
viewed Vatican II teachings as tentative, 33
*Mortalium Animos*, 94, 110
calls for return of non-Catholics to Church, 85
condemns ecumenical movement, 85
on corrupt Protestant version of Gospel, 95
on no salvation outside Catholic Church, 111
**Moss, David**, 123, 124, 125, 127, 128, 129, 130, 131, 133, 134, 135, 136, 137, 138, 139, 140, 143, 145, 146, 147, 148, 149, 217, 221
claims Catholic Church became sociologically Gentile 1800 years ago, 124
claims Church has denied Jews their collective vocation, 124
claims Church sociologically Gentile on EWTN, 134
claims Jews and Catholics live under same covenant with God, 125, 128
claims Jews cannot be what God made them in Catholic Church, 137
claims Jews must be corporate entity within Church, 135
claims Jews must stay out of Church to remain faithful, 135
claims Judaism still confers grace of faith, 130
claims New Covenant did not revoke Old Covenant, 125
claims St. Edith Stein died for Israeli state, 142
claims Vatican II corrected deficiencies of Church regarding assimilation of Jews, 124
denies Catholic Church is New Israel in place of old Israel, 138
featured by EWTN, 124
modernist double-talk by, 137
President of Association of Hebrew Catholics, 124
promotes Catholic Seder suppers on

EWTN, 146
promotes Hebrew Mass on Rosh
haShanah, 146
promotes Hebrew para-liturgy for
Hebrew Catholics, 148
promotes Zionism on EWTN, 142-143
rejects targeting of peoples for
conversion, 139
revises Sign of the Cross formula, 148
Moss, Rosalind
claims to be Catholic is to be Jewish,
121
EWTN celebrity, 124
rejects targeting of Jews for conversion,
140
**Mother Angelica**, 59
becomes totally detached from EWTN, 1
conflict with Bishop Foley, 3
conflict with Cardinal Mahony, 2
denounces liberal Bishops, female
Christ at Stations, 6
departure of, i
doubts Third Secret fully revealed, 1
drastically reduced role of, 2
likens New Mass to Protestant Liturgy,
7, 59
praised by *Remnant* newspaper, 6
resigns as CEO of EWTN, 4
returns to traditional nun's habit, 6
should have followed example of
Athanasius, 253
snubs Bishop Foley at Shrine
dedication, 3
suffers strokes, 1
surrenders control over EWTN to lay
board, 4-5
Mother Teresa of Calcutta
condemns Communion in the hand, 66
MTV
lauds John Paul II after death, 236
Murphy-O'Connor, Archbishop Cormac
rejects return of the dissidents, 102
Mystical Body, 76, 95, 117, 119, 121, 129
includes all nations, 138
is the Catholic Church, 126
is the New Israel, 129
*Mystici Corporis*, 95
on supersession of Old Covenant by
New Covenant, 118
Naaman, 257
Neo-Catechumenal Way, 220
heterodoxy of, 219
Judaized liturgy of, 219

promoted by *This Rock*, 219
New Church
definition of, i
distinguished from authentic Roman
Catholicism, 10
New Mass (*Novus Ordo Missae*), 9, 13, 36,
56
embodies demands of Protestant
"reformers", 57
English text contradicts Council of
Trent, 61
has harmed the Church, 56
never legally imposed on Church, 28
*New Oxford Review*, 195, 196, 199, 200,
201
criticizes theology of Scott Hahn, 195,
196
Newman, John Cardinal, 29, 162, 254,
255
on Arian crisis compared with current
crisis, 255
on limits of papal infallibility, 162
*Nostra Aetate*, 139
Oath Against Modernism, 46, 48
forbids view that dogmas evolve, 84
O'Neill, Edward, 195
Orthodox church, 102, 103, 105, 108
Orthodox churches
doctrinal differences with Catholic
Church, 107, 108
Orthodox rabbis
reject Israeli state as unbiblical, 143
Ott, Ludwig, 75, 194, 198, 199
Ottaviani, Alfredo Cardinal, 56, 177
Intervention of, 56
publicly criticizes New Mass, 56
*Pascendi Dominici Gregis* (Against
Modernism), 2, 6, 43, 45, 53, 69, 172,
260
censures enemies of any Church
tradition, 42
condemnation of ecclesiastical
novelties by, 209
condemns Modernist as reformer, 47
on Modernism as synthesis of all
heresies, 45
*see also* Modernism, Modernist
**Paul VI, Pope**, 23, 24, 28, 32, 33, 36, 38,
39, 41, 44, 48, 56, 58, 63, 64, 167, 168,
169, 171, 172, 176, 227, 246
admits he never forbade Latin Mass, 29
changes Mass, but not Rosary, 172
forbids innovation of Rosary, 167

laments opening to the world at
  Vatican II, 23
laments self-demolition of Church, 24
*Quo Primum* never revoked by, 44
rejects changes to Rosary proposed by
  Bugnini, 171
says smoke of Satan entered Church,
  24
Paul, St., 5, 11, 19, 20, 27, 118, 120, 123,
  127, 128, 130, 141, 142, 158, 169, 183,
  199, 252
  condemns Judaizers of early Church,
    120
  on abrogation of Old Law, 117-118
  on apostasy in Church, 251
  on Christ as fulfillment of promise to
    Abraham, 126-128
  on Christians as true heirs of Abraham,
    126-128
  on false Gospel, 27
  on Jews being grafted back into Christ
    by conversion, 129
  on passing away of Old Law, 126-127
  on passing of Old Covenant in favor of
    New, 117
  on superiority of celibate to married
    state, 183
  rebukes St. Peter, first Pope, 160
Peterson, Dr. William J., 54, 55, 62, 67,
  100, 101, 110, 112, 156, 157, 158, 212,
  228, 229
  employed by EWTN, 54
  fired by EWTN for questioning party
    line, 228
  on censorship of Mother Angelica, 228
  on collapse of missions due to
    ecumenism, 110
  on credibility of EWTN, 212
  on EWTN defending Pope kissing
    Koran, 157
  on EWTN's *a la carte* liturgy, 62
  on EWTN's defense of Assisi event
    scandals, 156
  on EWTN's elimination of kneeling at
    Communion, 61
  on EWTN's refusal to criticize any
    papal action, 156
  on hopes in Mother Angelica, 54
  on idolatry of Pope, 157
Pharisees, 13, 122, 128, 135, 214, 229, 250
Pius IV, Pope, 43
  profession of Faith of, 43
Pius IX, Blessed Pope, 36, 37, 43, 73, 74,
  81, 110
  condemns equation of Protestantism
    with Catholicism, 82
  condemns reconciliation of Pope to
    modern civilization, 37
  condemns universal salvation, 74
  on salvation outside the Church, 75
  Syllabus of Errors of, 37
Pius V, Pope St., 60, 166, 167, 168, 169,
  172
  canonizes Latin Mass in perpetuity, 44
  canonizes traditional Rosary, 167
  on exclusion of unbaptized infants
    from Heaven, 75
Pius VIII, Pope, 72
Pius X, Pope St., iii, 13, 36, 43, 45, 46, 48,
  53, 69, 89, 103, 112, 153, 172, 202, 207,
  209, 231, 242, 260
  Catechism of (on salvation), 73
  condemns Modernist as reformer, 47
  on adherence to ecclesiastical
    traditions, 42
  on Modernism, i, iii, 2
  on necessity of Orthodox reunion with
    Rome for salvation, 109
  on reunion of Orthodox with Rome,
    107-109
  would be horrified by New Mass, 9
Pius XI, Pope, 25, 87, 94, 95, 110, 111,
  115, 117, 127, 206
  condemns discussion of sexual details
    with children, 206
  condemns ecumenical movement, 85,
    110
  condemns idea that all religions are
    more or less good and
    praiseworthy, 110
  condemns pan-Christian movements,
    114
  forbids Catholic participation in non-
    Catholic assemblies, 85
  on corrupt Protestant version of
    Gospel, 95
  on figurehead Pope desired by world,
    236
  on Jews as former chosen people, 117
  on marriage, 175
  on no salvation outside Catholic
    Church, 111
  on primary and secondary ends of
    marriage, 185
Pius XII, Pope, i, 49, 57, 76, 83, 96, 118,
  216, 225, 227, 238, 246, 247, 256, 257

affirms Catholic doctrine on necessity
of return of dissidents to Church,
85
calls for Protestants to return to
Church, 95
condemns watering down of dogma
*nulla salus*, 76
defends Latin Mass against innovation,
39
links coming crisis in Church to Fatima
Message, 26, 255, 257
on supersession of Old Covenant by
New Covenant, 118
prophecy of crisis in Church, 25, 26, 36,
48, 246
says Protestants are separated from
Mystical Body, 95
strips Yves Congar of teaching
positions, 192
warns of ecclesial suicide through
innovation, 25, 48, 49, 56
Pontifical Council for Religious
Relations with the Jews, 120
**Popcak, Gregory**, 178, 179, 180, 181, 182,
183, 184, 185, 186, 187, 188, 191, 201,
202, 203
cites *Kama Sutra*, 184
claims carnal relations make places
holy, 185
claims NFP a duty, 187
claims sexual relations are a prayer,
179
EWTN celebrity, 178
likens lovemaking to Consecration at
Mass, 179
on monthly decision to conceive or not
conceive, 188
on sex as preparation for beatific
vision, 181, 182
on sexuality of priests and nuns, 179
promotes blasphemous analogy to Big
Bang, 201
promotes blasphemous interpretation
of marital relations, 180-181, 202
promotes NFP cult, 186
recommends boys charting mothers
and sisters, 186
sexualizes theology, 178
Poupard, Paul Cardinal
on mass unbelief today, 21
*Præclara Gratulationis Publicæ*
on necessity of reunion of Orthodox
with Rome for salvation, 106

processions of Holy Trinity
dogma of, 194
processions of the Trinity, 194, 195, 196,
197, 200
theology of undermined by Scott
Hahn, 195
*Professio Fidei*, 101
*pro multis* (for many), 59, 60
*Providentissimus Deus*, 89
*Quo Primum*
never revoked by Pope Paul VI, 44
not followed by Pope Paul VI, 172
**Ratzinger, Joseph Cardinal**, 26, 28, 29,
32, 33, 34, 35, 36, 37, 38, 39, 55, 59, 60,
160, 203, 225, 226
admits Latin Mass never forbidden, 29
admits process of decay after Vatican
II, 32
attempt to debunk Message of Fatima
by, 34
claims qualitative renewal of Church
despite decline, 241
criticizes attempt to suppress Latin
Mass, 26
election as Pope Benedict XVI, 235
on attempt to reconcile Church to era
begun at French Revolution, 38
on collapse of liturgy as cause of crisis,
35
on French Revolution, 37
on New Mass as breach in liturgical
history, 36
on Pope being subject to Tradition, 159
on Pope not being absolute monarch,
159
on Vatican II documents as countersyllabus, 36
on Vatican II wrongly treated as zero
hour, 35
upholds Pope Leo XIII's invalidation of
Anglican orders, 101
*See also* Benedict XVI, Pope
*Redemptionis Sacramentum*, 62
discourages Communion in the hand
where risk of profanation, 62
minimized by EWTN, 63
*Redemptor Hominis*
on freedom of Catholics to criticize
ecumenism, 112
*Remnant, The*, 6, 7, 29, 68, 176, 204, 229
praises Mother Angelica, 6
*Roarium Virginis Mariae*, 169
Roman Canon, 57, 59, 60, 226

*Rosarium Virginis Mariae*, 164
**Rosary**, 2, 6, 14, 82, 164, 165, 166, 167,
    168, 169, 170, 171, 172, 205, 219, 227,
    246, 254, 260
    change of by Pope John Paul II, 164
    damage to by addition of five new
        mysteries, 169
    Our Lady of Fatima on, 166
    traditional elements of, 168
    traditional form of, 166
    traditional triune pattern of, 169
    traditonal Fifteen Mysteries of, 166
**salvation**, 14, 27, 47, 60, 61, 71, 72, 73, 74,
    75, 76, 77, 78, 80, 81, 82, 83, 84, 86, 87,
    88, 91, 92, 94, 95, 96, 97, 99, 100, 103,
    104, 105, 106, 107, 108, 109, 110, 111,
    112, 113, 114, 115, 116, 118, 119, 121,
    126, 133, 134, 135, 140, 142, 149, 151,
    164, 168, 192, 197, 209, 225, 226, 241,
    245, 260, 261
    Council of Trent on, 70
    First Saturday devotion and, 164
    necessity of holding Catholic Faith for,
        42
    necessity of membership in Catholic
        Church for, 111
    no longer possible under Old
        Covenant, 118
    none outside Catholic Church, 71-74
    of Orthodox requiring submission to
        Pope, 108
    of souls, supreme law of Church, 31
    Pope Pius IX on, 74
    universal salvation as contrary to
        Catholic dogma, 70-73
    without formal membership in the
        Church, possibility of, 73-74
**schism**, 158, 232
    attachment to Tradition viewed as by
        EWTN, 113
    condemned by Council of Florence,
        108
    EWTN's double standard concerning,
        231, 248, 250
    Father Nicholas Gruner falsely accused
        of by EWTN's Colin Donovan, 210
    Great Western Schism, 106
    not recognized by EWTN except as to
        traditional Catholics, 103
    not seen as to true schismatics by
        EWTN, 112
    of Orthodox has not disappeared over
        time, 108

Society of St. Pius X not in, per Vatican,
    113
SSPX not in state of, per Cardinal
    Castrillon Hoyos, 113
term applied only to traditional
    Catholics by EWTN, 113
**schismatic**, 14, 102, 230, 231, 245
    American hierarchy described as by
        Cardinal Gagnon, 113
    *Catholic Family News* falsely accused of
        being by EWTN, 214
    Catholics falsely accused of being, 13,
        49
    cut off from Church despite baptism,
        106
    Father Nicholas Gruner falsely accused
        of being by EWTN, 112, 210
    must not be followed by Catholics, 105
    must reunite with Pope for salvation,
        107
    Orthodox churches as, 86, 103, 105
    Society of St. Pius X falsely accused of
        being, 113
    traditional Catholics accused of being,
        41
**schismatics**, 108, 109, 112, 226
    cannot be saved outside Catholic
        Church, 71, 72, 73, 80, 108, 134
    cannot have eternal life, 108
    Catholics falsely accused of being by
        EWTN, 209
    EWTN's indulgence of, 102, 103, 226
    EWTN's double standard concerning,
        112
    invited to use Fatima Shrine, 211
    mixed marriages with condemned by
        Pope Gregory XVI, 105
    objective state of, 108
    Orthodox status as, objectively, 109
    prayer in common with forbidden by
        Church, 87
**Schoeman, Roy H.**, 138, 139, 141, 142,
    143, 149
    claims Church erred in teaching on
        supersession of Old Covenant, 138
    claims Israeli state ordained by God,
        142
    claims Old Covenant will pefect New,
        141
    denies supersession of Old Covenant,
        138-139
Serpa, Father Vincent, O.P., 64, 121, 122,
    123, 131, 132, 133, 134, 217

claims Catholics are Jewish, 121
defends Communion in the hand for
    EWTN, 64
denies necessity of Jewish conversion,
    131
recommends Catholics celebrate
    Jewish holidays, 122
*Shanti Pa*
recited over altar at Fatima Shrine, 212
Sibley, Gordon
condemns Father Gruner, 212
fires Dr. Peterson at EWTN, 212
*Singulari Quadem*, 73
condemns universal salvation, 74
**Sister Lucy of Fatima**, 1, 25, 34, 36, 40,
    122, 155, 164, 166, 222, 224, 258, 259
on Consecration of Russia not being
    done in 1984, 223
on meaning of Russia's conversion, 222
on necessity of consecrating Russia to
    Immaculate Heart, 224
on not waiting for hierarchy to act, 258
Smith, Janet, 174, 175
on "reformulating" Catholic teaching,
    175
on supposed inadequacy of pre-
    Vatican II teaching, 175
SSPX (Society of Saint Pius X)
not in schism, per Cardinal Castrillon
    Hoyos, 113
EWTN less tolerant of than Vatican,
    113
Stein, St. Edith, 142, 145
Stickler, Alfons Cardinal, 29
reveals Pope John Paul II advised by
    Cardinal commission Latin Mass
    never forbidden, 28
Suarez, Francisco, S.J.
on conversion of Jews at End Times,
    129
Suenens, Cardinal
on French Revolution in the Church at
    Vatican II, 209
*Summa Theologica*, 19, 160, 166
on folly of changing traditions, 165
*Summo Iugiter Studio*, 73
condemns mixed marriages between
    Catholics and Orthodox, 105
Sungenis, Robert, 79, 203
*Supremi Apostolatus Officio*, 166
Talmud, 130, 136
Teresa of Avila, St., 43, 142, 145
*The Kingship of Christ and the Conversion*

*of the Jewish Nation*, 136
**Third Secret of Fatima**, 26, 34, 221, 225,
    247, 257, 258, 261
attempt to debunk by Cardinal
    Ratzinger, 34
Cardinal Ciappi on, 25
contents of, 25, 26, 36
Father Nicholas Gruner's study of, 221
not fully revealed, 1
predicts apostasy beginning at top of
    Church, 41, 247
predicts attack on Catholic dogma, 25
predicts crisis in Church, 1, 25
prophecy of Pius XII concerning, i, 25
warns of impending apostasy, 27
*This Rock*
calls for shunning of Father Nicholas
    Gruner, 219
calls Father Gruner a cult leader, 218
promotes bizarre ecclesial movements,
    218
Tomko, Cardinal
admits Pope told not to consecrate
    Russia specifically, 222-223
Torraco, Fr. Stephen F., 176-178, 186
claims NFP charting a mystical
    experience, 177
promotes NFP cult, 176
Tradition
defenders of impugned by New
    Church, 12
defined, 11
need to find existing sources of, 254
St. Vincent of Lerins on, 11
Trigilio, Father John, 99
says conversion merely brings
    "fullness", 99
**Turner, Dr. John**, 229, 230, 231, 232
denounces EWTN double standard
    concerning schism, 231
denounces EWTN for calling Father
    Gruner schismatic, 230
denounces EWTN for hypocrisy and
    false accusations, 229
renounces his former support of
    EWTN, 231
Vatican Council I
on limits of Church's doctrinal
    authority, 28
on papal infallibility, 161
on perpetual meaning and sense of
    dogma, 84
**Vatican Council II**

Cardinal Ratzinger on over-estimation
of, 35
crisis in Church since, i
did not announce new doctrine, 28
dilution of meaning of "conservative"
Catholicism since, 9
disclaimer of infallibility by, 33
drastic decline of baptisms and
conversions after, 109
likened to French Revolution by
Cardinal Suenens, 209
likened to Russian Revolution by Yves
Congar, 209
Modernist breakthrough at, 48
Msgr. Gamber on failure of, 38
Vennari, John, 67, 122, 211, 215, 218
on Fatima Shrine scandal, 213, 214
on World Youth Day, 67
Vigilius, Pope
condemned universal salvation, 71
Vincent, St., of Lerins
on duty to cling to Tradition during
Church crises, 11, 254

von Balthasar, Hans urs, 71
Vree, Dale, 200, 201
criticizes theology of Scott Hahn, 199
Weigel, George, 174
disparages John Paul II's pre-Vatican II
predecessors, 240
on theology of the body, 174
Weishaupt, Adam, 37
Weiss, Rabbi Yisroel Dovid
rejects Israeli state as unbiblical, 143
West, Christopher, 22, 23, 40, 174, 175,
223
on theology of the body, 175
World Day of Prayer for Peace-Assisi
(2002)
witch doctor at, 156
World Youth Day, 6, 67
sacrileges at, 67
Zoffoli, Father Enrico
exposes heterodoxy of Neo-
Catechumenal Way, 220
Zwingli, Ulrich, 59

## About the Author

Christopher A. Ferrara is a prolific writer on Catholic affairs whose articles and essays have appeared in *The Latin Mass* magazine, *The Remnant, Christian Order, Catholic Family News, The Fatima Crusader* magazine and many other publications, both in the United States and abroad. He is a regular columnist for *Fatima Perspectives* on the World Wide Web. Mr. Ferrara is co-author of *The Great Façade*, a renowned study of the post-Vatican II crisis in the Church and *Fatima Priest*, a biography of Father Nicholas Gruner, S.T.L. He has been a major contributor to several other books.

Mr. Ferrara is also an attorney specializing in First Amendment and civil rights litigation on behalf of Catholics throughout the country. He has handled a number of widely publicized cases, including the federal litigation on behalf of Theresa Schiavo and the landmark "Nuremberg Files" case, in which he continues to defend the First Amendment rights of Catholic pro-life advocates. He is a graduate of Fordham College ('73) and Fordham Law School ('77). In 2004 Mr. Ferrara was the recipient of the Edmund Burke Award of the National Lawyers Association.

Mr. Ferrara lives in New Jersey with his wife, Wendy, and their six children.